ON THE MOVE

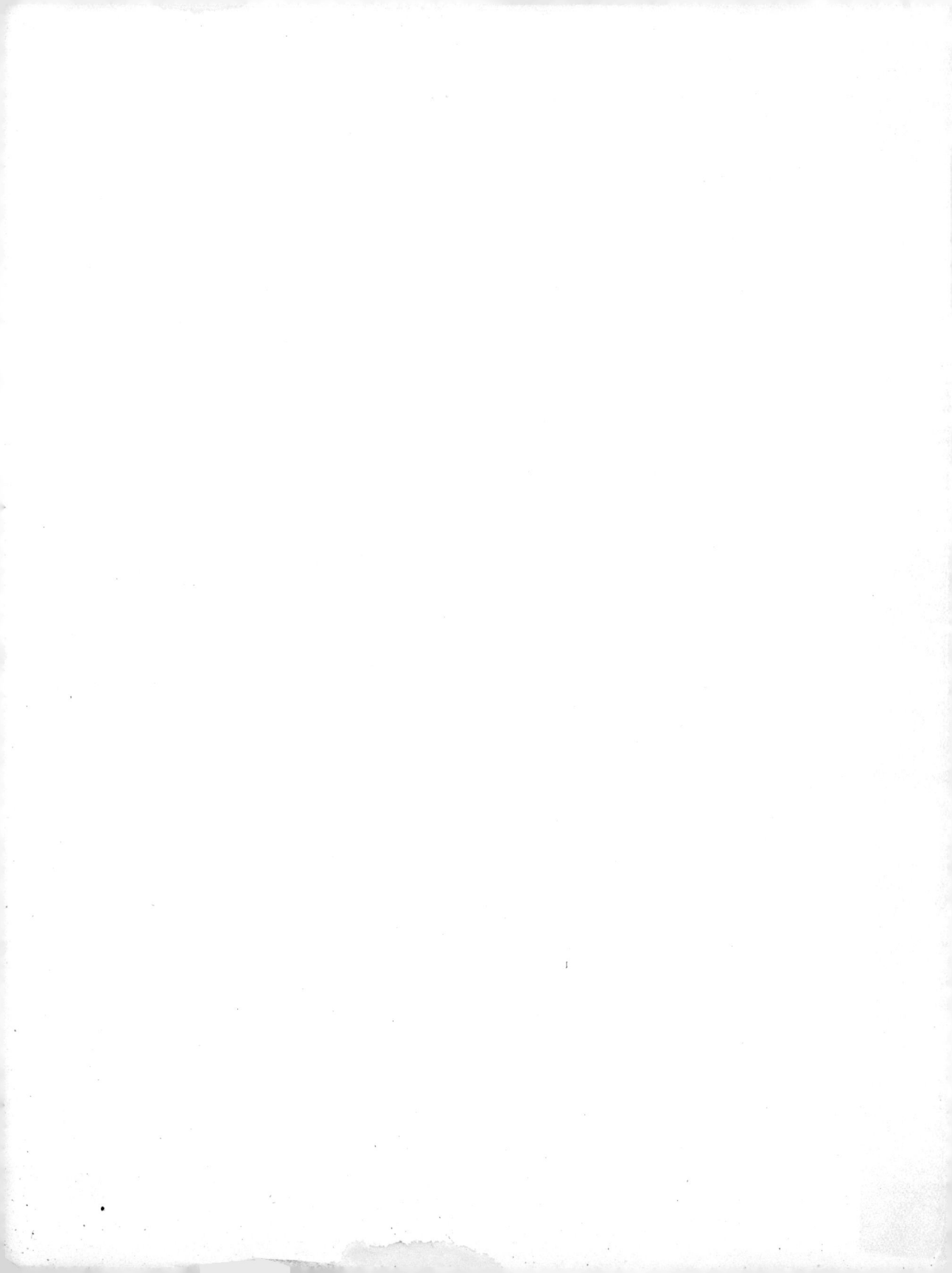

ANNE D. FORESTER
MARGARET REINHARD

On the Move

TEACHING
THE LEARNERS' WAY
IN GRADES 4–7

Printed and bound in Canada

91 92 93 94 95 5 4 3 2 1

Canadian Cataloguing in Publication Data

Forester, Anne D.
On the move: teaching the learners' way in grades 4–7

Includes bibliographical references.
ISBN 1-895411-35-1

1. Language arts (Elementary). 2. Language experience approach in education. I. Reinhard, Margaret, 1931–.
II. Title.

LB1576.F684 1991 372.6/044 C91-097169-2

Editor: Judy Norget
Book and cover design: Norman Schmidt

Peguis Publishers
520 Hargrave Street
Winnipeg MB Canada R3A 0X8

CONTENTS

5 AS READING ADVANCES SO DOES OVERALL LEARNING 153

**7 MOVING TOWARD COMBINATION CLASSES
AND THE NON-GRADED ELEMENTARY 239**

FOREWORD

MARG REINHARD AND ANNE FORESTER'S FIRST BOOK, *The Learners' Way*, guided many of us through the uncharted and threatening waters of whole language and holistic teaching. *The Learners' Way* was written for primary teachers and school administrators who were looking for a better, more satisfying way of teaching and learning. Marg and Anne showed us how integration of curriculum and teaching for thinking could be accomplished through creating a safe learning environment and establishing a "climate of delight" in the classroom.

Marg and Anne's current book, *On the Move*, extends the foundation built in the primary grades to the next logical level. Their ideas are based on personal experience and on collaboration with the entire staff at South Park Elementary School in Victoria, B.C. In particular, they worked with Sylvia Scott, Marne St. Claire, and Liz Hamblett – three of the most creative and innovative teachers with whom I have had the pleasure of working. Their intermediate, multi-age classrooms are examples of places where children are given the freedom and discipline to learn in an accepting, creative, and thought-provoking environment.

I hope this book will inspire many intermediate teachers to implement the learners' way with older children. The results will be twofold: teachers will feel empowered to be creative in their craft, and students will become independent, lifelong learners capable of contributing positively to a society in desperate need of solutions to environmental, moral, and social problems.

Trevor Calkins
Principal, South Park Elementary School
Victoria, B.C.

ACKNOWLEDGMENTS

ON THE MOVE IS BASED ON EVERYDAY WORK in intermediate classrooms. We could not have written the book without the generous contributions of students, teachers, and administrators. All of them extended the same support and encouragement to us that was evident in their classrooms. We are truly grateful for the enthusiastic support we received at every turn and wish to offer our special thanks, first to our collaborators at South Park School who brought their unique personalities and strengths to whole-language teaching: Marne brightened our work with music, art, and laughter and showed us how to create a climate of delight in an intermediate classroom; Liz charmed us as much as her students with her storytelling and the warmth and care she gives her students; Sylvia carried us along on the energy and joy for learning she radiates and transfers to her students. We have gained immeasurably from working and sharing with all three.

Research and learning went hand in hand as the entire staff of South Park School helped us at every turn. Trevor Calkins, the principal, not only gave us permission to do research in his school, but entered into our work with enthusiasm and warmth. Barbara Beukema shared her knowledge and expertise in the library and exemplified the benefits of making the library the heart of learning support. Anne Keay donated interview time, students' work examples, and her special insights into how to challenge students to extend their writing over time. Linda Picciotto shared her concerns for evaluating progress and offered valuable advice and examples of formats. Our warm thanks to all of the people at South Park for the help they extended to us.

At University Hill Elementary School in Vancouver, we received an open welcome and spent the day observing classes in progress, special library research, and outdoor work. From the principal to the students, everyone made us feel welcome. Interview time, students' work, special comments, and printed information augmented our records. We appreciate and enjoyed our visit. It validated and expanded our research at South Park. Thank you.

Interviews with teachers added further depth to our records. Hanne MacKay showed herself to be a learner in her own classroom. Her sense of humor, energy, and love of children's literature made her descriptions come alive for us. Vicki Green drew us into the learning for living in which she engages her students and kept us enthralled with her vivid metaphors and ways of inspiring children to learn. Judy Woodward's descriptions of her students' ingenuity in devising projects and carrying them out lent full weight to her comments that all of the curriculum areas are served in such imaginative work. Beverly Schreiber showed us how a dedicated teacher can turn learning around for students who have been labeled "hopeless." Anne Peterson demonstrated that there are different ways to convey knowledge and make learning fun and exciting. Val Carter shared her insights and her collections of natural science artifacts to affirm that students' curiosity draws them toward science and learning. And Malcolm Sneddan described in down-to-earth, yet exciting terms how to connect the study of science to students' everyday lives.

Each of these teachers made a unique contribution to our book. We experienced enthusiasm, wonder, and awe at the dedication and ingenuity they bring to teaching, and we offer our gratitude and admiration to each of them.

Special support came to us from Elaine Zakreski who shared her expertise and caring with us and with the teachers in her area. Anne Davies gave freely of her time and materials to address the difficult question of planning for an open system of learning while still fulfilling curriculum requirements. Our sincere thanks to them both.

Thanks are also due Judy Norget whose skill, patience, and tact in editing the manuscript have helped us smooth out the rough spots. She is giving the same meticulous care to *On the*

Move that she lavished on our previous book *The Learners' Way.* We appreciate that care, offer our tribute to it and our warm affection to Judy.

And finally there are the children who shared their learning and their work with us. They inspired, delighted, and surprised us. Seeing them work and evolve rekindled our energy. They gave freely of their work and their time and confirmed for us once again that they are natural learners whenever they are given the room to work their way. We thank them and salute them. In the schools in which we observed, they are definitely "on the move."

INTRODUCTION

ON THE MOVE IS ABOUT STUDENTS AND TEACHERS learning and growing together. It is about real classrooms in elementary schools here in Victoria and further afield and about students and teachers who are using whole-language ways of teaching/ learning. We will talk of our own experience and observations and those of other whole-language teachers to share the practical everyday work done in these classrooms and to give you a sense of the excitement, productivity, joy, and frustration that arise when students are on the move. We have experienced all those emotions – and many more – during the twenty years of our joint work with elementary-school and adult learners. Throughout the years, we have watched young and not-so-young learners come alive to learning. In the process, along with the joy, we have faced the anxiety, doubt, and antagonism that accompany moves into new ways of working. However, we have always been reassured and affirmed by the students themselves: by their joy and by the energy that they invest in their learning. We hope that *On the Move* will help you make the transition to whole-language teaching/learning, ease the concerns that come with change, and show you the excitement and positive energy that is generated when students are moving along.

Who we are

Margaret Reinhard is an elementary school teacher who for thirty years has been searching for better ways to help children learn. She is still doing so, and her teaching continues to change and evolve as she observes how the children in her K–1–2 class learn and respond. At times, even now, she agonizes over just how much input she should make and how much she should leave up to the children. But time and again, as she lets go, her students respond with yet more creativity and spontaneity. She is both a learner and a researcher in her own classroom, and as a result, her work is imbued with the same curiosity and eagerness that the very young bring to learning. By working with the children in ways that foster their way of learning, she has created a "climate of delight" in her classroom that eases even the most reluctant learners into confidence and productivity.

To share her practical experience and the how-to of whole-language teaching/learning, she has invited teachers and administrators to come into her classroom at South Park School to watch her and her students in action, secure in the knowledge that modeling and direct observations are the most natural and effective ways of teaching/learning. For those too far away to share this classroom experience, she has co-authored a guide to whole-language *The Learners' Way* for teachers of grades K–3, and she is kept busy on weekends responding to requests for workshops and inservice training. Teachers who either want to or who are required to move toward whole language respond to Margaret's solid experience and translation of theory into practice. They often tell Margaret that she has given them the courage and the concrete knowledge to work in new and joyful ways in their own classrooms.

Through the close contact with her colleagues at South Park School – our collaborators – and the hundreds of teachers who talk and share with her during her workshops, Margaret has expanded her expertise and concern into intermediate teaching. She visits classrooms, brings intermediate students into her own classroom, collaborates with intermediate teachers on projects, themes, and buddy work. Above all, she discusses and thinks about the translation of whole-language theory and practice into the intermediate grades and beyond. Her concerns about learning and the learner are as valid for the upper grades as for her own primary students, and, as her principal, Trevor Calkins, wrote in a note to Margaret: "As I watch the staff grow, I really appreciate how much your presence has contributed . . . Your extra effort, your professional attitude, and your professional example in and out of the classroom set a high standard."

Collaboration has been the guiding principle in all of Margaret's work as her entry into working "the learners' way" started through her partnership with me, Anne Forester, who almost twenty years ago came into Margaret's K–1 classroom as a researcher/observer. From the outset we shared our thoughts and feelings about fostering learning in positive ways, and merged my theoretical and practical knowledge of language learning and psycho-linguistics with Margaret's teaching experience and thirst for more effective ways of fostering learning.

Aside from being the writer-researcher of our team, I am the Reading and Study Skills Counselor at Camosun College, a community college that offers everything from basic literacy, to career training and university transfer courses. In my work helping adult students with their reading, writing, and study skills I build on the same principles of holistic learning that Margaret and I evolved, tested in the classroom, and then evolved further. As I work with my students, I continue to visit Margaret's classroom and note the parallels between the ways young and adult learners deal with learning when they are free to work their way. My excitement about open ways of learning often conveys itself to the students and to participants in the workshops I lead, and they begin to take an interest in the principles of learning that help them grow so effectively.

In writing *The Learners' Way,* Margaret and I drew together those basic principles of holistic learning. Primary teachers have been telling us that that book provided just what they needed most – a practical guide that was also based soundly on learning theory. So when intermediate teachers began to clamor for similar support, I returned to the kind of systematic in-class observations that set our partnership on its way. This time, I visited intermediate classrooms and, over a period of two years, spent much of my time with the three South Park School intermediate teachers who have become our collaborators and who have worked with us in the most supportive way.

Our collaborators

Our three collaborators teach at South Park School in Victoria, and each one made unique contributions to this book. Their individuality, personality, and backgrounds shine through their work and the ways in which they interact with their students. Like Margaret, they started their teaching in more traditional ways, and they, too, continue to grow and evolve as they work in their classrooms.

MARNE ST. CLAIRE

Marne is an artist at heart and her life is filled with music and artwork. Teaching music and art has given her full scope to express her creativity and spontaneity, but the structured programs required in language arts and content teaching were a frustration to her until she adopted whole-language methods in her grade 4–5–6 class. Now her classroom is alive with excitement as Marne brings her creativity to the full range of her teaching. Going into her classroom is almost sure to produce a surprise: beautiful singing, creative artwork, and the most delightful reading and writing. Learning is prodigious because Marne demands both discipline and dedication. She gets both, because her students know how deeply she cares for them.

SYLVIA SCOTT

Love for the outdoors and an unquenchable need to be active characterize Sylvia. Whole-language teaching is a natural outlet for her tremendous energy. It would be impossible to contain her inside the classroom day after day after day; she has to move out, take her students on outdoor field trips, to the museum, or to the playing field. Her classroom is lively and at times overwhelming to the casual observer, but Sylvia inspires her students to produce work well beyond that expected of the average grade 6–7 class – soulful poetry, projects to save the environment, a business venture planned and run by the students. Empowering students and having them care for and consider each other's feelings are Sylvia's ways of drawing productivity out of lively adolescents.

ELIZABETH HAMBLET

Liz captured the spirit of the whole-language approach through her professional reading and workshop attendance while she was working as an administrator. The promise held out by this philosophy, so different from what she had experienced in her early teaching days, was too hard to resist. So, while also filling the post of vice-principal, Liz is back in the classroom. She is definitely on the move. Visiting her grade 3–4 room was invaluable to us because she permitted us to see her struggles, her frustrations, and then her successes. Her courage to admit to herself and her students when things went wrong created wonderful learning opportunities, topped only by her obvious love of literature that revealed itself in her expressive oral readings. As they moved further into whole language and away from structures and worksheets, Liz and her students blossomed. Now, even the physical arrangement of her classroom has changed as she and her students work in ever more flexible ways.

Together, these three teachers have fifty-five years of experience. Their willingness to move away from the safety of traditional work has imbued the South Park team with a spirit of aliveness and collaboration that extends to the parents as well as to colleagues and students.

The hundred-year-old building that houses South Park School is a fitting place to contain all this excitement. It combines solid shelter with many unique features. Though its classrooms lack storage space, and the furnace – when it worked at all – used to shower coal dust throughout the school, South Park's wide hallways and spacious classrooms are well suited to the expansive ways of whole-language teachers who do not confine their students to their desks throughout the day.

The administrative structure, too, supports whole-language teaching/learning. Some years ago, South Park School rose

At South Park School collaboration is the byword

South Park School in Victoria provides a wonderful example of building new ways upon a solid foundation of tradition.

above certain closure when parents decided to petition for a special school in which they would have the chance to influence their children's education. Many of them had experienced the benefits of cooperative playschools and wanted a more child-centered environment than that offered in more traditional schools. Cooperation among parents, teachers, and administrators is still the guiding principle at South Park. At the same time though the school adheres to all of the rules and regulations set by the Victoria School Board.

South Park is a special place because all the people involved work as a team and support each other. At the time Margaret joined South Park, the teachers were ready to move into whole-language teaching. The supportive, child-centered atmosphere made it a fertile ground for new growth. Teachers were willing to take risks, and their principal, Trevor Calkins, encouraged them to be flexible and spontaneous in their work. According to him, Margaret gave the impetus for the change, but as the entire staff was ready and open to work and learn together, whole language grew to make the school even more special.

But what is whole language?

Whole language is the term used for teaching literacy skills by immersing children in literature, and using reading and writing for meaningful communication right from the very beginning. Children are trusted to learn to read and write in much the same way they learned to talk – by *doing*. That means that the usual sequence of teaching the ABCs first and reading/writing later is turned upside down. Story reading by the teacher, memory reading of familiar songs or rhymes, following recipes or directions teach children what it *means* to read first, and the learning of parts then emerges from that satisfying, meaningful whole-language foundation. Learning to write works in the same way. The teacher models meaningful writing at the chalkboard or around the classroom, to show that writing is meant to make sense, and then invites children to put their own messages into print. Out of their own wish to communicate arises the need for learning about letters, their sounds, and about spelling patterns.

Children thrive on this type of learning because it follows their own natural ways of learning. At home, they have learned to talk by talking. From the first days of their lives parents have surrounded them with meaningful talk – not as a lesson but a way of communicating. They are immersed in speech, and that speech is connected to meaningful activities around the home.

The learning of sounds and patterns of speech emerges from whole language used in meaningful ways. Parents trust their children to learn what they need simply by modeling meaningful talk. Parents *know* their babies are going to talk.

And baby talks. What's more he or she abstracts patterns of speech and grammar and by four or five has a good knowledge of how language works. Though parents do not give readiness tests or provide explicit instructions, children learn not only the parts of speech but sophisticated rules of grammar – word order, the use of pronouns, the formation of past tense and plurals. Though they can't talk about it, they understand and use meta-linguistic rules – rules *about* language. They have acquired that knowledge simply *through listening to models, engaging in prodigious practice, and receiving feedback that acknowledged and expanded what they said.*

The combination of those three – modeling, practice, and feedback – form the core of language learning at home, and now of whole-language teaching/learning at school. By building on the children's own ways of learning, we tap not only their self-acquired knowledge of language, but the system of learning that has served them so well at home. If we cut language into small parts with the intent of making learning to read and write easy, we actually do the opposite, because we strip language of its meaning. (See figure 1.) By trusting children to read by reading and write by writing (just as they learned to speak by speaking), we acknowledge that they are in fact highly effective and eager learners.

Trust in the learner is another core concept of whole-language teaching/learning. Whenever you come across a definition of whole language, you are sure to find the statement that it is an attitude or philosophy more than a method of teaching. The philosophy is based upon a set of consistent beliefs about the learner and the learning process. Whole-language teachers understand and acknowledge both the system of learning the children use naturally and the system of teaching that parents use at home. Because they do, teachers focus on learning more than on teaching, on strengths more than on errors, and on the students more than on the curriculum. They trust their students to learn, and they provide the rich learning context that allows the students to abstract patterns and parts *their* way.

FIGURE 1
Learning to speak at home compared with learning to read in a structured class

Speaking	Reading
The child learns to speak without formal speaking lessons.	Special reading instructions guide the learner.
Learning to speak is an integral part of everyday experience.	Reading is frequently taught as a separate skill.
Whole language and meaningful talk surround the learner.	Parts of written language are introduced one at at time.
A normal flow of language addressed to him/her and to others is available to the beginner as a model of fluent speech.	Little modeling of fluent reading is available to the beginning reader who listens only to his peers.
Familiar actions, concrete objects, and the context or setting give meaning to spoken language.	Context and practical applications are used minimally to help children make sense of initial reading.
The amount of oral language a child has available to model is varied and vast.	The type and amount of written language available to the beginner are often carefully controlled.
The child generates and applies rules of language.	Rules are introduced by adults.
The child decides when s/he is ready to move to a new level.	The teacher sets the sequence and timing for learning.
Gross performance with sounds and syntax is acceptable. (Few parents attempt to have beginning speakers correct their early language.)	Fine discrimination and accuracy are generally asked for. The teacher usually requires the beginning reader to correct imprecise readings of the text.
The child has ample opportunity to practice speaking.	Reading practice is often limited to minutes a day.
Meaning or the truth of a statement – rather than its form – guide the response of adults to the child.	Form – sounds and graphic symbols – are stressed more than meaning or the content of the message.
Parents confirm what the child has said, using feedback that expands and elaborates the child's words.	Use of feedback to confirm meaning is minimal in many classrooms.

(Note: The examples of structured, teacher-directed learning are based on our 1973 observational study.) From *The Learners' Way*, 1989.

AND NOW THERE'S WHOLE LANGUAGE IN THE INTERMEDIATE GRADES

Letting learning of parts emerge out of the context of whole, meaningful communication works equally well for more advanced students – those in grade 4 and beyond. Just as primary children have trouble relating to abstract concepts like letters, words, and sentences, so intermediate students have difficulty relating to the abstract concepts of paragraphs, literary analysis, or scientific principles. They do, that is, *unless* they have had the opportunity to do a lot of writing, reading, or hands-on science experience *first.*

Learning by doing really needs no justification. In sports, in crafts, and even in reading and writing, we know the benefits of sustained practice. But when we are used to lecturing to convey information, we sometimes forget that laboratory work and trial-and-error learning make far greater impact on students than any lecture or textbook.

Our classroom experience has revealed that if we trust learners to work their way, what they come up with will – more often than not – exceed our fondest expectations. Letting go of control and finding that trust are difficult at first, but once established, trust pays wonderful dividends. As students realize they are trusted to work their own way, they become creative and enthusiastic about their learning. The excitement of working on topics of their own brings forth that "climate of delight" that characterizes a true learning community.

After all, learning is social, and the more students can interact with each other and the teacher, the more your classroom will come alive to learning and true enquiry – students wanting to know for the sake of knowing, not because they need to answer test questions. If communication and quest for knowledge are important to you, their teacher, students will follow your model.

WHAT IS A WHOLE-LANGUAGE CLASSROOM LIKE?

As we indicated when we told you about Marne, Sylvia, and Liz, teachers – as well as students – have the opportunity to express their own individuality in whole-language classrooms, so whole-language classrooms are as varied as the teachers. But there are definite shared characteristics that spring from the whole-language philosophy of seeing students as active, competent learners who can be trusted to direct their own learning and become researchers – researchers in the very areas that many intermediate teachers now worry about when told to move into more holistic methods of teaching.

Here is what you are likely to find in intermediate-grade whole-language classrooms:

- Learning is child-directed. Students set their own pace and have a choice within parameters set by the teacher.
- Literature-based teaching expands reading skills. Students read novels, stories, poetry, and non-fiction instead of basal texts, discuss their reading, and write book reports and responses to their reading in reading response journals instead of answering prepared questions or doing structured exercises.
- Writer's workshop is the dominant way of expanding writing skills. Students do both creative writing and report writing, and discuss their writing and editing with both teacher and peers.
- Projects and themes are used extensively to cover content material required by the curriculum and/or requested by the students. Students do active research and report writing and often use original methods to present their findings.
- There is much integration of all the subjects. Students use reader's and writer's workshops to gather and record information for their projects. They read and write copiously in connection with their content studies.
- Time lines are flexible during each day and for the duration of a project. Students have the freedom to spend an entire day immersed in a special project, or extend work over several days (or even weeks) to do in-depth study or move through several stages in their work.
- Learning centers and hands-on work are key elements of everyday learning. Students incorporate such things as artwork, science experiments, and a wide range of reference sources in their learning.
- The classroom is active and frequently abuzz with noise. Students are free to move around, find their own space to curl up with a book, or confer with their classmates. Complete silence reins only during specified periods of reading or during writer's workshop.
- The energy level is high. Students work energetically and purposefully. They participate freely in discussions.
- Evaluation of progress is ongoing. Students rarely have to write tests as they and the teacher keep track of their reading, writing, math, and project work on an ongoing basis.

• Modeling is the dominant mode of instruction. Students learn by following the lead of the teacher.

The mode of teaching is perhaps the most rewarding aspect of whole-language teaching/learning. Modeling learning behaviors – thinking out loud, genuine enquiry, reading/writing, participating in projects – turns you, the teacher into a learner in your own classroom. Instead of grinding through the same prepared lessons year after year, you will find it as intriguing as your students to engage in original research instead of following the textbook, and to use literature to study an era or region rather than memorizing facts and figures. As they note your curiosity and enthusiasm you are that much more effective as a model for them and there is a mutuality of learning that keeps everyone on the move.

How to use this book

Learning by doing and observing the learners are key components of whole-language work. Apply these two in using this book. Once you have a feel for the overall philosophy and are comfortable with some of the activities we are describing, begin by trying out those that sound most appealing to you. Then observe what happens. If you are already doing writer's workshop, compare your students' interest and enthusiasm – and results – with the interest and enthusiam generated by more structured exercises, such as combining sentences, answering teacher-generated questions, writing about topics supplied by the teacher. Fill your room with interesting books and watch students gravitate toward reading after giving them glimpses of interesting pages and chapters. Experiment with keeping time schedules more flexible to capture the momentum of energy of students at work at an engaging project, or to end a session early that has clearly become a bore.

Throughout, observe both your own and the students' reactions. How are they working? Are they doing more, learning more? And are you enjoying the change? Instead of evaluating whether students are doing what you expected them to do or what they "should" do, learn to describe what they are actually doing – discussing, experimenting, looking things up, drafting. We have found that when we suspend judgment and examine dispassionately what is actually going on, the students are generally on task – and we learn something about their learning styles or ways of problem solving at the same time as we keep track of what they are doing.

Discuss the changes you are making with your students and invite their comments. They will respond with honest feedback when you show real interest in their reactions. Sharing your thoughts and observations with them becomes another step toward giving the students genuine choices and a degree of control over what happens from day to day. Note how they rise to the challenge of responsibility and independence. Sometimes they need more time, but most often you will find that they are eager to take charge of their learning.

Describe the changes and observations you are making to other teachers, particularly those who are also launched on whole-language work, and ask for their input. Compare notes, exchange ideas, bolster each other's morale if things seem to go slowly. Most often, we have found that such sharing takes on an air of excitement and anticipation, an eagerness to see what will happen next.

Above all, be kind to yourself and acknowledge that learning is a gradual process. None of us abandoned our more structured ways of teaching overnight. Instead, we adopted one or two new ideas at a time and built our trust in the learners slowly but steadily. When teaching the whole-language way, there is always something new to explore and discover. Learning continues to evolve for you as well as for the students.

In writing this book we hope to convey the excitement and joy that arise from watching students learn effectively, without anxiety or stress. The teachers who have collaborated with us and those we have interviewed have all expressed their delight and amazement at what their students are capable of producing when given a chance to work their way. By adopting what these teachers have found to work for them, you will find that your classroom, too, will be on the move.

YOU CAN DO IT!

1

THE MOST IMPORTANT, and at the same time the most satisfying, part of whole-language teaching is its *can-do* philosophy. As you move into new ways of interacting with your students, that can-do feeling will pervade your day. As you change your style of teaching, you will experience a building momentum that carries you and your students along new paths of learning.

But entering new paths and moving into unfamiliar territory, though exciting, can be scary. You will need maps and guides to chart your way and to reassure yourself that you are not lost in some unproductive wilderness. The following chapters can serve as your guide to make the transition into productive whole-language teaching. There are suggestions for creating a learning climate; for shaping your day; for innovative ways of teaching reading, writing, and assessing progress; for conveying solid subject information in ways that diverge from traditional carefully arranged lesson plans. But here we want to talk about the more subtle, yet most important, aspect of making the transition to whole-language teaching – that of capturing the philosophy behind it.

The can-do attitude of whole learning springs from accepting that your students are effective learners who can be trusted to develop their potential in productive ways. Of course, that growth derives from their natural learning as nurtured in a supportive environment that makes it both safe and natural to take risks and to engage freely and joyfully in trial-and-error

**The priority –
creating a
learning climate**

learning. And so your first and foremost priority in making the transition to whole-language learning is to develop a climate of delight in your classroom.

As you start your year, set aside for the moment your concerns about meeting the curriculum and help your students get settled into their new environment. Make it your first priority to create an atmosphere that draws them into learning and exploring, that invites them to participate, to get involved, to become curious and excited about what the year will hold. Concentrate on lots of hands-on, manipulative activities; artwork; science experiments; phys. ed. games; field trips; and anything else that will capture their imagination. Be sure to draw on your own talents and preferences – music, phys. ed., history, science, literature, whatever they are. Your interest and enthusiasm will be contagious, and students will join you in genuine enquiry and experimentation.

Imagine the pleasure of pursuing your own special interests, and compare that feeling with your reaction to reworking – for the umpteenth time – the same lesson plans about . . . . The freshness of learning will not be lost on your students who are more than aware when your questions are merely tests to see if they can guess what you want to hear. They are equally aware when you are genuinely interested in hearing what they have to say. Build on the students' interests as well, and invite them to bring in related materials and books to fill the classroom.

Involve your students in planning their year. Do some fast-paced brainstorming sessions to get ideas flowing. Give them some broad outlines of curriculum areas they will need to cover during the year and ask for their suggestions for working within those guidelines. If you are studying cultures that year, explore those eras and geographical locations that interest students. If the focus is on science, ask about resources that students have available at home or that can be found in the community. By asking for their input, you make students active partners in developing a resource base. Bring in your own collections, examples of student projects from years past, books, science supplies, and materials for making displays, and encourage students to share their own treasures with the class. Above all, acknowledge your students' input and demonstrate to them that they are your partners in planning their learning. If they know you truly value their suggestions, they will contribute more ideas than you can possibly cover in one year.

FIELD TRIPS

SEPT. 8   ART GALLERY

SEPT. 21   DAYSPRING SOYA
SEPT. 29   VICTORIA FLYING CLUB, AIRPORT TOWER
OCT. 12   CLIMB MT. DOUG (Aerial Photographs)
OCT. 27   CLIMB MT. FINLAYSON (Salmon)
NOV. 3   ART GALLERY (Lino, Inuit, Carr, Tapestries)
NOV. 9   BIG EYES (Owl Study) at the Museum
NOV. 24   SWAN LAKE

JAN.   TREE-MENDOUS at the Museum
FEB.   INUIT ART SHOP
FEB.   ROCK SHOP

MAY   WITTY'S LAGOON
MAY   SIDNEY SPIT
JUNE   BEAVER LAKE

Veterinarian's office
Butcher
Farm w/some milking cows
Chief Paul the carver at the Museum
Fatt's Island Poultry Farm
Architect's office
Museum taxidermy

Students in Liz's class brainstormed possible field trips and saw most of them materialize as the year progressed.

With this mutuality of planning, you will unleash your own creativity and that of your students. Your room will bubble with activity and the momentum of learning will accelerate. Students will help you set up learning centers and plan special projects. They will decorate the room with their artwork and displays of special books and artifacts. As the room takes on a personality created by you and the students, the feeling of being "at school" will disappear and a feeling of being in a special place for learning will emerge. Just as their younger classmates will convert their playhouse into a space station, a hospital, or a medieval castle, so your students may convert their classroom into a "museum" or a "jungle," as one grade 5 class did using special displays for the former and the cultivation of lush plants for the latter.

Perhaps we should sound a warning at this point. Once you are launched along this course, you will not be able to turn back. Excitement and activities will snowball and roll along, gathering momentum. You and your students will be moving along together, and if you return to your old ways of carefully designed and sequenced lessons – as you may wish to do from time to time – you will find that they will fall sadly flat. While you may feel the loss of the old ways at first, soon you will find that the enthusiasm, good feelings, and productivity compensate you tenfold for what you have given up. As your actions and the learning climate you create will proclaim to your students that you perceive them to be responsible, capable learners, they will view themselves that way, and their learning will blossom. All of you will be on the move.

MAKE READING AND WRITING NATURAL PARTS OF YOUR DAY

In creating a learning climate that affirms the students' natural ways of learning, reading and writing will be integral parts of everything they do. If you make your classroom a place where the written word is as natural a part of communication as talking, then language and learning will become rich and varied. Model the uses of reading and writing every day, and even your most reluctant readers and writers will follow your example.

Set the tone right from the beginning of the year by reading aloud to your students. Make your selection from every genre, and never underestimate your students' interests and abilities. Be daring – put your basal readers on the back shelf. Instead, bring in books and reading materials of every description. (Take a look at our suggestions in chapter 5 about filling your classroom with books.) If the topics are interesting and varied, your students will open their minds and hearts to reading. Read them humorous or exciting books, poems, stories, non-fiction, newspapers, parts of interesting journal articles, scientific reports – anything that interests or delights you. If you begin by sharing *your* favorites, the students will sense your interest and pleasure and will respond by bringing in their own. Reader's workshop is a natural outgrowth of these read-aloud sessions as students will be eager to carry on reading.

Writing works in much the same way. If you begin by modeling the many uses of writing – making lists, composing letters, writing poetry, recording news, noting ideas generated during brainstorming sessions – students will follow your example. They will use writing as part of all their learning activities and will eagerly join author's circle to share their own work. Instead of having to coax a few lines out of reluctant writers, you will get groans of protest if you have to curtail writer's workshop. The change may be gradual at first, but as the year progresses all your students will move toward fluent, expressive writing. So hang in there and trust. They will love to write and you will love their writing.

SPECIAL PROJECTS AND THEMES
ADD NEW LIFE TO CONTENT TEACHING

Perhaps the best news for intermediate teachers is the reassurance that, far from destroying the integrity of their favorite subject or discipline, whole-language teaching opens the way to enriching and broadening it. Instead of having a fixed hour or two once or twice a week to devote to science, social studies, or math, you will have the opportunity to draw the students into projects that extend over time and move across the curriculum. These projects will include library research, report writing, art, and oral presentations, along with the physical examination of specimens, collecting of evidence, careful experimentation, and hands-on work.

Here again, you can trust your students to rise to the challenge. When they know that they are engaged in actual fact finding and true research, their curiosity and energy will be boundless. They will become keen workers who take their research questions home, involve their parents and other adults, go to the library or even the archives, and search the TV newscasts for all available information on their topic. You are sure to find that their energy moves them far beyond the realm of your former lessons and the assigned textbooks – so much so that you will find yourself learning along with the students and sharing their excitement.

When the language arts are integrated into the content areas, the benefits are reciprocal. The language arts flourish because students read and write for purposes that are important and meaningful to them; research flourishes because students are freely using their reading, writing, and oral communication skills. All of these skills evolve jointly. If you are used to gauging progress by watching for the development of specific component skills, then at first you may think little progress is being made. But if you watch instead for the evolution of thinking, the growth of reading, writing, and listening, you will find that your students are moving right along.

But am I doing the right thing? Are they really learning?

Doubts, fears, and worries about "doing the right thing," about the students "really learning what they need to learn" are natural parts of making a change and natural parts of being a responsible, concerned teacher. Just don't let them get you down. Instead, develop a whole repertoire of ways to reassure yourself. Begin by acknowledging that there will be times when your best-laid plans won't work out the way you thought they would, when special lessons or projects will fall flat – *just as some of them did when you were using traditional methods.* In other words, don't expect to be Superteacher, and, at the very least, allow yourself the same leeway that you gave yourself under the old system. Taking risks and being creative include finding out what does and what does not work with your students, all of whom are unique, individual learners.

To affirm for your students that trial-and-error learning is an important and viable part of growth, you must accept that it is for you too. Enter into the spirit of adventure that pervades your students' learning, laugh at some of your misadventures, and never feel guilty when a particular activity does not work the way you thought it would. Instead, discuss with your students what happened, what went wrong, and what, if anything, could or should be done to forestall the problems you encountered. Your students will be thoughtful, resourceful advisers, and the sense of community and co-creative learning will flourish.

Talking to other teachers is another powerful way to ease your concerns and shore up your confidence. Sharing your worries will quickly show you that you are not alone. Each of us has suffered the agonies of doubt and self-questioning about "doing the right thing," about "turning too much over to the students," about "not building skills fast enough". . . . The list is long and varied, but behind it always lies genuine concern for the welfare of students, and that is what all good teaching is about. So pat yourself on the back for being a concerned teacher, talk to kindred spirits, and tell yourself, "I *am* doing fine!"

Whole-language teachers are supportive of each other, enthusiastic, and sociable. They will talk and meet anywhere. Seek them out in your staff room, go into their classrooms, meet over potluck suppers, have picnics together, organize special in-service workshops, and talk to each other on the telephone. If you are just starting to teach the whole-language way, you may feel panicky at first and in dire need of reassurance that all is well. Margaret and all of our collaborators have gone through such phases. All continue to question how their work affects their students. They continue to observe and reflect.

As you become accustomed to watching students' progress, your self-questioning and your calls for help will gradually lessen. You will require only simple confirmation that the steps forward you are observing are right and natural. As the year progresses and you keep in touch with your fellow teachers, your enthusiasm, and that of the students, will increase, and your messages will shift to eager reports about your students' successes and about the marvelous work they are producing. Sharing that excitement is just as important as sharing your doubts. Learning is social and, just as your students revel in sharing their work with other students, so you will thrive on sharing your pleasure in your students' growth and accomplishments with other teachers.

Collaboration and sharing are hallmarks of whole-language teaching. As you establish a learning climate in your classroom, your students will model themselves after your supportive and cooperative ways of interacting. (Visitors to Margaret's classroom immediately pick up on the remarkable spirit of cooperation.) Competition and strife dissolve and mutual support and genuine caring take their place. High productivity, excellence of performance, and creativity are the by-products of that collaborative spirit, and will nourish you as much as the students. Your adult whole-language network will further enhance that feeling of being part of a productive, positive community. Together you will be sharing information, sharing resources, brainstorming new ideas, developing joint projects, planning buddy work for younger students, or talking about the joy of being free to work as a competent professional in the classroom, with time to develop themes and projects fully.

Sharing books and other printed resources becomes another bonus of keeping in close touch with like-minded teachers. As soon as one of the group has discovered a new and exciting article, book, or conference package, the word spreads and the rush is on to get a copy, to try out new ideas, and then to get together to compare notes. Now that whole-language teaching is entrenched in elementary schools in many districts throughout North America, articles about whole language are appearing in all the major reading and education journals, and presentations or workshops on whole language are offered at conferences. So you will not be without resources in making your transition. Instead you can pick and choose among the many ideas offered and decide, "This looks like fun," or "I could adapt that for my students," or "They can certainly do that!" When you are no longer tied to basal readers and page-by-page textbook work, your own interests and needs as well as those of your students become the guiding principles in satisfying the broad requirements of your district's intermediate curriculum.

Once you have established your "climate of delight," work on the curriculum proceeds smoothly

If you are worrying about the "wasted time" that you spent on building the learning climate, you will quickly discover that the eagerness and energy that whole-language students bring to their work more than makes up for any lost time. As you launch into projects, themes, and specific skill building, you will have teams of students take on research tasks and fact finding. Their work will be fueled by their own curiosity and desire to know. So instead of questions like, "How much do we need to write?" or "Are we going to be tested on this?" students will seek you out as a resource person and information-giver who can help them discover, and then structure, information.

As you observe their work, you will note that not only are they developing all of the higher-order skills of reading comprehension, research, and report writing, but they are also engaging in genuine hypothesis testing, inference drawing, and synthesis of data. In short, their learning transcends and surpasses the accumulation of facts from textbooks. They are becoming junior scientists, careful observers, and effective researchers. Their thinking and communication skills are developing as they work to satisfy the concrete curriculum requirements. You have unleashed their natural learning.

Whole-language learning builds on strengths

When using the whole-language approach you build on strengths – your own and those of the students. Since you begin the year with lots of physical activities and hands-on work, the frustrations and hostility that often accompany more traditional work vanish. Students feel free to expand into new realms. Often those students who have done poorly academically reveal special skills or knowledge in practical areas – gardening, the outdoors, sports, or artwork. If you think of the personal strengths you bring to whole-language teaching, you will experience the same source of energy as your students. Here is a checklist to help you discover how much you already teach the whole-language way. Be sure to congratulate yourself for every *yes* answer.

TO WHAT EXTENT AM I ALREADY DOING WHOLE-LANGUAGE TEACHING?

When teaching, do I
• Model reading, writing, thinking, social behaviors?
• Give lots of positive feedback?
• Encourage students' ongoing learning?
• Value and acknowledge the products of learning?
• Provide ample time for students to practice?
• Encourage students to develop their own learning styles?
• Listen with care to what students are saying?
• Make eye contact when talking to students?
• Show myself to be a learner in class?
• Reveal that I, too, make mistakes and can be uncertain?
• Make learning safe – see mistakes as stepping stones?
• Trust students to learn and develop at their own pace?
• Observe the same rules of courtesy and respect that I would follow with adults?
• Involve parents in their children's learning – in class and at home?
• Draw on all available resources – libraries, field trips, materials?

- Call in volunteers to help – parents, students, people from the community?
- Hang in there when some students take a long time to evolve?

To foster independence of learning, do I
- Turn over as many tasks as possible to the students?
- Give genuine choices – for tasks, topics, books, partners, participation?
- Teach students strategies to settle their disputes?
- Acknowledge and celebrate students' good ideas?
- Set flexible guidelines so that students can move easily from job to job?
- Give students enough time and space to generate their own ideas?

In language arts, do I
- Use literature to teach reading?
- Watch for teachable moments to build on students' interests?
- Work with individual students and with flexible groupings?
- Encourage individual writing – have writer's workshop?
- Integrate reading and writing with science and social studies?
- Foster peer teaching?
- Model the uses of reading throughout the day?

In math, do I
- Make lots of hands-on materials available?
- Encourage students to manipulate, measure things, make patterns?
- Make problem solving an important part of the day?
- Provide open-ended activities that involve arithmetic?
- Connect math with everyday living/learning?
- Ask students to estimate answers to problems?

In science or social studies, do I
- Give students genuine choices within the framework of the curriculum?
- Use concrete demonstrations and materials as well as books?
- Encourage students to bring in books and articles?
- Enter into the excitement of discovery learning?
- Invite visitors to enrich my lessons?

To foster thinking, do I
- Encourage students to solve day-to-day problems themselves?
- Give serious consideration to students' ideas/suggestions?
- Value and acknowledge students' opinions?
- Model enquiry behavior (as in "I wonder about . . . .")?
- Talk about thinking and solving problems – *metacognition?*
- Think out loud to model thinking behaviors?
- Encourage and value problem-solving strategies?

If you have given yourself credit for absolutely everything you already do, you are probably well on your way to being a whole-language teacher. Since you are basing your teaching on discovering, and then building upon both your students' and your own strengths, there is always more to be discovered. Your classroom will never be dull or repetitive in its work, because each year you will be working with a new and unique group of students who bring their own personal talents with them. Your whole-language network will keep your talents expanding as well, and you will find yourself drawn into a circle of dynamic, positive co-workers both in class and out.

WHAT YOU WILL GAIN FROM
BECOMING A WHOLE-LANGUAGE TEACHER

New energy, interest, and enthusiasm are generated when you launch into whole-language teaching. You are sure to have moments of doubt and panic as you worry about trusting the learners with yet more freedom, but if you observe them closely and keep your eyes on all steps forward, you will be reassured. As your students grow, so will your professionalism. Each year you will gain more confidence and self-assurance. Because your students engage in genuine research, your own knowledge and subject area expertise will expand, as will your perceptiveness. That can-do attitude of regarding your students as competent, knowledgeable learners will affect your self-image as well, and will make your transition into whole-language learning both positive and effective. So, when doubts assail you, *hang in there. You can do it!*

ESTABLISHING A CLIMATE FOR LEARNING

2

CREATING A NEW LEARNING CLIMATE in your classroom involves change, and change – even change for something you want – takes effort. But in this case you will find that the effort pays wonderful dividends. As you observe your students and their ways of learning, you will gradually move away from structuring lessons for them and will give them greater scope for taking the initiative for learning. As you do, you will build a climate of interactive, cooperative learning that will involve you as much as the students in new discoveries and in the excitement that those discoveries engender. As you gradually transfer more and more responsibility for learning to the students – abandoning your lesson plans of old – you will observe a new surge of energy and productivity in your students that will exceed your highest expectations.

But change does not come by itself. Though you are greatly reducing the time spent on structured lessons, your role in the classroom actually becomes more important than ever before. Your leadership role will be that of an effective manager who increases productivity while building mutual trust and respect. You will set the tone for learning and spark the students' interest, at the same time ensuring that they maintain a high level of social responsibility. As a "lead teacher" you will establish a climate of delight for learning and a climate of responsibility and caring for social interaction.

Sparking interest in learning

Enthusiasm, curiosity, and excitement about new discoveries are contagious. If you show yourself to be a learner in your classroom, your students will join in, some immediately, some with a bit of encouragement, and some only after holding back awhile. But if your interest in topics is genuine, you will spark interest in the students as well. The best way to start is to bring your personal talents and interests into the classroom.

Sylvia is an outdoors enthusiast. She began her school year with an overnight camping trip to the Carmanah Valley, a place of beauty where huge ancient trees are threatened by logging. Starting the year with a field trip set the tone for the entire year. Environmental concerns and thoughtful writing on the topic pervaded much of the year's work.

Liz brought the excitement of traveling to exotic places into her classroom. Her trip to Thailand yielded stories, pictures, and special guest presentations. Lively oral descriptions, photographs, and travel guides made the study of geography personal and interesting and led quite naturally to the use of maps to locate other places discussed throughout the year. The high point of the study of Thailand was the production of Thai masks based on pictures found on posters and in books. Creativity and imagination flourished and involved everyone, even the self-proclaimed "non-artists."

Marne's life is filled with music. She sings with her own students and often involves the entire school in choir singing and concerts. Rounds, familiar children's songs, even Schubert's Lieder sung in German, enliven her classroom from the first day of school. As children open their voices and hearts in song, so they open themselves to the other activities throughout the year. A warm, vibrant feeling pervades the classroom, yet Marne demands discipline in social interactions as well as in singing. The exuberance of song and fun is not marred by silly antics, sloppy singing, or roughhousing. Quality moves hand in hand with total involvement and social responsibility.

If you bring your own interests – literature, crafts, sports, hobbies, gardening, drama, music, art – into your classroom, you will be modeling genuine interest, curiosity, and commitment that students will sense and then emulate because you clearly value and enjoy your learning. Students read their teachers' every mood, so to demonstrate passionate involvement with reading, bring in books, stories, and articles that you enjoy. Read them in your read-aloud sessions, talk about your feelings about them, and invite children to bring in their own favorites. They will quickly take their cue from you and share their interests and books with you and their classmates. Involvement that comes from the heart will help to establish your climate of delight.

IT'S THAT FIRST STEP
THAT MAKES THE DIFFERENCE

Students will cheerfully launch into new projects when they are given time to talk things over, get input from others, and let ideas roll around for a bit. Helping them catch that spark of interest will fire their imaginations and will quickly move them past that initial barrier – not knowing how to start. Can you remember the agonies you suffered in school when you were suddenly put on the spot to say, write, or produce something? What was the quality of your work at times like those? In our own writing we continually come up against that initial blank, that horrible feeling of, "I don't have anything to say!" To get past it, we get together to talk, brainstorm, and reminisce about class-room experiences – and then move on.

To help your students move beyond that initial blank, your way of sparking their interest will make the difference. Whether you want them to write, draw, select a book for silent reading, or engage in special research, simply telling them to "go ahead" will elicit little more than blank looks, reluctant shuffling, and slow starts. If, instead, you provide a lead-in that stirs their emotions, connects materials to their lives, injects some challenge or suspense, students will eagerly set about the new task.

In chapter 5 we tell you about Margaret and Marne jointly sparking a poetry-writing session. The same kind of exchange launched students into a session of creating get-well cards for the custodian of the school, who was in hospital at the time. The suggestion to send cards to Ted produced only stunned silence. So to infuse life into writing and artwork, Marne and Marg interacted much as they did for the poetry session. Asking the students to voice their feelings and accepting all suggestions left the room abuzz with children eager to get started.

MARNE: *Let's take a minute to think what we would like best if somebody sent us a get-well card. Lee, you were in bed with the chicken pox not long ago. What would you have liked to have seen on get-well cards you received?*

LEE: *Something to make me laugh.*

MARNE: *Aha, so laughter and fun are what you want. How about the rest of you, what kinds of things would you like on get-well cards?*

From that point on, suggestions poured in: something beautiful, interesting stories, riddles, funny language, a pretend pay raise, puzzles and mazes, word games, even interesting math problems. Marg and Marne kept acknowledging and elaborating on the suggestions, then simply stood back to let production move along. Recess had to be shifted to a later time to make room for the full expression of all the ideas. And Ted received an amazing array of get-well cards to keep his mind off his illness.

Sylvia's Carmanah field trip was a way of triggering the production of writing and projects, as were Liz's lively descriptions of Thailand. When Marne wanted to inspire children to draw and paint, she brought in an armful of iris. Instead of simply asking students to "look and draw," she spoke of the care that had gone into planting and growing the flowers and the love with which they had been given to her. What the students had in front of them was not simply a beautiful bouquet of flowers but a symbol of love and caring. They put the same kind of love and caring into their artwork. And though individual iris lay on desks, on the floor, and on counters, not one was crushed.

Providing a lead-in that sparks interest enhances artwork as well as writing.

PROVIDING A FRAMEWORK FOR LEARNING

Turning control for learning over to the students does not mean that the teacher simply stands back to let the students fend for themselves. Though it is not always readily apparent to students or visitors to the classroom, the teacher creates the rough framework within which students function freely and creatively. We give more specific examples in chapter 6 about setting frameworks for projects, but here we are concerned with setting a climate for learning. We will limit ourselves to comparing two field trips: one an outing to a nature sanctuary by a lake, the other a visit to the local museum that features an outstanding section on the culture and artifacts of the native tribes of the west coast.

Since the students were well launched on a project that included studying all aspects of west coast native culture, the teacher felt that students already knew what they needed (and wanted) to look for at the museum. Groups of students were working on cooperative projects studying such topics as legends, transportation, food, and housing. The museum displays offered a wealth of information on all of these topics, but during their visit to the museum students ambled around aimlessly, looked at unrelated displays, and generally treated the experience as time out. No doubt, in the long run, they derived some benefit, but the real value of the visit was lost because there had been no prior discussion to stir interest and feelings, and to set a framework for research.

The trip to the nature sanctuary produced quite different results. With the help of naturalists at the nature center, the class split into three groups that rotated to give everyone a chance to dip nets into the lake, to examine the contents in their special classroom, and to look at the displays – including some live animals – inside the center. In this instance, brief talks about the delicate balance of nature in that micro-environment, careful examination of a live turtle and questions about its characteristics – are the hind legs the same as the front legs? – kept students on task and totally involved. To raise consciousness about the different housing needs of various animals, the leader asked children how many different kinds of homes *they* lived in – apartments, townhouses, semi-attached and separate houses – and then displayed the homes of bees, birds, and small animals that lived in colonies to emphasize the fact that animals, too, have variety in their homes. (See page 30.)

LAKE LIFE NAME _____

PLANTS

Sketch a lake plant	Draw another plant
What is it?	What is it?

ANIMALS

Draw an animal	What is it?
	Draw a line to show its size
	How does it move?
	What colour is it?
	How does it breathe?
	Any special observations?

Draw another animal	What is it?
	How does it move?
	How does it breathe?
	Draw a line to show its size
	What colour is it?
	Any special observations?

Involving students' concern for the environment, connecting information to their own lives, and setting a few specific tasks made the nature sanctuary field trip a much more focused and productive one than the visit to the museum. Even though the outside setting offered ample invitation to treat the field trip as a romp, the framework provided by the teacher and the naturalists created a learning experience that offered fun and excitement as well as interesting information.

A lively group discussion prior to the museum visit probably would have served as framework for much more serious work than the actual visit elicited. Asking students to talk about their knowledge of the displays at the museum, speculate about the authenticity of life-sized dioramas, explore feelings about the past and the loss of many things that are now only seen in museums would undoubtedly have set quite a different tone to that field trip. Group brainstorming about information needed

SCAVENGER HUNT
AT THE ART GALLERY

In the CASTLES AND CHURCHES
What three pictures show cows?
1. Artist _____   Title _____
2. Artist _____   Title _____
3. Artist _____   Title _____

Please look at the quay-side harbour in "Peel Castle, Isle of Man" by Wm. Stanfield.

How many people are there in "Tintagel Castle, Cornwall" by Marmaduke Langdale? _____
What award did the Royal Academy give this painting in 1865?
_____

Can you find a dragon in WEST COAST REALITY · THE PAINTINGS OF JIM McKENZIE? _____ Where is it? _____

In EXPLORATIONS IN CANADIAN ART
In what town is the Roman Aqueduct by Joe Plaskett? _____

In THE HUMAN FIGURE IN MODERN CHINESE PAINTING
With whom is Zhong Gui playing the game Go? _____

The large head of Buddha is chiselled out of _____ _____.

In ART RENTAL
Elizabeth Kerfoot's white cows are in a _____ orchard.

Turning a field trip to the art gallery into a scavenger hunt set a framework for attentive information gathering that extended beyond the specifics being asked for.

to expand upon in-class research, and determining what specific information each group was to focus on, would have assured a much stronger focus on gathering information and enjoying the displays. Turning the trip into a kind of treasure hunt, challenging students to see how many different facts they could gather for their specific project, might also have injected a different spirit into the rather listless group that wandered past displays full of items pertaining to their very topic without giving them a second glance. They were much more interested in a special museum display that invites young visitors to open drawers to find information on a wide variety of natural science topics; the mystery of the unknown and being asked to explore had the entire class excited. Providing a bit of mystery and the invitation to make discoveries will spark lively activity among otherwise apathetic students.

Personal involvement in learning fosters independence and social development

Encouraging students to develop their special interests, hobbies, or talents will enrich your classroom and create a climate of co-creative teaching/learning.

Clubs build social skills as well as learning

While you may want to provide some examples and information, let students take the initiative to form clubs to fit their interests. Suggestions include the following:
• Drama Club
• Poetry Club
• Ski Club
• Stamp Club
• Computer Club
• Chess Club

Participating on the student council creates awareness

Students learn about
• Committee work
• Fiscal responsibility
• Democratic principles
• Leadership qualities

- Taking minutes
- Public speaking
- Voting/consensus
- Group decisions
- Considering minorities
- Persuasion
- Debating

*Students' hobbies can be shared
in ways that benefit the whole class*

Demonstrating the knowledge and skills developed in connection with their hobbies helps students build self-confidence and gives their classmates the opportunity to learn about such things as
- Camping
- Model building
- Knitting
- Cooking
- Gardening
- Stamp collecting
- Photography
- Animal husbandry
- Weaving

CAPTURING TEACHABLE MOMENTS

One way to generate enthusiasm for learning is to listen for interesting questions or suggestions from students and to build on these teachable moments. As you keep musing aloud about how those totem poles were held upright, which one of the optional ways of spelling a word is most appropriate, how to find information on . . . , students will take their cue from you, become inquisitive, and ask, "How did they make the colors to paint the totem poles?" "Why is that town named 'Prince Albert'?" "Do animals really have special ways of signaling to each other?" At that point some (or all) of them will be eager to take you up on the suggestion to do some research on the matter.

The questions or comments raised by students often provide wonderful openings that lead into the very topics you are required to cover in science or social studies. Students' environmental concerns can lead quite naturally into discussions of health, nutrition, and the effects of pesticides. Comments on the novel being read by the group or remarks in reading response journals may trigger discussions of family relations and cultural differences. The key here, as in most learning, is to spark interest in a way that involves students on a personal level. Learning and searching for answers are not just a matter of accumulating bits of information but a way of involving the learners personally.

When Marne had her class sing four bars of Pachelbel's Canon in D as a round, she built on the children's experience and simply wrote the first letters of the notes on the board:

    s s l s l s l s
    m r m m f m f r
    d t d t d d d t
    d s l m f d f s

After a bit of practice singing, "so so la so la so la so . . ." Dylan asked, "Why don't we write some words for this?" Marne responded, "Wonderful idea!", and immediately interrupted the singing practice to act on the suggestion. To set a framework for getting started she asked the students to hum the bars to themselves, close their eyes, and experience the "feel" of those notes. "What does the melody make you think of and feel?" she asked. After a bit of humming and reflecting, the students suggested nature, the ocean, the sky looking down on nature below. From there they moved into groups to develop their theme and find specific words.

A music lesson and the fun of singing rounds turned into very exacting writing. Students extended the work over several days during writer's workshop time. As each group completed its version, writing was enlivened by singing that group's lyrics. To complete the job, everyone entered the round in the special music notebook kept by each student in Marne's class. At no time did Marne comment on the need to fit the music to the notes, to keep all the bars the same length, or other such mechanical details. She had provided the spark of interest by that first question about the theme or feel of the music, and then she left the young writers to their creative endeavors. She trusted them to do the job and provided the necessary time and encouragement to complete it to the fullest. And they did!

Learning flourishes in a climate of trust

New learning involves entering new territory. Fear of the unknown, of missteps or failure can slow or even stop the journey.

Zoë / Kirstin / Naomi / Morgan / Brooke

S L S   L   S   L   S   L S
Waves are roll - ing up, and down

M R M M F M F R
Birds are soar - ing in the sky.

D T D T D D D T
Roaring is wind through the moonlit sky

D S L M F R F S
Stars are shining every where

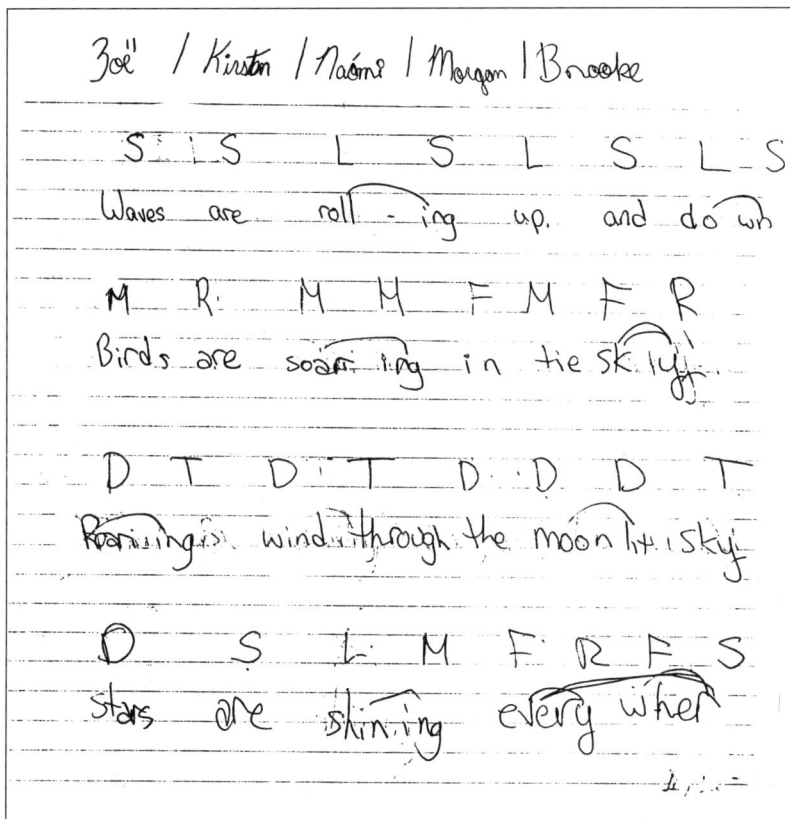

As students become creators of lyrics they evolve their sense of language, of rhythm, and of correct musical notations to guide their singing.

Building a feeling of trust in the classroom is key to establishing a good climate for learning. Whole-language learning has been developed on the foundation of the language learning young children do at home. Parents' trust in children's ability to learn to talk is one of the factors that makes learning to speak so effective and seemingly effortless. At home no one frets about babies' ability to talk, and in that climate of trust babies *do* talk, in their own good time and their own way of moving toward ever-more-accurate ways of emulating what they hear around them.

TRUSTING LEARNERS
TO LEARN IN THEIR OWN WAY

As a teacher you can build the same climate of trust in your classroom. Most important is your own attitude toward students. If, like the parent at home, you make up your mind that *all* your students are going to move forward, *all* are going to learn, then that confidence will pervade your interactions with students and they will work to merit that confidence. They will know that you do not regard their need for extra time or practice as a sign of their inability or unwillingness to move ahead at the same pace as their more advanced peers. The knowledge that they are free to engage in trial-and-error learning, that you trust them to move gradually toward a finished product that reflects their best effort, will inject life and enthusiasm into the classroom. Over years of observing students and visiting many classrooms we have found that trusting learners implicitly is a key ingredient to creating a climate of delight – a climate for maximum learning and enjoyment.

LOOKING FOR AND ACKNOWLEDGING STEPS FORWARD TO BUILD TRUST

Watching for steps forward, instead of focusing on errors in students' work, is another crucial way of building trust – in you and in the students. Throughout the day, look for and note your students' every step forward, no matter how small: coming to school on time, getting settled more quickly than the day before, writing a few lines more, having more words spelled correctly, selecting reading material without undue deliberation, speaking up in class. These are not big events, but if they represent improvement over past performance and you notice them, then you will begin to build trust in your students' ability and willingness to learn and grow. Students sense your attitude toward them and their work, and they, too, will begin to trust their own ability to learn. Adolescence is a time of tremendous change and uncertainty. If you can make these pre-adolescent students aware that you trust them, recognize their steps forward, and confidently look for yet more improvement, they will begin to internalize that trust and will gain in confidence and self-assurance.

TURNING JOBS OVER TO THE STUDENTS MAKES TRUST MANIFEST

Demonstrating your trust will soon pervade your day: standing back and letting students do the work, affirming that there is a *gradual* refinement of skills over time, acknowledging drafts and revisions as essential parts of arriving at finished products, handing over responsibility for routine work that needs to be done without nagging or worrying. If students have accepted responsibility for watering the plants, carrying out the compost after lunch, or keeping the roster of students who are going to band practice, library, or enrichment classes, let them carry out those tasks and trust them to be responsible. If there are lapses, discuss them in the same way that you would with an adult – get *them* to suggest ways they can improve.

TRUSTING THE LEARNERS TO DO WHAT THEY NEED OR WANT

When Vicki Green, an experienced intermediate teacher, agreed to pilot Ginn's *Springboards* series she walked into her classroom with a large stack of grade 4 and grade 5 readers and teacher guides. Wondering just how she could move through that much material, she found that she could turn the matter over to her students.

Sylvia's students set up, arranged, and staffed their booth at Victoria's Environmental Fair, and do not hesitate to explain their displays to Her Honor the Mayor.

I walked into the room with a stack of books. But I also walked into a room full of real learners and participatory helpers, and that was great because most of the time it seemed I needed a lot of help. The kids asked, 'What have you got?' Well, I told them, 'These are new readers, and right away they asked, 'Can we look at these *Springboards?*' And then they asked, 'What are these other ones with the coil binding?' And when I told them, 'Those are the teacher guides. They are for me to read so I will know how to use this stuff,' they asked, 'Can we look at them?' 'Of course,' I said.

That became one big eye opener. The fact that they were let into something that was 'The Teacher Book' made it exciting and a mystery, and as a result they brought a critical eye to the job. Right away they started to comment: 'This is a *good* idea!' 'This would be really fun.' 'We should try *this.*' 'Oh, I don't think that would work well.' 'This sounds kind of boring.' And they ended up going through each story, checking what the authors wanted the teacher to do with it, and then they'd try out different things.

So that became a way of approaching that seemingly overwhelming job. Here were twenty-six kids who were ready to look at all the books and suggestions and were able to come up with their own ideas. They took over and piloted *Springboards* their way.

TRUST IN STUDENTS PRODUCES QUALITY WORK AND COOPERATION

If you are concerned that trust seems to be an invitation to chaos and inappropriate behavior in class, relax. We have found that, on the contrary, students rise to our expectations. One of the early research findings during our in-class observations was that Margaret needed to call children to order more often during the periods when she was teaching formal lessons than when children were working at the learning centers where they were free to choose their own tasks. Once Margaret shifted to holistic methods of teaching reading and writing that showed the children that they were trusted to do their own work their own way, she found that both productivity and creativity blossomed. Where writing had been a matter of "doing what the teacher said," once they felt trusted to work their own way, students used their imaginations and drew on their personal experiences to write creatively and profusely. In short, trusting the learners and letting go of the need to control their every move not only improved the social climate in the classroom but enhanced both the quality and quantity of work done. The same holds true in intermediate classrooms. Teachers comment again and again how their students surprise and delight them. When they have been given the opportunity to work their own way their creativity and productivity blossom. Vicky Green's account of her students piloting *Springboards* is a prime example of this. Judy Woodward, a grade 7 teacher, says much the same thing, "I would never be able to come up with the creative ideas that the students do." Her units on building a dream house and studying ancient Greece and Rome that are described in chapter 6 show the energy and ingenuity students will invest in work that affirms their ability to make intelligent choices.

**Your leadership
style is the key
to learning
cooperatively**

In our quest for quality, what we need to strive for is students setting their own standards for quality, not just doing well on tasks the teacher assigns . . . . There is always the fear in education . . . that too great a concern with quality means that students inevitably cover less ground . . . that as quality increases, productivity declines, but the opposite occurs. *(Glasser 1990)*

Like the teachers we observed and interviewed, William Glasser in his article, "The Quality School," talks of the very real benefits that accrue when we change our styles of leadership and share responsibility. Drawing upon a management model, he speaks of the changes that came about as a result of managers who shared responsibility for production with the workers, trusted them, and were concerned with the climate in the workplace. He offers a comparison between "boss managers" and "lead managers" that can readily be applied to classroom management styles.

BECOMING A "LEAD TEACHER" BUILDS COOPERATION AND PRODUCTIVITY

Figure 2 sets two classroom management styles side by side. Boss teachers keep tight control in the classroom and focus most of their attention on the curriculum; lead teachers are concerned with the classroom learning climate and focus their attention on the needs of the learners. For the former, product is the main concern; for the latter, people are central to all decisions. Not surprisingly, productive learning flourishes best when human needs are the prime concern. The pleasure and challenge of connecting the students' own concerns and needs with the body

FIGURE 2
Using a management model to compare teaching styles

The Boss Teacher	The Lead Teacher
Decides what will be taught and how it will be learned.	Sets the framework for learning but leaves room for options.
Keeps strict control of all aspects of the classroom.	Encourages students to make choices about their learning.
Decides on the rules and how to enforce them.	Discusses reasons for rules and asks for students' input to formulate and enforce these rules.
Keeps a strong focus on the curriculum to shape lessons. Is more concerned with the *what* of learning than the *how*.	Observes learners, their needs and interests to foster learning that fulfills students' needs as well as curriculum requirements.
Tends to use the lecture format to convey information.	Models the skills to be learned and uses experiental, hands-on work.
Relies heavily on Cazden's (1988) IRE model – teacher **I**nitiation, student **R**esponse, teacher **E**valuation.	Engages students in discussions about the relevance and quality of work undertaken in class. Makes information sharing reciprocal.
Tries to have all students work on the same job at the same pace.	Offers choices that fit the work to students' interests, abilities, maturity, and experience.
Generally has students work by themselves.	Often uses teamwork and cooperative learning.
Generally is the chief information giver and initiator of jobs, themes, or projects.	Encourages students to share information and to initiate projects.
Relies on outside motivation – grades, praise – to urge students to work hard.	Relies on students' inner motivation to excel. Trusts them to work to the best of their abilities.
Sees education as serious business that needs to be shaped by a knowledgeable leader – the teacher.	Sees learning as exciting, fun, and arising from the students' own needs and curiosity, which has ŀ stimulated by interesting work.

FIGURE 2 (continued)

The Boss Teacher	The Lead Teacher
Generally feels that students must be closely supervised to ensure that they will do the work.	Trusts students to work in their own ways and at their own pace.
Relies largely on tests, worksheets, and exams to evaluate students' progress.	Uses informal observation and ongoing anecdotal records to evaluate students' progress and to enrich information derived from exams.
Generally sees record keeping and evaluation as being the teacher's job.	Has students keep many of the records and uses students' self-evaluations to augment teacher observation.
Holds the power in the classroom.	Empowers students to work freely on academic tasks while observing social rules that have been established cooperatively.
Focuses on the end product of learning.	Focuses on the process of learning.
Manages the curriculum.	Manages people.

Derived from Dr. William Glasser's article on the work of Dr. W. Edwards Deming, which dramatically changed and improved the Japanese economy. (Phi Delta Kappan *1990*)

of knowledge they are supposed to acquire add new interest to teaching. As Judy Woodward puts it:

Sometimes the assumption is that you just turn control over to the kids and that's it; but that's not it at all. If you have a kid in your class that just wants to do hockey, hockey, dinosaurs, and then more hockey, that's not good enough. Somebody has figured out that there are things an educated citizen needs, and that's fair. You have to give the students those parameters to start with. Then you can give them lots of choices and make the work really fun, flexible, and practical. If I had left it strictly up to them, my students would never have studied ancient Greece and

Rome. As it is they loved it, and because they discovered and shared the information, they learned a lot in the process. *(See chapter 6.)*

Whether dealing with questions of studying or getting along in class, the lead teacher "emphasizes that problems are not solved by coercion; they are solved by having all parties to the problem figure out a better way that is acceptable to all. If the first solution doesn't work, the problem is addressed again" (Glasser 1990). In that kind of climate, inner motivation and excitement about learning become factors that control students' work, as well as their social interactions. In chapter 3 we give examples of students participating in setting rules and solving disputes. Their input and the teachers' willingness to listen respectfully to their concerns created harmony and mutual respect rather than clashes of words and negative feelings.

If it seems hard to relinquish the controls traditionally held by teachers and to shift to a lead teacher style, then it becomes important to observe closely how students react when they are actively involved in and consulted about the work to be done. When they feel that their opinions are valued and that they are working on tasks that have importance to them, they will strive to do their best. When the teacher takes the trouble to set the framework for learning as described above, then students will recognize that learning and working hard have their own rewards, or as Glasser points out:

> What all of us – workers and students alike – do when we do high-quality work is to evaluate carefully what we are doing and come to the conclusion that it is worth working hard because it feels good. What few managers realize is that coercion prevents this necessary self-evaluation, because the workers and students spend most of their time and effort evaluating the boss instead of evaluating their work. *(Glasser 1990)*

BUT WHAT ABOUT DISCIPLINE?

Glasser confirms what we found. Students who are trusted and are given the freedom to work will take pleasure and pride in their projects. But it is important to be clear that by giving them freedom to work freely and creatively, we are not giving them license to behave in any way they choose. In other words, the cooperative, learner-centered ways of lead teaching *do not mean chaos* in social terms. The distinction is crucial because we often take an all-or-nothing attitude towards control: If we control in-class behavior, we also keep strict control over learning activities; if we relinquish control over learning, we tend to be lax in social control. But the two are separate issues. Unfortunately, they are sometimes lumped together in unproductive ways.

THE CONTRADICTION OF CONTROL

Linda McNeil (1986) speaks of the "contradiction of control" and points to the difference between *knowledge control and management control.* In the American high schools in which she made close observations, teachers and administrators attributed the boredom, frustration, and consequent acting out on the part of the students to lack of control. Students faced with having to learn uncorrelated facts that seemed to have no relevance or use became restive, sullen, and eventually rebellious. The administrators then advocated and/or instituted even more stringent controls over classroom management. Instead of fostering freedom of physical movement, teamwork, projects, and individualization through contract work, there was a reversion to lectures and whole-class assignments. McNeil comments:

After being processed through worksheets, list-filled lectures, and short-answer tests, the cultural content, regardless of whose interests it may have served before, comes to serve only the interests of institutional efficiencies.

McNeil speaks of the barrenness of in-class work compared to the lively subject-area discussions she had with the high school teachers. Ironically, when both teachers and students are bored and frustrated, the resulting tensions suggest the need for *more* control when in fact an opening of the classroom to the excitement of learning is actually what is needed.

FREEDOM TO LEARN
BUILDS RESPONSIBILITY AND SUCCESS

Again and again, intermediate teachers tell us that when the students are captivated by work that involves them personally, the "problem of control" vanishes. Freedom to learn and to take responsibility for work produces social responsibility as well as productive learning. Success in one area builds success in others as well. Talking about a student who has difficulties with concentrating, Brenda Laurie, a Learning Support Teacher at Brentwood College, comments:

Jim is an outstanding athlete, but because he has some difficulties academically, administrators felt that we should curtail his sports activities. But I disagreed with them. His successes in sports are gradually helping him to build concentration, first on the rowing machine practicing for a rowing meet, then in class doing academic work. The pleasure and successes he gets from his sports are essential to his overall progress.

Lead parenting is a good model for success

The question becomes how to meet the dual need of giving students freedom to learn and maintaining discipline in the classroom. Once again parenting offers a solid answer. Diana Baumrind's 1983 studies of parenting patterns identified ways of parenting that give freedom and support to children but leave the parent in a solid leadership role that is neither overly bossy nor overly indulgent.

At first glance some of the parenting patterns of lead parents shown on figure 3 may seem contradictory. How can you encourage independence and individuality when you also set definite rules? How can you model assertive behavior and at the same time provide loving support? How can you trust children to perform when you set high standards? The answers to these challenges lies in maintaining open communication and having a genuine give and take in discussions. Children who are listened to and who know that their points of view will be heard and seriously considered will accept their parents' authority. Children need and respect order and require definite guidelines. The ambiguity and uncertainty that often characterize the behavior of indulgent parents – often parents with the best of intentions – create doubts and uneasiness.

DEMANDING MATURE BEHAVIOR IS A WAY OF AFFIRMING THAT CHILDREN ARE GROWING UP

Setting high standards of mature behavior, far from thwarting children's independence, allows them to "be like the big guys." At the same time, lead parents do not try to curtail children's natural playfulness, instead they provide guidelines that make that playfulness safe and enjoyable. Mature behavior implies consideration for others, the acknowledgment that adults and children alike have rights and responsibilities. Regard for others and their needs develops attitudes of caring and self-control.

The independence and confidence that grow from clearly defined outer rules – both at home and in school – and emerging inner control become the solid foundation on which children

FIGURE 3

Lead Parenting	Usual Effects on Children's Behavior
Lead Parents	*Children of Lead Parents*
Are loving and supportive of children's goals.	Strive to succeed and are achievement oriented.
Maintain open communication, listen to children's points of view, encourage verbal give-and-take.	Are willing to speak up, state their points of view, and discuss them.
Encourage children's independence and individuality.	Act with independence and confidence.
Establish definite rules and enforce them consistently.	Are well socialized and aware of others' needs.
Set clear standards for mature behavior and expect compliance with those standards.	Show responsibility, self-control, and self-reliant behavior. Accept standards of behavior and strive to meet them.
Model consistent, assertive behavior.	Become self-assertive and confident.
Demonstrate caring and concern about children.	Are outgoing and friendly.
Set high standards of performance – have high expectations and trust children to meet them.	Have high aspirations and persistence in pursuing goals. Are willing to take risks in learning.

Based on the work of Diana Baumrind 1983 (see Bibliography)

build new learning. They are willing to explore, venture forth, keep trying, and look for ever-expanding horizons. Parents' and teachers' firmness and assertiveness become models for children to build their own assertiveness. Since rules are not laid down as edicts from on high without discussion or recourse, children are not daunted or made rebellious as they might be under overly authoritarian parents or teachers. Because there are discussions – at times stormy – there are no pent-up feelings of anger to give mixed messages, nor is there occasion to build resentment about commands to "be quiet and do as you are told." Such commands have no place in a leadership climate. Instead, the firmness of leadership becomes internalized imperceptibly as children model themselves after their parents and teachers and build their own confidence.

Seen in this light, there is no contradiction between setting and enforcing rules of mature behavior and fostering independence and high standards. When communication is open, rules become a mutual concern and a solid framework for self-reliant behavior.

Here comes trouble! – or . . . ?

Watching students lead their peers into all the wrong behaviors can be a real challenge, as Early Childhood Consultant Elaine Zakreski found in her in-class work in her district. Though Elaine's story of Colin deals with a grade 3 student leader, its message is ageless:

Last year I worked at a school to help implement an integrated primary. Children from K to year 3 were assigned to groups with a year 3 student leader. It was my job to work with the group leaders and to observe them. Their first task was to create a group story based on a familiar story pattern. Colin's group was having a wonderful time – doing everything *but* the assigned task and not doing anything quietly. 'Oh, great,' I thought, 'this is all I need to confirm to anyone who happens to drop by that consultants create more problems than they solve.' I struggled to keep my mouth shut and myself from taking control, which could have further confirmed that consultants not only create problems but then do nothing to solve them.

At the end of the assigned time I mentioned to Colin that I needed his evaluation of his group's performance. He looked a little shocked but stayed there to face me. I then asked him, 'How do you rate your group's performance on a scale from one to ten – one being the lowest and ten the highest?' 'One,' he said without the slightest hesitation. 'And how do you rate yourself as a group leader?' I asked. 'One,' he replied.

'Interesting, isn't it, that you and your group have the same rating. Why do you think that is so?' I asked. 'Oh, I was acting like a jerk and they all did what I did.' 'So you're a pretty strong leader. What do you think will happen tomorrow?' 'Oh, we'll do a lot better,' he said, and indeed they did.

Colin became our strongest and most effective leader. His teacher could hardly believe the change in him. He was a new kind of kid, happy and full of confidence. His attention-getting, off-task classroom behavior disappeared.

When I interviewed him about his experience as a leader, he said, 'You know, Mrs. Zakreski, I really didn't know how to act to get kids to like me before; now I do.' When I asked him how he would feel when someone else was chosen to be the leader, he replied, 'Good, 'cause maybe he'll learn as much as me!'

Standing back, being non-judgmental, giving the student the chance to self-evaluate and then self-correct are key factors in this success story. But central to it is the acknowledgment of strength and leadership qualities in a student who was, for the moment, creating havoc. Seeing beyond the immediate behavior and its negative effects is a wonderful skill, and one that is well worth cultivating. It has its foundation in trust in the learners and is a powerful tool for making learning safe, not only for all the Colins but for all the other learners in your class.

How does all this look in a *real* classroom?

When observing in both primary and intermediate classrooms we have found time and again that lead teaching produces not only a climate of mutual respect but enthusiasm for learning and exploration. Margaret certainly will not countenance destructive or unruly behavior, yet her classroom is filled with the joy and excitement of exploring, learning, and achieving.

Marne's ready laughter and feel for music and art make her classroom a lively, stimulating place, yet she is adamant about mature, responsible behavior. While students are free to gaze into space when collecting thoughts for writing or to talk freely while working on group projects, Marne demands their undivided attention and complete quiet during mini-lessons or lectures. She models attending behavior when working with students in conferences or similar situations that demand her full attention, and during writer's workshop she enforces the rules for being quiet with adults and students alike. No one is in doubt about what is and what is not acceptable behavior in her classroom. Within that framework of well-established, reasonable rules, learning flourishes and students evolve not only academic knowledge but social skills and aesthetic appreciation. They are self-confident and willing to speak up. Above all, they are excited about learning and growing.

In Sylvia's class, students participate in generating and enforcing rules. After a regrettable lapse in classroom deportment, Sylvia told them in no uncertain terms about her disappointment and disapproval of such uncaring, irresponsible behavior. She then invited the class to discuss the need for courteous, responsible behavior, and together they generated a list of items that would help to build trust and respect. (See page 68.) Building upon those self-generated rules, students in her class enjoy the freedom to work on projects, to choose how to group their activities – such as doing math once every day or in one or two blocks – and to interact with their peers. Sylvia's enthusiasm and readiness to adjust her plans to fit the moment make for an easy flow, and projects get done with a depth of involvement that is rarely evident in classrooms run along more structured, teacher-directed lines. Her willingness to negotiate with students about marks (see page 298) is a perfect example of her genuine openness to two-way communication and consistent firmness in the face of persistent cajoling. Making certain that the personal hurts of individual students are addressed (see page 69) leaves no doubt in students' minds about their teacher's caring for each and every one of them.

LEAD TEACHING PRODUCES TANGIBLE BENEFITS

Liz's class and those of other teachers we have collaborated with have shown the same positive effects of lead teaching. Students develop both independence and self-confidence when they are working in a climate where rules are arrived at democratically and enforced consistently. In the supportive, caring environment they feel safe and are willing to venture into new territory. Because their teacher trusts them to do well and is firm in the belief that they can achieve, students set high goals and persist in moving toward them. Like the teacher, they are friendly and outgoing. The open communication and verbal give-and-take make for co-creative teaching that fosters a climate of delight.

Making it safe to venture forth into new learning

Learning can be fraught with doubts and fears. If students have been accustomed to a classroom management style that has focused attention on their errors, then your efforts to remove the fear from learning will bring noticeable benefits. If you remember your own anxieties over doing well, passing exams, and doing assignments correctly, you will understand that making learning safe for students is an important part of creating a positive learning climate.

A FOCUS ON STRENGTHS MAKES LEARNING SAFE

Looking for progress – "steps forward" – is an integral part of whole-language teaching. Whenever you observe your students' classroom behaviors, keep track of their reading, or look at their writing, what you are looking for are steps forward. Making students aware early in the year that looking for these steps foward will be your central focus will help them relax and get on with their work. There is far less likelihood of students coming up against blocks and blank-outs when they know that errors are natural parts of drafts – not black marks against them.

WHEN ERRORS BECOME STEPPING STONES LEARNING EVOLVES

With the focus on progress and gradual development, students will find that errors often lead to more insightful learning. In the classroom we speak of standard spelling versus non-standard spelling to avoid the dichotomy of right-wrong, and as a result students learn that thinking about their non-standard spelling in analytic ways helps to move them toward greater accuracy. Recognizing that there are a number of spellings for *there,* and trying to figure out which is which, create awareness and memory of the correct usage far more than correction marks on a spelling test.

Going over students' drafts with them in your conferences will reveal gaps and false starts in non-threatening ways and will lead to more effective composing. Seeing math as a way of exploring numbers and their relationships, and trying to figure out *why* that answer was not the one that was expected may lead to understanding how to approach that particular type of problem. As long as errors are little more than red marks to be hidden in desks and feared at report-card time, the relaxed explorations of *why* something did or did not work have little chance of emerging. But once students realize that "errors" or false starts merely offer the opportunity to stand back to examine what happened and to decide what to do next, then they will feel safe to tackle whatever new work comes their way.

HAVING CHOICES EASES TENSIONS

Choice and voluntary participation are two effective ways of making learning safe. Even if you have set the topic – studying Japan, working on a display for the year 2000, reading a novel – you can leave the what and how of working on the topic wide open. If students know that they can select those parts of a project that interest them most, they will eagerly choose their jobs. If they have choices in partners and in modes of demonstrating their knowledge, they are free to draw upon their best learning style. You simply stand back and observe as students find their niche in the overall project. If you remember the agonies you suffered when you were required to work on jobs you found incompatible with your learning style and then had to face being graded on that work, you will understand why the freedom of choice opens new possibilities for your students. Because they are not obliged to do so, they will quite often try their hands at ways of work that they have shunned in the past.

VOLUNTARY PARTICIPATION BRINGS FORTH VOLUNTEERS

Just as freedom of choice in the jobs they do has beneficial effects on students' work, so does voluntary participation. Creating situations in which students have options leads to their independence and enhances, rather than reduces, willingness to come forth and participate. Students who know they are free to pass when called on to share their writing, to make a statement in a discussion, or to participate in a given project lose their shyness and will speak up when they want to make a point or share their work. Giving options to pass is not a matter of telling them, "You don't have to do this," but rather one of conveying the message, "I won't put you on the spot. You have a right to your privacy." At times a bit of reverse psychology helps those who would like to take voluntary participation to its extreme.

Reminiscing about her grade 4 class in Armstrong, B.C., Vicki Green tells of having a new student come to her class and announce, "I don't do any work!" Instead of arguing or cajoling, Vicki immediately replied, "Oh, great, then I won't have to do any work at home for you." Somewhat puzzled the boy asked, "Do you mean you take that stuff home to work on?" "You bet," Vicki replied. "Every night I spend some time on each student's writing. But now, when I come to yours, I won't have to do a thing. I can just sit back and have a cup of coffee." "Not tonight, you won't," he shot back. "Tonight you'll have to look at a whole lot of pages in my book." And so she did!

COURTESY MAKES FOR SAFETY

Responding to students in adult ways and observing the same rules of courtesy that you would accord an adult open the way to genuine give-and-take in discussions and sharing. Looking at videotapes of our early in-class observations revealed many instances when teachers were unnecessarily rude to students. We observed lots of non-listening behavior in which teachers laid down rules or lectured but failed to listen attentively to students' input or points of view. There was often impatience or insufficient time for students to formulate and state their answers. At times, we found abruptness in the teachers' ways of talking. In short, there were many ways of interacting with students that failed to follow the rules people usually observe with adults.

So one way of making the classroom safe for learning is to consciously apply the courtesies that you would accord your adult peers. We have found that tensions and anxieties ease when the tone in the classroom is one of courteous give-and-take. When students know that neither you nor anyone else in class will make disparaging remarks about their work, creativity has a chance to blossom. Patience and a matter-of-fact tone of voice will help a lot. Students are sharp listeners and will hear accusing undertones no matter what the teacher's words may be. So the important thing is to develop an inner attitude in which you acknowledge that all your students want to do well and are young people whose feelings matter. When your interactions with them reflect that inner attitude, they, too, will show consideration for others. Of course there will be lapses, and it may take time to establish these habits of courtesy in your students, but in the meantime, if you model attentive listening (complete with eye contact) and discuss their drafts and projects the same way you would discuss work with an adult, your students will follow your example.

FOLLOWING A MODEL IS A SAFE WAY TO LEARN

Providing students with a model of the behaviors you would like to instill works well not only in social interactions but also in demonstrating learning behaviors. When we began our work we noticed that teachers rarely modeled enquiry behavior in class.

There were lots of questions directed at students, but they were really pseudo-questions or tests. The teachers already knew the answers. In fact they were testing to see if the students could come up with the desired answers. Under that kind of questioning "wrong answers" often create uneasy feelings and students get little practice engaging in true enquiry.

Shifting to whole-language ways of teaching opens the door to modeling learning behaviors and genuine inquiry. As you join students in seeking answers to questions that arise from classroom work, you will be modeling ways of finding information, raising additional questions, musing aloud about possible answers, seeking alternative answers, looking at the probability of something working. Since your information seeking is genuine, it will not arouse anxiety or uncertainty but will spark the students' interest. You and your students are co-learners, and they will build on the modeling you do.

If you encourage group work and cooperation in the completion of projects, students will also have the opportunity to observe their peers' approach to class work. Often students who have trouble following oral directions will find it easier and less threatening to model their work after that of a classmate. In nongraded classes peer modeling becomes particularly effective as younger students look to their older peers as models. But even in regular one-grade classes, following the lead of a more experienced classmate becomes a safe way to try new or difficult work. There is also the fun of sharing and comparing, and copying is not simply a case of plagiarizing another student's work. Following the leader leaves lots of room for individual variations-on-a-theme, and students feel free to build on what has worked for their peers. When the classroom climate encourages cooperation, students feel free to explore not only their knowledge but their feelings as well.

Feelings are important to the learning climate

When discussing subject-area learning, there are often remarks about the need for retaining objectivity: "Facts should not be cluttered up with opinions or feelings; researchers need to be objective if their work is to be accepted." The trouble with that attitude is that it strips work of the passion that comes out of genuine enquiry. Researchers who are dedicated to their work are passionately involved in their search for knowledge. Why would they spend hour after hour in a laboratory or the library if the answers were of little interest or consequence to them?

In the commendable effort to do rigorous work and not to let our findings be clouded by our sentiments, we sometimes bend too far backward to strip factual enquiry of its emotional content. Being interested, curious, excited, perplexed, delighted, bemused are all feelings that form natural parts of learning. In fact, they are the steam that drives enquiry. If we want students to become lifelong learners who are passionately involved in searching out answers to questions that face them, then we need to ensure that the learning in our classrooms is invested with feeling. We have to find ways to connect learning to students' own interests and lives, show our own enthusiasm for learning, invest new learning with mystery and excitement, and make sure that students understand that the learning has relevance to their own lives.

PERSONAL FEELINGS NEED TO BE ACKNOWLEDGED

Just as feelings about the work in class are important factors in learning, so too are the personal feelings of students about their interactions with classmates, with their teacher, and at home. The years leading up to adolescence can be stormy. Uncertainties, strange new feelings, and new ways of interacting are all part of the process of physical maturation. The boy-girl attractions that emerge between students may take the form of new feelings for male or female teachers. If learning is to proceed, then we cannot ignore these feelings or pretend they are of little importance. Just as we as adults have difficulty functioning effectively when powerful emotions are stirring within us, so students experience difficulty in focusing on their learning.

This is not to suggest that all students are beset by strong emotional upheavals, or that we should focus undue attention upon feelings. But ignoring personal feelings does not make them go away. If ignored, undercurrents of unrest, resentment, and anger will pervade the classroom and disrupt learning. If you adopt the stance of a lead teacher who is willing to have open give-and-take in class, then students' feelings and uncertainties can become powerful lessons in effective communication and mutual trust. The important thing is to acknowledge that you notice and respect students' feelings. Using the counselor's approach of reflecting back to students what you perceive leaves them the option to deny or acknowledge what you say, but also shows them that you care. "I sense that you are frustrated [angry, sad, worried]" leaves the door open to the student to confirm, deny, or to elaborate on the feeling.

WORKING WITH FEELINGS CAN BE PRODUCTIVE

As students learn that you will acknowledge their feelings and admit that they have a right to them, they will become more open and willing to voice their feelings. At the early stages you may need to help them to explore just what it *is* they feel, because they may only be aware of a vague feeling of discomfort or uneasiness. Encouraging them to write about their feelings, to express them in journals or poetry, to act them out in drama, or to explore them through reading books and stories on the topics that trouble them, can be very releasing. Aside from their own problems, students often face difficulties at home – divorce, violence, drinking, drug abuse, the loneliness of coming home to an empty house each day.

Acknowledging feelings does not mean that you will encourage or allow violent outbursts or destructive behavior. In chapter 3 we discuss conflict resolution and ways of turning misbehaviors into learning experiences. You can go a step further and help students explore the origins and patterns of their strong feelings. Faced with a hostile, disturbed little girl in her class, Margaret had to deal with periodic violent temper tantrums. Margaret dealt with them by staying very calm and quiet, telling the child that she understood she was upset, but at the same time restraining her from being either destructive to property or hurtful to others. Allowing the child time to cool down a bit helped. Margaret did not match screaming with screaming but instead used a composed, firm voice. After each outburst she would chart the onset and course of the storm in her notebook. She described what the child did, what preceded the tantrum, and how long it lasted, and then she discussed the outburst with the child to see if they could detect some pattern.

With more mature students the possibilities for dealing with tempers are much broader. Quiet discussions about the possible causes of the angry outbreaks, charting or graphing outbursts, their intensity and duration, and behavior patterns could reveal a lot. This could be the same kind of productive work that Trevor, South Park's principal, undertook when asking a troublesome student to develop a list of ways to interact positively. (See page 67.) Students may not even be aware of underlying causes of their outbreaks of anger, and if they are encouraged to explore and then voice them, a lot of pressure will be released, often to the point that the outbursts cease. Such an approach to strong feelings can lead to students' self-awarness, social responsibility, and feelings of being taken seriously.

The students who act out will benefit, and the overall classroom climate will improve. Strong feelings – even when unspoken – can be almost tangible in a group of students. If these feelings are freely expressed in appropriate ways, and both students and teachers learn to respect each other's feelings, than the hidden agendas and undercurrents of distraction will be minimized. Hanne MacKay, a grade 4–5 teacher at M. V. Beattie Elementary School in Salmon Arm, B.C., goes so far as to have a daily class meeting that gives everyone a chance to voice personal concerns. She finds that having such a public forum not only allows those with problems or concerns to voice and explore them, but also teaches caring ways of listening, acknowledging feelings, and helping the troubled student. By allowing time to air personal concerns, students find that they are not alone in facing problems. Those with similar ones may also have suggestions or personal support to offer. From that personal support, buddy work and solid learning emerge.

TEACHERS, TOO, HAVE FEELINGS

Acknowledging and sharing feelings in class are not limited to the students. While it is important to work at being calm and centered when teaching, denying feelings is as distracting for teachers as it is for students – and just as destructive. Students read their teacher like a book. A smile pasted over feelings of anger or frustration will come across as a mixed message, or worse still, as hypocrisy. Students need to trust their teacher if their learning is to be free and open. Though it may seem counterproductive to share your feelings of worry, sadness, and anger as well as more positive feelings of happiness and excitement, the expression of genuine feelings nevertheless serves as a model of openness and clears the way for learning. Rather than respecting their teacher less for showing genuine emotions, students will value the teacher more. And the students often will become more considerate in the bargain. When feelings are accepted and welcomed as natural parts of classroom communication, spontaneity, curiosity, and creativity are free to blossom.

LEARNERS NEED TO KNOW THAT
WHAT THEY LEARN HAS RELEVANCE TO THEIR LIVES

One of the maxims of adult education is that materials taught must have relevance to the learners and must be directly usable in the learners' lives. It has long been our conviction that the only reason for making this a maxim of adult education is that, unlike elementary school students, adults are not a captive audience. Adults who perceive lessons to be boring and useless are free to leave – and frequently do so! If we look at the statistics for school drop-outs, particularly for those of minority groups who relate to the standard curriculum even less than the rest of the students, then we have to acknowledge that young learners, too, need to know that the learning they do has relevance to their lives. The suggestion is not that we should abandon our responsibility to teach students the basics they need and that are incorporated in the curriculum. But we find that when teachers go to the trouble of building upon student interests and creating frameworks that show the relevance of this new learning, students become engaged in ways that assure that they *retain* what they learn beyond the weekly quiz – because what they learn has meaning.

To be concrete about linking learning to students' lives, we describe a number of projects that have captured their interest – and that have produced a surprising depth of learning. Literature that pleases and intrigues students can be an introduction to the study of history, geography, and human relations. Field trips, both in town and further afield, can link environmental concerns to the students' own living space. Delegating real jobs teaches more about responsible collaboration than any simulation or textbook. Looking at exercise and nutrition in light of the students' own current needs – skin problems, fatigue, growth – makes the study of health and human physiology both personal and useful. Instead of looking at problems of modern society in the abstract, look at problems facing students and their families right now.

Physical involvement is essential to learning

When we wrote about primary students in *The Learners' Way* we stressed the importance of physical movement to full development, not only of the body but of the brain as well. Brain research has demonstrated that active physical manipulation and involvement of all the senses are both essential to the stimulation of full growth of the brain. That same research also points to the fact that active involvement continues to create new white (glial) cells in the brain. Growth does not stop. So even though students at the intermediate level are more mature, they still need physical movement to allow them to develop fully.

If you think of your own intellectual functioning, you will be aware that simply sitting still in front of a book, a piece of paper, or a computer can go on for only so long. At a given point the brain shuts down and gives the signal, "I am saturated. I need something quite different to give me time to program what you have been feeding in." The wise person stops at that moment, takes a walk around the block, goes into the cafeteria for a chat with colleagues, or retires to the garden to commune with the soil. The need to regroup may take no more than a few minutes, or may require half an hour or more. But almost invariably, a break and shift to physical activity exerts beneficial influence on the completion of the intellectual task at hand.

Students in elementary school are no different; in fact, they probably need physical movement even more than we adults do to stimulate their learning fully. It may seem desirable to fill their every moment with useful, productive table work. But their brains, like ours, will give the shut-down signal, and at that point any further intake is either blocked altogether or slowed down to an agonizing pace. So it makes good sense to allow students to move about in class, to sit or lie on the floor while reading or writing, to work at the chalkboard, or to do some drawing during writer's workshop. In addition, it helps to intersperse table work with more active ways of studying – building things, movement games, drama, physical education, clean-up work around the classroom, a brief walk around the block, anything that adds physical movement to intellectual work.

If your students are restive and you perceive that they come in charged with more nervous energy than the classroom can contain, you can begin the day with a run or an active game. But remember that quiet exercise, deep breathing, or slow-motion bending and stretching can also have wonderful effects, especially when done to music and when students are free to improvise. Good feelings and a sense of freedom and choice and fun are key factors in interjecting physical movement and reaping its full benefits. As in other areas of learning, flexibility is key. Observing students as they work will tell you when they need to move and when they are so absorbed in their work that you need to extend their reading or writing time.

The climate of delight is marked by co-creative teaching/learning

When teaching the learners' way both you and your students have freedom of movement, freedom of choice, freedom of expression, and freedom to work in individual ways. The commitment to learning is based upon the mutuality of learning. Neither you nor the students are ever quite sure what the day may hold – interesting books brought in by students, a new discovery in a project or experiment, a shift to capture a teachable moment. The boredom and stress of working through prescribed textbooks page by page give way to the delight of exploring new learning together. The climate of delight is marked by co-creative teaching/learning that is productive for teacher and student alike.

CLASSROOM MANAGEMENT – THE SHAPE OF THE DAY

3

WHOLE-LANGUAGE CLASSROOMS are fairly bubbling with excitement and activities, and there is no saying in advance what the day is going to bring. Yes, there are the blocks of time allocated to writer's workshop and reader's workshop, but there are always new interests that add extra life and variety to these sessions. We will be describing some typical days, but in general terms only. Since flexibility of planning and freedom of choice are two key aspects of classroom management, those plans are subject to change at a moment's notice. Projects that students find absorbing may prove to be more time-consuming than expected, or teachable moments may suggest a shift in direction. Since students make their input into the planning, and teachers listen to requests for change, there is a fluidity of planning that occasionally even transcends the recess bell. If important work is in progress or students are absorbed in finishing a task, the teacher may decide to postpone recess until a later time. (At South Park School such flexibility is workable as the venerable old brick structure affords maximum sound insulation, and extra stairways allow quiet entries that do not disrupt other classes.) While such flexibility seems to ignore the demands of good organization, it gives a strong message to students that the work they do is important and that their needs are paramount. As a result, responsible behavior and on-task work habits flourish.

Fitting activities to the needs of the students

Fitting classroom management to the needs of the students means making room for the wide range of interests and abilities they bring to their studies, whether they attend regular classes or the combination classes that are becoming more prevalent as many schools make the move toward the non-graded elementary. In chapter 7 we give more specific examples of working with family groupings in combination classes, but any teacher – whether working with one grade or a combination class – needs to accommodate not only different levels of performance but also different learning styles.

Using a wide variety of teaching/learning methods assures that all students have the opportunity to work in the mode that suits them best. Presenting material to the whole group – talking, showing pictures, demonstrating – works well for children who are used to listening to careful directions and explanations at home. But for most students, even at the intermediate level, having skills and behaviors modeled produces more learning. If the teacher models expressive reading, thinks aloud for students, or demonstrates how he or she would go about finding the spelling of a difficult word, students will pick up on the example and try to emulate his or her ways.

Peer modeling and small-group interactions augment the teacher's work. Hanne MacKay describes how her grade 4–5 class mathematics sessions begin with a brief introduction of the concept to be learned – place value, adding strings of numbers. Next, Hanne asks the students to work out the problems with concrete materials, such as Dienes blocks. At that point, the students get on the floor with large sheets of paper and crayons, and after working with the blocks get into groups of two or three to talk over what they have learned. Some students will have the lesson down pat, others may be quite at sea, but the interaction between peers, the hands-on manipulation, and the large-scale drawing/writing help those who could not follow the teacher's presentation in the abstract. Watching their more mature buddies and having them explain what it is they are doing will generally move most students to an understanding. Closing the lesson with a written representation of the problem helps to draw the concrete, interactive work into the symbolic world of mathematics.

Talking to each other, manipulating materials, drawing, comparing notes, watching the teacher, trying out various ways of arriving at answers all combine to make for understanding. A time factor is also involved in this kind of approach to teaching/learning, one that makes ample extra time available for those students who find it difficult to grasp one-time instructions or to listen in a large group.

As Marne puts it:

Some children – often those who are not very verbal – have trouble processing material that is presented or discussed when they are in a large group. They don't seem to have as much trouble with small groups where the options are simpler. These students just fade away in a big classroom. They simply check out. They are the ones who need the small-group interactions and the one-to-one work with their buddies or the teacher.

The important thing to realize is that this failure to absorb information in large-group settings is not a matter of lack of intelligence but one of personality or background. Several of the quiet students in Marne's class developed excellent creative writing skills and became quite vocal when they discussed their work in one-to-one settings. For them it was important to individualize their learning.

Make your classroom an active hands-on workplace

Recent brain research has confirmed what teachers have always known, that learning by doing works best. To be more specific, research provides neurologic evidence that appropriate physical activity enhances mental development as well as overall well-being. We have observed the concentration and joy of students doing hands-on work. Here are some examples of the kinds of activities that students respond to well. (By observing your own students you will quickly expand on this list.)

Provide or build mechanical equipment
- Old appliance motors to disassemble
- Crystal radio sets, burglar alarms, door bells to assemble
- Old typewriters, calculators, cash registers, adding machines to use
- Meccano and/or Lego sets
- Computers – large and small
- If you have the space, an old car to disassemble
- Video cameras or regular cameras on loan for special events

Encourage crafts
- Carving, whittling
- Sculpting and clay modeling
- Knitting, sewing, crocheting
- Painting with oils, pastels, acrylics

Invite students to handle projects independently. For example, have them set up their own art show
- Display works
- Do their own bookbinding or picture framing
- Set up a "frame-it" shop
- Offer art for sale
- Keep account books on the value of items on hand, expenses, income . . .
- Produce a catalog
- Set up a haunted house at Hallowe'en and sell tickets to rest of school

Make students responsible for the care of animals and plants in the classroom
- Hamsters, birds, turtles . . .
- Aquarium
- Terrarium
- Ant farm
- Flowering plants
- Chicks that hatch in the classroom

Do math for real purposes
- Play cards (cribbage is great for math)
- Add scores
- Deal with money
- Do measurements and layout for construction of playground or building of models

READER'S AND WRITER'S WORKSHOPS MAKE FOR PRODUCTIVITY

For both reading and writing, the workshop approach creates a wonderful climate for on-task learning. Setting aside large blocks of time – an hour or more each day – gives students the opportunity to become immersed in their reading or writing. Since they are given a wide range of choices in their reading materials and the topics about which they write, there is no problem with attention spans. In fact, loud protests often greet the occasional announcement that workshop time needs to be curtailed that day.

The fact that students are free to move out of their seats during workshop times enhances the relaxed atmosphere that makes for ease of learning. Rules of courtesy keep noise levels

down, but here, as at other times, communication with others
becomes an important part of teaching/learning. Reader's workshop includes written dialogue with the teacher by way of
"reading response journals," and it also makes room for sharing
at the end of the day when students talk about particularly
enjoyable or exciting books they have been reading. As a result,
students are often influenced to pick up the book described,
without any input from the teacher. In writer's workshop, peer
conferences are part of the ongoing work, and the specially
designated corners for quiet consultation are rarely empty.

PROJECTS INTEGRATE LEARNING

Projects that draw together reading, writing, artwork, crafts, and
research in the pursuit of some special topic are ideal for giving
students of varying maturity and interests the opportunity to
participate fully at levels that are comfortable and appropriate
for them. Students become totally engrossed and the classroom
is abuzz with activity as they make masks as part of the study of
Thailand, create dioramas of the "environmentally safe home,"
study Canadian literature as a way of learning Canadian geography, or participate in a field trip that points to the pollution
created on beaches by storm sewers.

The choice of specific topics for reading/writing, artwork to
be incorporated, and the extent of the project are governed by
individual students' interests and maturity. Acknowledging
their contributions to a group project includes appreciation of
students' artwork, personal knowledge, or academic research –
in equal measure. Quite often the artistic work falls to the less
verbal partners, whose work is given as much appreciation as
the work of the writers. The level of involvement also varies with
personal inclination. In the case of the special field trip to view
the pollution created by storm sewer outlets, James continued
to ponder the problem of heavy-metal pollution for the rest of
the year and was busy thinking of improved designs for car
engines that would prevent such pollution in the future.

Work connected with projects not only makes for such
personal commitment, but also provides practice in research.
Finding sources in the library, looking things up in reference
works, and pulling together information in organized ways are
effective when students work in teams. Gaining interviewing
skills, listening to the news, involving parents in projects, and
learning about current events are some of the important side
effects of project work. Students become aware of the processes
involved in information gathering and become ever more independent in their learning.

DISCUSSIONS BUILD BOTH
CONFIDENCE AND SKILLS

Projects and research demand discussion, and group interaction again becomes a key factor in learning. Whether the teacher leads the discussion or small groups of students work as teams, successful interaction has to be guided by the rules of courtesy described in chapter 2 under the heading "Making Learning Safe." Rejecting remarks or opinions out of hand – whether by teacher or fellow students – quickly stops genuine discussion and, depending on students' temperaments, leads to hurt, sullen silence, or angry arguments. Discussions that acknowledge all input, and then weigh its accuracy and/or importance in relationship to a particular issue, show students that their thoughts and research efforts are valued and lead them to thoughtful ways of evaluating information and opinions.

Quite often we find that students whose writing is less than fluent have valuable information to contribute to discussions about concrete issues. Often they are interested in nature, in sports, in the work their parents are doing, or in a particular issue that has been widely discussed at home. Making sure that these students are heard during discussions adds depth to the information and shows them that they are valued.

Along with idea sifting, discussions are invaluable in teaching problem solving and careful listening. Marne's description of her "debriefing" session after "buddy time" provides solid evidence that time spent on discussions can teach lessons more valuable than any "facts" listed on curriculum guides. Here she is talking about the regularly scheduled visit of her grade 5–6 students to Margaret's K–1–2 class and the problems encountered by her own student, Alexis, when trying to relate to her young buddy, Michaela:

We'd take the big buddies down to meet the little ones, then when the big kids came back into our classroom, we'd debrief. Going right down the class list I'd ask, 'How did it go for you?' They'd listen to each other, and they could relate to the problems, because some of the little ones are regular tyrants. Poor Alexis really had to struggle to stay in there with little Michaela. (Michaela knows what she wants and goes for it.) But it really helped Alexis to talk about it. The class speculated about why the little ones did what they did. That led to, 'Does anyone have any ideas for Alexis to help her deal with Michaela's bossiness?' So the discussion became a wonderful opportunity to talk about 'getting along.' As a result, the older kids really got close to their younger buddies, and they became aware *why* these children might do what they did. In a sense, once they articulated the problems, they were much more understanding. The older kids *loved* going down to Marg's class. It did wonderful things for them – their learning, their self-concept, and all those social skills.

At times visitors to South Park School have questioned the amount of time spent on lengthy discussions – particularly in the intermediate grades when there is so much "material" to be covered. But by observing learners closely we have come to the conclusion that the mental explorations and soul searchings that go on when students are free to voice their feelings, thoughts, and opinions make for some of the most important learning of all. They affirm that students have both inner and outer resources to draw upon whenever they need to find answers. That knowledge and confidence in their own ability to approach all kinds of questions and problems becomes the core of any learning they will do as they move along.

Involving students and keeping lines of communication open may be time-consuming, but an atmosphere is created in which problems become something to be solved jointly, hence more

Resolving conflicts – maintaining discipline

Marne's grade 5–6 students give their young buddies in Margaret's K–1–2 class their undivided attention.

How to make room for fun and play

Few will question that young children learn through play, but we find that play does wonders for older students as well. They relax, explore, learn, and have fun. No doubt you know lots of games that your students will enjoy, but here are some general suggestions to bring play into your classroom as yet another way to enhance your students well-being and learning.

- Have a dress-up box full of all kinds of clothes. Call it your "drama box" or "costume box" and watch students use the clothing as inspiration for new plays.
- Provide a make-up kit for plays and games.
- Have a good supply of Lego blocks for building models of items/houses that students have designed.
- Suggest that students design a playground for younger children.
- Have regular "buddy time" when your students play with the "little ones" in ways that would not "be cool" on their own – using the sand table, the water tank, working at the train center.
- Invite students to build a doll house for their young buddies – choosing decor, colors, and layout; weaving doormats; connecting electric bells to batteries; creating items for the kitchen out of plasticine.
- Extend their drama work to include costume and set design and creative movement.

solidly than when settled by edicts handed down from on high. Modeling cooperative behaviors and calmly but firmly setting down rules go a long way toward establishing mature behaviors. In chapter 2 we talk about the benefits of taking the stance of a "lead teacher" as against a "boss teacher" and about the "contra-diction of control" in which boredom with learning materials is misinterpreted as a discipline problem. Here we want to offer some specific examples of positive and successful ways of dealing with conflicts and maintaining discipline.

STUDENT INPUT MAKES RULES MEANINGFUL

Just as academic work that asks for student opinions and feelings makes for more solid learning, so asking for student input in setting rules results in more willing compliance and thoughtful behavior. At South Park, the principal, as well as the teachers, practiced student involvement at all levels. Faced with a particularly violent outburst on the part of a student, Trevor Calkins decided that some solitude and careful thought were needed to ease those violent feelings into more socially acceptable channels. After some discussion with the student, he informed her that an in-school detention was called for to give her time to develop some thoughts on how to settle disputes in a more reasonable way. He then supplied her with pen and paper and told her that he was really interested in seeing what she could come up with.

Instead of simply making the detention a punitive measure that would likely exacerbate the violent behavior, Trevor turned it into a highly productive reflecting/writing session. He then proved the sincerity of his interest by publishing the result in the *South Park Newsletter,* which goes out to all parents and staff. Here is what appeared under the heading "Principal's Report":

This week Laurain, Karen, Marie, and I had occasion to discuss ways of disagreeing while still respecting the other person. Laurain produced this marvelous list. If you would like to have a poster of this list, please bring in $1.00 and we will produce you one on the Macintosh.

How to disagree in an agreeable way

1. Understand both sides of the story.
2. Try to get your point across without being disrespectful.
3. Don't always argue against the other person's side.
4. Try to respect the other person's feelings.
5. Don't assume your side is the only one that is correct.
6. Give the other person your full attention (eye contact).
7. State your side without putting the other person down.
8. Try not to let the situation get out of hand by making the other person angry or upset.
9. If you get too mad, ask for "time out" to get control of your emotions.
10. If the person says, "That made me angry," instead of saying, "Oh, that's stupid," say, "I understand how that makes you feel."

The same newsletter contained a note by Sylvia about her grade 6–7 class:

We are now operating on a system of privileges and responsible behavior. The latter includes working on task, working quietly, producing quality work, cleaning up, and showing respect for people and property. Privileges include eating, wearing hats, chewing gum, working outside, and listening to Walkmans or the stereo. We are expecting to enjoy our last weeks at South Park while maintaining a strong work ethic.

Like Laurain's list, Sylvia's enumeration of responsibilities and privileges was the outcome of discussion and student input. If privileges like chewing gum in class and wearing hats seemed an invitation to disrespect, the attendant responsibilities kept work in class on a even keel and ended the year with good feelings for both teacher and students.

Earlier in the year the class had brainstormed a list of "trust and respect" rules as a result of bad behavior when Sylvia was away for a day and the class had made life thoroughly unbearable for her substitute teacher. Talking to her students about her disappointment and asking for their input settled the class into more reasonable ways, and the list became a reference poster for the rest of the year, often referred to at first, then simply there as a silent reminder, one that was noticed and commented on by visitors to the class.

How to build trust and respect

1. Listen to rules and obey them.
2. Respect school property.
3. Respect other students and their property.
4. Respect the teacher and substitutes.
5. Go to the washroom one at a time.
6. Ask the teacher before leaving the classroom.
7. Don't wander inside or outside the school.
8. Don't run in the halls.
9. Do work as assigned.
10. Be a good role model for the rest of the students in the school.
11. Stay in your desk at lunch.
12. Don't go to the staff's or boys'/girls' washrooms without permission.
13. Go outside at 10:10 and 12:20. Do this promptly and cheerfully.
14. Don't go to the store without permission.
15. Use the library, computer room, and telephone only with a pass. Please return the pass to the classroom.

HELPING STUDENTS SETTLE THEIR OWN DISPUTES

The fact that teachers have become careful observers of students and their behaviors makes students more open to noting behaviors too. In Liz's class, talking about respect for others in concrete terms first produced neutral descriptions, then some specific thoughts on settling disputes. Both Martin and Alex can be fractious in their own ways and getting them to describe what happened and then work together on a list of conflict strategies produced much better results than scolding had in the past. (See page 71.)

When they are allowed to express themselves freely, writing can also help students vent feelings of anger and frustration. When Marne noticed that Christian was taking out some pent-up anger by damaging things in the classroom, she took him aside to make him aware that he needed to find another way to let go of whatever it was that made him angry. Over a period of time, Christian's writing reflected some of his violent thoughts, but his classroom behavior settled into friendly, sociable patterns.

When feelings stem from being hurt by fellow students, writing and sharing ease the hurt and make others aware of it. Sylvia invited Thor to read his poem to the class, then added her comments to make certain that the students really heard what he was saying. Once she announced the reading, the entire group became absolutely silent, and there was no question about the total attention students gave to both the reading and to Thor's expression of his feelings.

SYLVIA: *For those of you who weren't here yesterday, Thor wrote a poem. He may choose to do a little more work on the rhythm in the middle of the poem later on, but the reason he loses a bit of the rhythm is because he's really focusing on what he's trying to say, and I think it's essential that we all hear his message and take it to heart.*

THOR: *O.K. It's called "People."*

>*If you all thought of a person as a big rubber band*
>*If you stretch it too far, it will break*
>*But if you let go, or hold it too loose*
>*It will drift away like a dumb old moose.*
>*But if there was a person – let's say his name was Fred –*
>*And you bugged him all day,*
>*You've stretched the band almost to the end.*
>*And Fred would shout and scream and rave and rant.*
>*Be careful, watch out, listen to what I say.*

If you stretch it too far, snap, crack, it will break.
That'll be the end of your funny games.
This is no threat or no lie.
Fred might have had it with the way he's been treated
He'll fight back against you to the very very end.
[applause]

SYLVIA: *What's the main feeling in that poem?*

CHILDREN: *How Thor sees us.*

SYLVIA: *Yes. The question was, what's the main feeling in that poem – the primary emotion? Zoe?*

ZOE: *He doesn't want to be teased or hurt.*

SYLVIA: *Right. And the feeling? . . . the feeling, Juliana?*

JULIANA: *Hurt.*

SYLVIA: *Hurt. Exactly. And the message is, he does not like to be teased. And I think even more than that – that there is a limit to how much he can take. So be sensitive to that please. I really appreciate the way he wrote about this. To be able to express that in a poem and to share that with the class is a really positive outlet for frustration when you're feeling strung out and you're reaching your limit.*

SHOWING RESPECT FOR THOUGHTS AND FEELINGS REAPS RESPECT

The message that comes across at South Park is that both teachers and administrators respect the thoughts and feelings of others. They model cooperative behavior and they are careful listeners. The staff room and halls are filled with animated talk and laughter, and students know that getting along is not just a matter of "Do as I say, but not as I do." Preparing their report card for their teacher (a frequent assignment at South Park), Caitlin and Devon noted under their heading "Buddy Time": "Marne and Margaret [their teachers] love to play together!" And so they do. The light-hearted, enthusiastic interactions between the two teachers set the tone, and students work at following their teachers' example. Marne and Margaret clearly like and respect each other (see page 72), and when exchanging ideas or suggestions during buddy time, *no* is not in their vocabularies. Students thrive in that atmosphere of mutual respect, and when lapses are dealt with positively, calm is re-established more readily and with more lasting effect.

Martin

At lunch recess, I was playing soccer with some other people in my class (including Alex and Brendan) Alex got angry when all of my team, sort of as a joke, crowded into our goal when he was about to take a penalty shot. After a few minutes the game was resumed, but Alex started cheating and after a while, when Danny kicked the ball out by accident, he ran to get it when it was not his team's turn to have possesion of the ball.(That is, it was some-one on his team that kicked it out, Dan-ny asked for it back, but Alex wouldn't give it to him, Danny finally decided that that was the last straw and said "Let's not let Alex play, he's been eating chocolate." Then Paxton came up and asked him if he would give the ball back. "Try and make me" Alex said, and we all tried to get the ball back from him, He bit me on the thumb, and (I think) put all his weight on Brendan's foot. Louis eventually got the ball back from him and he, Paxton, Sam, Michael, Danny, and everyone else who had been playing, restarted.

We were playing soccer the ball got kicked out i went to get the ball. Daniol W. tried to get the ball from me and i scrached him.

martin. would say : Alex took the ball and wauant give it back.

Brenden would say. Alex would not give the ball back

LiLyx saw me biting and puell brenden And martins hair and then puling my hair ant biting me.

Alex

ITHINK — I've got a problem

PLAN — CONFLICT STRATEGIES

☆1. NEGOTIATING — Talk and discuss.
☆2. COMPROMISING — Both parties give up something.
3. TAKING TURNS — One goes first - second
☆4. APOLOGISING — Saying you are sorry
☆5. INTERVENTION — Ask for adult's help
☆6. POSTPONING — Wait for another time to talk
7. HUMOUR — See funny side
8. CHANCE — Flip a coin
☆9. SHARING — Share Fault
☆10. ABANDONING — Forget the whole thing

DO —

Look Back — did my strategies work

Writing out descriptions of what happened becomes the first step. Out of it arise strategies for resolving conflicts.

Marg's report card
South park school by
Marg is nice.
Marg likes caitlin
playing with and
Devon
Marne. her Best
freind is the Marne.
She is Good in
class. Marg
is. Good at
Lisinen to storys.

Writing a report card for the teacher is a natural part of the open give-and-take of the classroom.

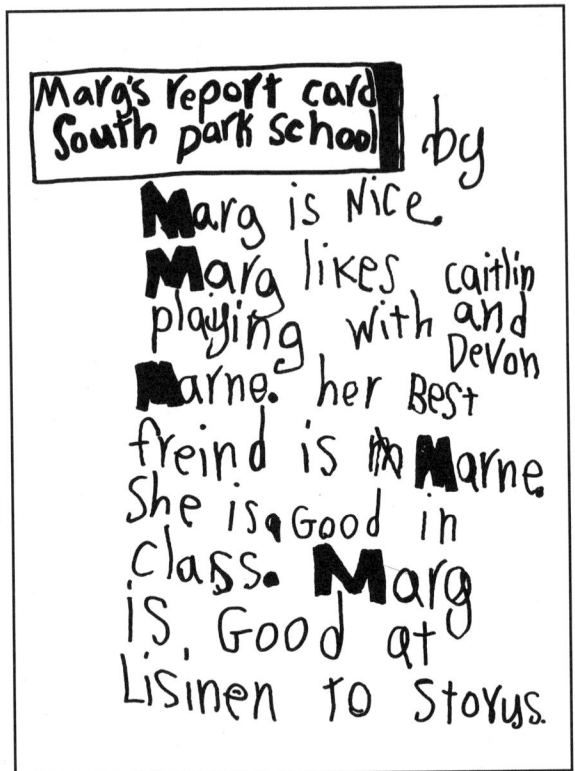

Margs report card
card South park
School by
caitlin
and
Devon

trun
page
to read
to
Report
card.

The intermediate learner

The move toward independence and autonomy is perhaps the central issue for students in the intermediate grades. They want to assert themselves in new ways: be more independent from family and teacher; move toward greater peer interaction; find their own taste in clothes they wear, in choosing friends, in the kind of topics they want to work on and study. Emotions can run high as hormones start to percolate and boy-girl relations become important. Personal problems come to the fore for those students who suffer the consequences of a poor homelife, divorce, abuse, loneliness. Issues involving ethics, substance abuse, and sexuality need to be aired and taken seriously. Choices, decisions, contracts, and attendant bargaining enliven academic work.

SATISFYING THE DEMANDS
OF THE LEARNERS AND THE CURRICULUM

Being in tune with both the learners *and* the curriculum is the balancing act we saw teachers perform as they worked in open ways with their students, yet stayed in charge of discipline and the general area of learning. Flexible planning, responding to sparks of interest, capturing teachable moments, setting interesting frameworks for learning, offering choices, and keeping work concrete and relevant kept both interest and productivity high. Chapters 6 and 7 will provide specifics of meeting curriculum requirements in reading, writing, and content areas.

Acknowledging students' maturity and their ability to make meaningful decisions establishes a climate of mutual respect. Joint planning of projects, group brainstorming to establish rules of conduct, handing routine tasks over to students give them a feeling of control over their lives. Active participation in social and academic situations establishes a feeling of community and empowers students. When students themselves have helped shape the rules, discipline problems are less likely to arise, and curriculum demands are met more readily when students have choices about the ways in which they will work.

The shape
of the day

Plans for the intermediate day are as versatile as the teachers with whom we worked and whom we interviewed. As the year unfolded, it became obvious to us that while there is an underlying pattern to the day, both teachers and students are flexible enough to make time for special occasions, for visitors who have exciting material to present, or for completing a task that is well underway. The philosophy behind this flexibility is that it is learning and the learners that are of prime importance. Timetables are merely there to give a general framework and stability to the day-to-day work. Students need – and feel secure with – a fairly predictable daily routine, but they also thrive on having their needs accommodated. Here we describe a number of different teachers' daily schedules to give you a feel for ways in which you can organize *your* day. Ultimately, your own preferences and the needs of your students will shape your day in class.

MARGARET'S DESIGN
FOR AN IDEAL INTERMEDIATE DAY

"Imagine having a free hand in designing your program and shaping each day to fit you and your students. If you gave your imagination free rein and worked unhampered by thoughts of the 'shoulds,' the budget restraints, or considerations of space and resources in your school, you could generate wonderful plans for your intermediate day. Then you could brainstorm to see how you could carry out what you have created, regardless of the fact that 'We have never done it this way.' In South Park School, we have experienced that creative power and developed, then implemented, truly productive plans that at first seemed quite out of reach."

Bearing that process in mind, Margaret has given her imagination free rein, and aided by her years of experience and extensive contact with intermediate teachers and students, has designed her ideal "intermediate day." The time frames suggested are flexible and will vary with each class.

Morning

"If I was a phys. ed. teacher, I might start my day with a fast-paced game of kick ball or some such activity. But since my specialty is language arts, I would start my day with a ten-minute edit – work on a piece of my own writing or a student's writing that needed it. (See top of page 75.) Or I might have a mystery search – getting the students to look for something in a book or story that we were studying, "Find the _____ (whatever)." I would make these activities fast-paced, fun, and challenging to get the habitual latecomers interested in getting there on time, and to get everyone started on a high-energy level." *(Opening session – 10–15 minutes, more if students are keen.)*

"From there I would go to a class rap session to plan the day or to talk about feelings, long-range plans, field trips, or whatever else came up. I would make sure the tone was kept positive and would resist turning it into a gripe session. To draw everyone

A Ten-Minute Edit

A "ten-minute edit" is fast-paced, fun, and almost competitive as children stumble over each other to be the first to find the mistakes or problems in the piece of writing. Discussions/arguments follow as to who has the best ideas for changing or clarifying sentences. Students turn to each other to give better examples and interact with one another to set up perfect sentences and paragraphs.

On the chalkboard before students arrive:

The two commun concerns that every speaker was: to like youre career. Cause if you just choosed a career and wasnt happ it wouldnt be right.

There would be argument and discussion over such things as the colon, how to clarify "every speaker was," and so on. Apostrophes are always good for discussion that explores the reasons why they are necessary. The whole key to this work is to keep it fast-paced and fun.

together, I would then read aloud to the students – a chapter, story, or poem." *(Rap session – approximately 15–45 minutes.)*

"On most days, I would have a writing session – writer's workshop – as the first major activity. The students would initiate something new, finish off a chapter, or do project writing, such as writing up an experiment they just completed. The length of time we would spend on the writing would depend on the level of students' involvement. If work was really flying along, a whole block of time or even a whole day might be filled with writing to keep a theme underway or to complete a project. My day would definitely integrate science and social studies with the writing and reading activities, and I would schedule five or six writer's conferences each day to make sure that I saw each student at least once a week." *(Writer's workshop – approximately 60 minutes.)*

"Next I would have a block of reading – reader's workshop. Most of the time I would keep the focus on reading for pleasure with students able to choose their own materials and settle down to quiet enjoyment. Out of this block of reading time might come reader's theater, a puppet show, read-alouds, or drama." *(Reader's workshop – 30 minutes, more if interest holds.)*

"A skill-building session would follow next. Sometimes I would work with the whole class, but more often I would gather small groups to work on specific needs – paragraph building, poetry writing, spelling, critical reading strategies, story mapping, or other work with literature – whatever needs had arisen in the course of the ongoing work." *(Skill-building session – approximately 20–25 minutes.)*

Afternoon

"I would open the afternoon with another read-aloud session and would then go to math activities. But I would also make sure that math, measurement, comparisons, planning, or estimating were always viable parts of ongoing projects and day-to-day work." *(Read-aloud – 10–20 minutes; math – 30 minute block and throughout the day.)*

"After math, I would have choosing time (much as I do now for my primary children). Observing intermediate students during buddy time has convinced me that many still need and want to have hands-on 'play' time, so I would give them the opportunity to move around the classroom to work with games, bricks, craftwork, art, sewing, small motors, or, for that matter, more reading and writing, so everyone would have a chance to be active. I know students love that freedom and respond to it with all their beings." *(Choosing time – approximately 40 minutes.)*

"Toward the end of the day I would have a twenty-minute catch-up time to allow slower students to complete work or to get some extra help from their teacher or classmates. That extra time avoids the upset of having to miss music, art, phys. ed., or choosing time in order to keep up.

"To close the day, I would have an evaluation in which my students and I would compare notes on how the day went, what felt good, what needed improvement, and what we could pat ourselves on our backs for. Drawing all the students together for that final session sends them home with good feelings and the knowledge that they are part of a school community in which their thoughts and feelings matter." *(Catch-up and evaluation of day – approximately 30 minutes.)*

"In all my teaching, I would stress solving problems as they occur. The development of research skills is high on my list of priorities, and I want to foster discovery learning, curiosity, reflective thinking, independence, and joyful learning.

"Since phys. ed. and special subjects like French or music have to be scheduled at predetermined times of the day to fit everyone's timetable, I would like to see all of these subjects grouped together on one day, so that the rest of the week could flow without interruptions.

"If I was a specialist in music or art, I would want to give these areas prominence in my overall planning because my own enthusiasm would then carry the students along. Entire weeks might be set aside for special art projects that integrate with the topics under study in science or social studies, or we might choose to have art for art's sake for a whole week. Students thrive on these right-brain activities – and they learn that much better in all areas of the curriculum.

"My days also would be enriched by frequent field trips, by visitors and special speakers, and by audio-visual presentations. Health topics, the environment, family living, and special science topics would form part of the ongoing work in class.

"Above all, the atmosphere in class would acknowledge and celebrate each student's unique abilities and strengths – a beautiful singing voice, a sense of humor, a flair for poetry, artistic talents, a green thumb, love of animals . . . whatever. As a result, the classroom would be filled with fun, productivity, and respect for one another. The can-do feeling would pervade."

DAILY PLAN FOR LIZ'S GRADE 3–4 CLASS

Morning

Silent reading opens the day. As students come in they sit down at their tables to read books of their choice. Liz plays a tape of quiet classical music to provide a calm, pleasant atmosphere to start the day. *(Silent reading – approximately 10 minutes.)*

A read-aloud session of a part of a novel or some poetry follows the silent reading. Liz puts her verve and humor into these readings and students are all ears as she reads. At times she will read non-fiction material that is relevant to what the students are studying. Special books brought in by students augment

Liz's own store of reading materials. *(Read-aloud – approximately 15 minutes.)*

"Language in action" is next. This is a time for sharing books that the students have read and want to recommend to others, for sharing ideas or learning, for sharing some writing done at home, and for discussing news. *(Sharing time – approximately 20 minutes.)*

On most days there will then be a reading mini-lesson in which Liz will work with a page from a book that has recently been read aloud. Using an overhead projector to show the page, Liz will draw the students' attention to ways in which the author makes his or her book enjoyable, easy to read, suspenseful. She may look at interesting vocabulary, special uses of punctuation, spelling, sentence structure, or anything that would help students make the reading/writing connection in their own written compositions. Quick, snappy work and student involvement add liveliness to these sessions, which end as soon as the students start to fidget. *(Mini-lesson in reading – approximately 20 minutes.)*

To conclude the reading segment, Liz's students write reactions to the books they are currently reading. But this is a flexible period – some students may be busy making covers for their latest publication, completing a project, or working at a learning center of their choice. *("Flex time" – approximately 25 minutes.)*

Recess

Writer's workshop begins with a quick check on the status of students' writing and sometimes a mini-lesson that addresses a need that has revealed itself in a number of the students' writings: good opening statements, questions of punctuation or spelling, a point of grammar, or a suggestion based on a particularly good example of student writing. Writing and conferencing take up the bulk of most workshops with sharing time concluding the session. Students who need help or advice read their work to the group and gather ideas and suggestions. *(Writer's workshop – approximately 50–60 minutes.)*

Project time builds on suggestions generated by the students. Students research and discuss topics in small groups or on their own. They take responsibility for becoming expert in an area of their choice and prepare both written and oral reports, or create a diorama or play. *(Project time – 30–35 minutes, more if a major project is underway.)*

Afternoon

The afternoon begins with silent reading followed by a read-aloud session. *(Reading – approximately 10–15 minutes.)*

A mathematics session follows. The use of manipulative materials, model building, sharing, problem solving, and discussions enliven this work. *(Math – approximately 30 minutes.)*

Then comes a flexible period of the day that involves creative expression. The students engage in music, art, physical education, social studies, science, or health education, although these areas are also integrated into the day during reading, writing, and project times. Whenever possible there is some free choice during this period to give students an opportunity to do whatever interests them at the time, including some free play. *("Flex time" – approximately 30–40 minutes.)*

A summing-up ends the day. Everyone gathers around to talk about what went well that day, what went wrong, and how to make things better. Sometimes the students share something significant that happened to them during the day. The summing-up also includes a look ahead at the next day. *(Summing up – approximately 10–15 minutes.)*

DAILY PLAN FOR HANNE MACKAY'S GRADE 4–5 CLASS

Morning

As children come in, Hanne greets them and listens to their personal news and chit-chat. It is her way to "take the temperature of the group," to gather ideas for the day, and to strengthen her bond with her students. To teachers who spend the first minutes of the day scrambling to get ready for the first lesson, Hanne's advice is, "Drop everything and greet your students!"

"Buddy reading" opens the day (not to be confused with "buddy time" in which older students work with younger "buddies").

Students get together in groups of two and three and read together. At the beginning of the year Hanne selects fifty to one hundred books for students from the school library. From then on, two to four students take on the task of exchanging the stock of books for a new supply each week, keeping in mind the varying interests of their classmates.

To add variety to buddy reading, song sheets of popular folk songs, campfire songs, and the like make for valuable reading practice as everybody joins in to sing. These song sheets are collected in binders, and by the end of the year students have a wonderful collection. Even reluctant readers do a great deal of reading without really being aware that they are engaging in reading practice. *(Buddy reading – approximately 10–20 minutes.)*

Charting the plans for the day follows. Using the chalkboard, an overhead projector, or flipchart, the group charts activities including band practice, challenge programs, and whatever else is coming up that day. *(Charting the day – approximately 5–10 minutes.)*

For a change of pace there may be a quick mental math exercise ("3 x 2 + 4 x 6 is how much?") or a two-minute mystery reading to spot "Who took the hammer? What gave the clue to...?" Both are fun ways to sharpen listening, attending. *(Quick math – approximately 5–10 minutes.)*

Circle time expands on the daily plans. Students sit in a circle (or two concentric circles if the group is too large) to take a look at school-wide activities, special events, the start or completion of projects. If the weather is noteworthy, it may receive descriptive comment in talk about cumulus clouds and cold fronts or high pressure areas.

Circle time includes a brief check on news items that students want to share. At the beginning of the year students sign their names in their very best script on pieces of cardboard, and those name cards are used throughout the year for drawing lots to make sure everyone gets a turn. But there are no command performances, and students are free to present news or to pass when their names are drawn. Usually students are eager to participate, and news time provides another opportunity to tune in to their interests and concerns – environmental concerns, teenage conflicts – sports, drugs, children in crisis, getting along with parents and peers.

Since Hanne loves poetry, she closes the morning talking/ listening time by reading one or two of her favorite poems to the students. *(Circle time – approximately 15–25 minutes.)*

Language arts period incorporates science and social studies. Students are reading and researching for definite purposes. Non-fiction reading addresses questions the students have raised, such as "Where did the dinosaurs go?" "Why is there salt in the ocean?" The study of literature draws on the personal concerns brought forth by the students during discussion times. *(Language arts – research and reading for content learning – approximately 60 minutes.)*

Recess

A read-aloud session draws students together after recess. Hanne chooses books that are slightly ahead of the students' reading levels to stretch their vocabulary and concept building, to stimulate interest, and to introduce new authors or expand on the current theme or topic in science or social studies. *(Read-aloud – approximately 10–20 minutes depending on topic.)*

Math time includes the use of hands-on materials and peer teaching. Students use such materials as Dienes blocks for place-value problems and work in pairs to maximize discussion about the problems to be solved. Hanne introduces the concept to be studied that day, and students work together to explain their understanding of the work to each other. Large sheets of paper and crayons aid the working-out/explaining. Hanne ends the session by summarizing and writing the problems on the chalkboard in standard math notations. *(Math work – approximately 20–40 minutes.)*

A brief spelling practice session also draws on teamwork. Drawing words that need review from students' writing ties the spelling work into their daily concerns. Students take turns thinking of funny or memorable ways to remember the spelling of words – "There's an EEL on my REEL" – and then share their discoveries with each other. Fun, and the need to think about words, their structures and meanings, make the work easy and effective.

Afternoon

A class meeting brings everyone together in a circle again. This is the most important sharing time of the day. Personal issues or concerns, disputes, worries, or plans for the future can and will be raised. Students who have a strong need to be heard can place their names on the agenda for the day to make sure there will be time for them. The meeting opens with a group brainstorming session to come up with three things that are going really well – (1) student research on the current project is producing lots of material, (2) plans for the field trip are progressing, (3) the latest batch of books from the library is great. Next comes the airing of personal concerns. The meeting closes with another brainstorming session to find three good things that have happened as a result of the meeting. Careful listening and sensitive responses set the tone from the beginning of the year, and students learn to air their joys and grievances in productive ways. The level of trust built during these class meetings does wonders for the overall classroom climate. *(Class meeting – this period is very flexible and may take 10–60 minutes, or even more, depending on the concerns aired.)*

Reader's workshop gives everyone the opportunity to read material of his or her choice. Hanne does her own professional reading at that time and covers a lot of ground as the weeks and months progress. A brief sharing time ends the personal reading period. *(Reader's workshop – approximately 30–60 minutes.)*

The remainder of the day is taken up by physical education, fine arts, music, and any special topic or project that is pending. *(Special topics – length of time varies from day to day.)*

Before leaving school, students write some thoughts on the day in their journals or learning logs and then compare notes on what the day held for them. Doing such reflecting at the end of the day recaptures the high points, and students take those feelings of accomplishment home with them. *(Summing up – approximately 5–10 minutes.)*

If there is time, Hanne may end the day with yet another story or with a "break for beauty" during which she shares something aesthetically pleasing with her students – a picture, a piece of driftwood, some flowers, anything she has enjoyed that day. *("Break for beauty" – fitted in, at end of day or earlier, as time allows.)*

Positive feelings, a sense of accomplishment, and personal involvement pervade the day and accompany the students on their way home.

DAILY PLAN FOR MARNE'S GRADE 4–5–6 CLASS

At the beginning of the school year, Marne promises her students that they will have time for reading and writing each day, and she fulfils that promise by setting aside large blocks of time each morning for writer's workshop and reader's workshop. Both of these sessions integrate work on projects or specific research arising out of science or social studies. The day is liberally interspersed with on-the-spot changes of pace to sing, talk, hear a story or a play. Marne sets very definite parameters for on-task behavior and quiet courtesy when students need time to think and concentrate, but, in her words, "My classroom bubbles like a brook" with lively talk when students are working together on group projects or team problem solving.

Morning

Welcoming students and taking a look at the events of the day draw students together. Discussions of plans, sharing ideas, and general housekeeping chores (collecting money for field trips, checking attendance, deciding whose turn it is to . . .) clear the way for the quiet time of writer's workshop. *(Welcoming and housekeeping – approximately 5–10 minutes.)*

Before the class settles down to writing, Marne may lead a singing session or have a ten-minute drawing session in which students express their thoughts through art or use their drawings to illustrate what they derived from their current readings. (See page 84.) *(Optional music or art session – approximately 10 minutes.)*

After a quick check on the status of everyone's writing, the classroom becomes very quiet as everyone settles down to writer's workshop. Gathering information, brainstorming ideas, planning new work, drafting, redrafting, editing, and polishing are all part of the individual work. In the specially designated conference corners, students consult with each other in hushed voices. Once enough students have brought their work to a final-edit stage, Marne may move into the hall outside the classroom to conduct her conferences so those who need quiet time to write are not disturbed. *(Writer's workshop – approximately 50–70 minutes.)*

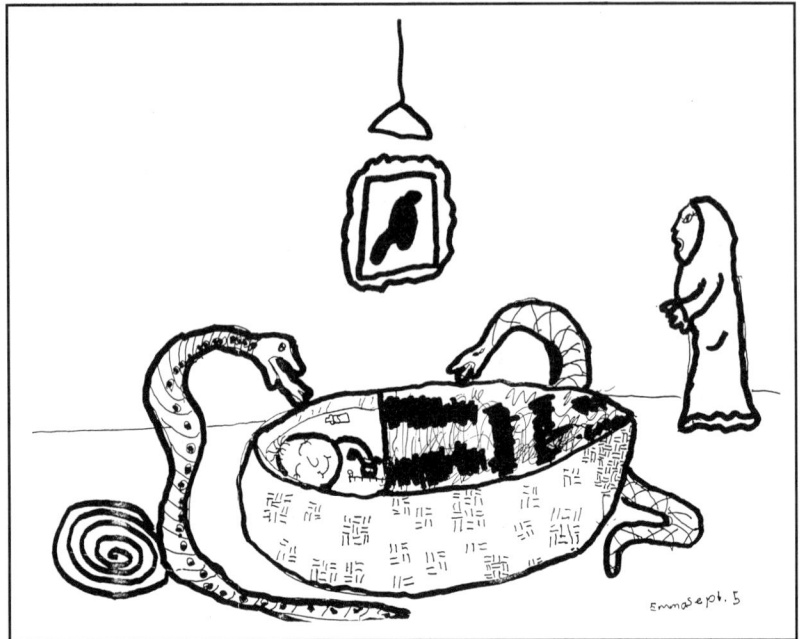

To lead into the ten-minute drawing session, Marne may read a short selection. Here the students depict what they derived from the story of Hercules.

Recess

Reader's workshop follows recess. At the beginning of the year Marne will read chapters or sections of novels or non-fiction works to capture students' interest, and will display these and similar books prominently to give students the opportunity to choose them for their personal reading. Later in the year, once sharing is underway, students build their reading choices on peer recommendations as much as on teacher input.

Entries in the reading response journals and a brief sharing of feelings about the reading material end the session. Students may choose to speak to the entire class about a particularly exciting book or to share with partners or in small groups. Preferences about the kind or length of sharing vary from day to day, and sharing does not become a marathon listening session.

Project time may follow or be part of reader's workshop. If Marne has shifted the focus of reading to non-fiction material for the time being, then the reading leads quite naturally to projects, and the time before lunch integrates reading and project work. *(Reader's workshop and project time – these often merge to fill the after-recess period.)*

Afternoon

The afternoon is filled with math, science, social studies, physical education. Projects, hands-on manipulations in math, and student-initiated research keep the time flexible and action-filled. *(Content learning through projects, themes, and problem solving involve almost the entire afternoon. See chapter 6.)*

Looking back and looking ahead close the day. *(Closing the day – approximately 10–15 minutes.)*

DAILY PLAN FOR SYLVIA'S GRADE 6–7 CLASS

Student involvement, studying in blocks of time, integrating work through projects, and giving students responsibility for their work are the key factors in Sylvia's ways of managing her grade 6–7 class. She encourages students to voice their preferences and make choices, and offers students the opportunity to choose alternative topics or ways of working if they find it impossible to relate to the main topics under study. For example, if the curriculum calls for learning about the democratic process in government and a student has trouble relating to any of the readings, Sylvia will discuss the curriculum goals with that student and invite him or her to find alternative ways of meeting those goals – watching relevant TV programs or videos, interviewing people in government or elected positions, going to a Legislative Assembly meeting (students living in Victoria have that option open to them), or arranging for an election in the class/school.

At the beginning of the year, students participate in a brainstorming session to generate possible topics for study – transportation, the environment, sports, travel, animal studies. That list of themes becomes a starting point for blocks of study that run for six to eight weeks. Last year opened with the Carmanah field trip and ensuing environmental studies mentioned in the introduction. Recycling projects and dioramas on the environmentally safe home built on that beginning. The study of various countries and a unit on ancient Rome and Greece fulfilled curriculum requirements. A unit on oral presentations and news reports built speaking and listening skills (also a curriculum requirement). Writer's workshop and the production of newspapers concluded the year and enhanced the writing and research that students had done throughout the year.

Mathematics, physical education, and music are threaded into the blocks of study on a continuing basis. But even though these topics are the subject of daily or weekly lessons, students have the option to complete their work in blocks. The requirement is to complete specific tasks by each Friday. Students may opt to do their work each day or in a block toward the end of the week. They are responsible for the completion of the assignments and learn to accept that independence quite well.

Students work well when they have the choice to focus on one major topic at a time, and six-week units are about the right length of time to keep interest and involvement high. Getting ready for oral presentations or working on projects requires teamwork and extended research. Being able to do sustained work over a period of time produces both good work and independent students. The level of commitment is high and students rise to the challenge of taking charge of their work.

Expanding on the amount of responsibility given over to students, Sylvia has drawn up guidelines for a number of classroom committees. Students are asked to be in charge of a number of areas ranging from classroom organization to computer room maintenance. Although she has drawn up the basic guidelines, students decide on rules for the class, select books from the library, and see what equipment is needed. As the senior group in the school, students are placed in a position of leadership, and the duties fulfilled by the committees transcend the grade 6–7 classroom; service to the entire school becomes part of the committee work.

Flexibility of planning, integration of skill building and content area learning, and the encouragement of independent work – all part of whole-language teaching – are the basis of Sylvia's day-to-day class management. Her open ways of interacting with the learners work because she demands that students show the same considerate behavior that she accords them. (If Sylvia's six-week units offer too little structure for you

Bring the community into your classroom

When the focus of learning rests too much on academic skills, students may feel that they are learning only to accommodate the teacher or school requirements. Connecting classroom work with the community outside of school helps students apply what they learn in class to their everyday lives and to understand the usefulness of the skills they are acquiring.

Plan field trips that involve the community.
Take students to see
• local businesses – the corner store, garage, bakery, pet shop . . .
• municipal offices – planning department, police station, fire station, city/town hall . . .
• art galleries, museums, public libraries
• the airport, heliport, harbor, train or bus station
• local farms, nurseries, flower shops

Encourage research/work that is based in the community
• Become involved in local issues – redevelopment of parts of the city or rural area, traffic patterns, road building plans, parks . . .

- Visit a local hotel to find out about the jobs required at the hotel and what they entail (we had an entire class bake cookies in a hotel kitchen)
- Follow special reports in the local newspaper

Do projects that will be of use to students beyond school.
Plan a trip to Europe, the Far East, Australia
- Develop the itinerary
- Consult a local travel agency about transportation
- Do cost estimates
- Check into local accommodations
- Research the history of countries to be visited
- Brainstorm ways of raising money to take the trip

Study the school cafeteria
- Menu planning
- Costs
- Services
- Waste disposal

The chef at a local hotel turned an in-town field trip into a very special event.

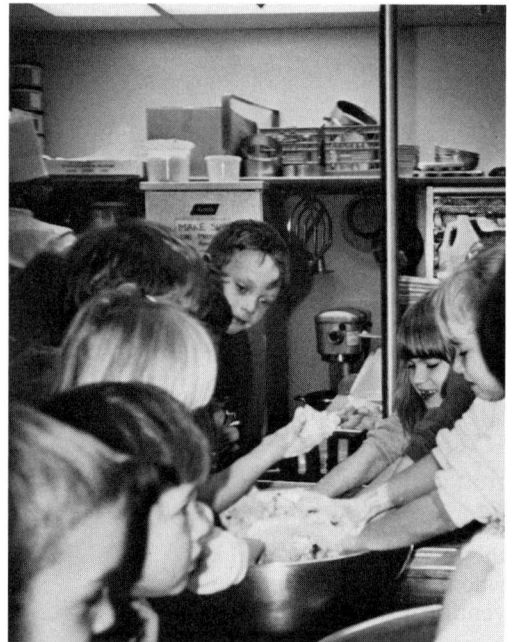

to feel comfortable, the overall plans for the day outlined by Hanne and Marne work equally well for grades 4–7.)

Letting go of control and genuine sharing in the classroom can flourish only if there are feelings of mutual caring and trust. The thought that students should take charge of their own learning may sound like a call for chaos, but our experience has shown the opposite to be true. The more responsibility we turn over to students, the more independent and responsible they become. Trust is built gradually as both students and teacher learn new ways to interact, but the open climate is more satisfying and more productive for both. Having arrived at that attitude of complete trust, Vicki Green, who used to teach a grade 3-4-5 class, speaks of her regret about having waited so long to develop that trust, and of wondering why it took her so long to accept that learners need to select their own menu of learning.

You almost feel you want to apologize to your students and tell them, 'I'm so sorry. I thought I knew. I thought I could present this and control all the variables to create optimum learning. It never occurred to me that it was really up to you. I thought I had to give the dinner party.'

I feel I used to work like that. I set the menu for the students, I practiced making the meal, I cleaned the house – I did everything. But one day I decided to let the kids have a smorgasbord with food prepared by them. However, I still controlled the menu – I didn't trust them to bring the right things. I felt I had to tell them, 'You bring the salad, and you bring the potatoes – you bring this and you bring that.' Until one day I wondered, why don't we go with potluck? Because even if they all bring salads, the probability of them all being the same kind of salad is remote. They'll bring chicken salad and fruit salad and potato salad. We'll get the entire dinner done. And everybody will make comments or ask questions like, 'How did you make your salad? Why did you add that? That looks good.' And the combination will be incredible! So we just have to trust them, and trust our own knowing.

Reflecting on the varying needs of students and the changes that come about as children move through school, Vicki adds:

By the time they get to grade 4, I find many kids don't trust any more (if they ever did). So to be fair you have to provide some structure for those who want it. And for the ones who want to leave the firm base and venture out, you have to suggest some paths that they can consider.

People often have to get back into that feeling of being safe in order to start again and be trusting. For example, defining a topic for kids when you first start out helps them find their ground. Although you certainly elicit topics from them, you wouldn't ask them to 'choose whatever you want.' Who can make a choice when it's unlimited? But if you say, 'Here's the way I think this should happen,' or 'Here's something you can try,' they can ask, 'Can I change that?' Then they get a choice, and the work comes from some kind of negotiation to alter the task to suit them. For example, through discussion and negotiation students might decide to study one explorer and follow his life in detail, rather than studying about several explorers. Or kids might opt to do a cooperative project, rather than an individual one.

Once again, observing students is the key to success. Letting them set their own menu will produce better, more nourishing dinners for the entire class. But just as you don't ask an absolute novice to prepare dinner for a group of thirty, you don't ask your students to take over jobs for which they are unprepared – emotionally or intellectually. Make learning safe. Set frameworks within which students can work. This will give you – and them – time to build the trust that leads to open planning and cooperative classroom management.

LEARNING TO WRITE – WRITING TO LEARN

4

IN THE OPEN INTERACTIVE ATMOSPHERE of whole-language classrooms, writing is as much a part of communication as talking. Students interact with each other and with the teacher through writing conferences, letters, sharing sessions, and joint work. They communicate their thoughts and feelings about the books they have read, and they use writing to explore new fields of interest. Constant practice in a relaxed, supportive atmosphere makes writing a joy instead of a dreaded chore. Students explore new ways of expressing their thoughts, melding artwork with language, and using models from their reading to create their own published works. They cherish writer's workshop as an important and enjoyable part of their day, and become totally absorbed in the process of committing their thoughts to the page. Writing pervades the day. Though the block of time set aside for writer's workshop is the most significant part of writing practice in most intermediate classrooms, projects, writing connected with other studies, and incidental writing provide further meaningful practice throughout the day.

Writer's workshop

In the classrooms we observed, writer's workshop was largely modeled on Nancie Atwell's book *In the Middle.* Like so much of whole-language teaching, her work is based on observing how learners actually work and on noting what helps and what blocks learning. In that spirit, Nancie Atwell and her fellow teachers looked back to their own writing development as they collaborated to find new and better ways to help their students write. They discussed openly what had helped and what had hindered them as they learned to write. One of them commented, "Teachers were overly critical, and I learned to dislike writing. When a teacher was interested in what I had to say, I began to write." From that kind of reflection about their own writing and that of their students, Nancie Atwell's group developed their approach to writer's workshop (Atwell 1985).

CREATING A CLIMATE FOR WRITING

Setting the climate for writing and "making it a way of life more than a program" have been the key factors in the success of writer's workshops. Like Atwell and her group of teachers, we find that if we abandon the thought that writing is a neat, linear process and instead accept its messy, fuzzy beginnings, sporadic spurts forward, and periodic slowings down, then we acknowledge how thinking and writing really work. By looking back at our own struggles and successes with composing, we can readily understand that students learning to write need the freedom to work in that same open way. When we cater to the needs that Atwell and her colleagues defined, then we find that students' writing thrives.

WRITERS NEED TIME

To develop their writing, students need to have time to develop their thoughts and move through a number of notes and drafts to polish their original rough ideas. Abandoning fixed time lines for completion of a piece of writing opens the way to a relaxed exploration of ideas and the opportunity to polish special gems to a high sparkle. Since you check on the status of everyone's writing each day, you will be aware of those who are stuck or those who keep shifting from topic to topic without finishing. Open time lines for writing do not mean that your class procrastinator will never finish a piece of writing. As with other learning, we find that open-ended writing produces both quality and quantity. Students become deeply involved in their work and will often take writing home to continue it after school. After a buddy poetry-writing session we overheard two of the girls whisper their plans for recess: "Let's take this outside and sit under the steps so we can keep on working on this poem."

Giving writer's workshop a prominent place in your day and devoting a significant amount of time to it are key factors to success. We have found that at the beginning of the year twenty minutes may be the span of time that students are comfortable with. But very quickly that time needs to be expanded. As students settle into the routine of writer's workshop and become involved in their writing, concentration becomes intense, and students enjoy longer sessions. If we have to end a session before the usual time, students often complain loudly and ask for extra time later on. Thirty, forty minutes – even an hour – will not be too long for writer's workshop once your students have experienced the excitement of working on topics of their choice. If you take your cues from your students' absorption in their writing, you will know when to extend the session or when – as sometimes happens – their restlessness suggests that it is time to ask them to finish up what they are doing.

WRITERS NEED TOPICS
AND FORMATS OF THEIR OWN CHOICE

When you keep the focus on communication and invite students to write about topics of their choice, writing takes on new life. Personal knowledge or experience, special interests, feelings of frustration, sadness, or joy will infuse life into writing. Imagination and fantasy will play large parts in your students' creations. If you leave the choice of format open and encourage students to choose one that fits their topic, the range and expressiveness of writing will expand. Descriptions, narratives, poetry, research reports, and even plays will emerge. Noting that James had difficulty writing even though he was most expressive when he spoke, Marne suggested that he do his "writing" by recording his compositions on tape. The result was the creation of a series of radio plays complete with sound effects, voices to fit the characters, and a narrator to hold the story together. At intervals, one or two other students joined James, and the entire class responded enthusiastically to his plays.

WRITERS NEED TO INTERACT
WITH OTHERS AS THEY WRITE

Having an audience for their writing adds fun to the writing process and convinces students of the need for careful editing and for accuracy of spelling and grammar in the finished product. Having a teacher make a few perfunctory comments at the bottom of a finished product simply is not enough if writing is to become a way of capturing students' innermost thoughts

Encouraging a student to do his writing with the use of a tape-recorder ended his writer's block and produced excellent results that enticed classmates to join in.

and feelings. As a piece of writing moves through several stages, conferences with classmates and teacher give writers opportunities to read their work aloud, to hear what their writing sounds like, to get the reaction of listeners, and to answer questions or receive suggestions. If it is made quite clear that writers have control over their own finished writing and are under no obligation to incorporate suggested changes, then conferences become both fun and valuable. Roughness of structure or style, and poor punctuation or paragraphing show themselves readily when the author reads a piece of writing aloud or lets others read it. If the writer's use of the mechanics of writing interferes with the effectiveness and enjoyment of the sharing, then the author will be eager to make corrections and learn how to avoid similar pitfalls in the future.

WRITERS NEED TO LEARN
THE MECHANICS OF WRITING IN CONTEXT

Giving personal feedback or basing mini-lessons on specific problems of mechanics as they arise is a good way to capture teachable moments. Talking about misplaced pronoun references in the abstract is not nearly as effective as pointing to their funny effects in a specific context.

MARNE: *Here the man comes out, and you describe "him" as "spotted."*

LISA: *Yeah!* [both laugh]

MARNE: *Acne, I assume?* [both laugh]

LISA: *There's a dog in a carrying kennel in the first draft.*

MARNE: *Ah . . . So you could make it clear that it's the dog that's spotted.*

LISA: *I just got tired of rewriting this.*

MARNE: *Don't rewrite it. These little clarifications can go in without rewriting the whole thing. Your paragraphing is perfect and all of your punctuation is looking great – there is no reason to rewrite. You might spell* finally *and* stopped *accurately, O.K.?*

With the permission of the author, such on-the-spot comments can become mini-lessons for the entire class on accurate usage or refinement of style. They are remembered and applied because they are based on a concrete model.

*During writer's workshop
the designated conference
corners are rarely empty.*

WRITERS NEED MODELS

If writing is to be more than talk written down, then writers need to be readers. Listening to the writing of many different writers and reading a wide variety of works become pleasurable ways to develop a feel for the different writing styles of narrative, description, poetry, and reports. As the students evolve their writing, they will be ever more conscious of the reading-writing connection. As you respond to the students' comments in their reading response journals you will have the opportunity to draw their attention to any particularly interesting and effective ways an author has used to tell a story, to involve all the senses to make a story vivid, or to make dialogue realistic.

Quite early in our research we found that even primary children become sensitive to the need to adapt their writing styles to their topics. Fairy tales they invent have "once upon a time" beginnings, sports reports definitely sound like sportscasts, and research reports are modeled after the books the students use as sources. Intermediate students take their adoption of book language a step further and extend their vocabulary to become rich and descriptive. Noting the importance of fitting names and vocabulary to the setting of her story, Alexis searched books on India for names and descriptions. The satisfying sounds of fantastic invented words capture students' imagination, and they often make up their own special words to add color to both poetry and prose.

In chapter 5 we describe how reading a variety of poetry to the buddy group provided the inspiration and the models that students needed to create their own poetry. Giving them written patterns to emulate can be equally effective. Building on the personal experience of visiting the Carmanah Valley, Sylvia's class collaborated on producing a volume of special poetry. Many adapted their own impressions to a model provided by Chief Dan George, but others used his poem as a springboard for more individual work. All of them invested their poems with their feelings and perceptions. The visit to the forest had touched their souls and Chief Dan George provided a model for giving voice to the deeply felt impressions. The resulting poems leave no doubt about the value of pattern writing. The Carmanah poems expressed each student's own experience; they were not a writing exercise done for the teacher but personal statements. (See pages 98 and 99.)

Carmanah

The power of the trees
The freshness of the air
The rushing of the river
   Speak to me.

The brightness of the stars
The flying sparks of the fire
The shining of the sun
   Speak to me.

The coolness of the breeze
The smoothness of the rocks
The steepness of the hills
   Speak to me.

The softness of the moss
The clearness of the sky
The greenness of the forest
   Speak to me.

And my heart soars.

Andrew

Carmanah

The beauty of the trees,
the softness of the soil,
the boldness of the leaves,
   speak to me.

The freshness of air,
the heating from the sun,
the coolness of the breeze,
   speak to me.

The refreshing water from the creek,
the warmth of the fire,
the whispers of the wind,
   speak to me.

The intensity of my sleeping bag,
the dampness of the fire,
the closing of my eyes,
   speak to me.

And my heart soars.

Oriole

Trees

The beauty of the trees,
The freshness of the air,
The pureness of the water,
    speak to me.

The color of the sun,
The twinkle of the stars,
The sparkle of the dew,
    speak to me.

The raindrops on the creek,
The falling of the leaves,
The fragrance of the spruce,
    speak to me.

The sizzle of the fire,
The whistle of the wind,
The richness of the soil,
They speak to me

And my heart soars.

Bronwen

Big trees,
A little black squirrel,
Nibbling on an acorn.
And my heart soars

Dead trees,
Little black ants
Crawling along the wood.
And my heart soars

Baby trees,
With their green leaves
growing along the fallen logs.
And my heart soars

Hemlock trees,
Smooth soft needles
The underside is white.
And my heart soars

Spruce trees,
Big sweeping branches,
The giants of the forest.
And my heart soars

Crooked trees,
Split tops
Planted by careless hands.
And my heart soars

Burned trees,
Disgusting, ugly, stumps,
Jumbled on the forest floor
Where they will live no more.

Staci

*Through following the
pattern of poetry provided
by Chief Dan George,
students express their own
feelings about their field
trip to an ancient forest.*

Sept. 18

Dear Marne,
I am reading The Enormous Egg by
Oliver Butterworth. My grandparents
know Oliver and my mom used to
play with his daughter! My grandmot-
her says that everyone in the Butterworth family has red hair! (at
least everyone that she ever knew.)

The First time I read the enormous
egg I kind of began to think that
a dinousaur realy could hatch out
of a hen's egg. I am in the middle
of chapter five and I can't wait
for the exciting part were they
go to Washington! I've read this
book many times before and I
enjoyed it so much I wanted
to read it again! I've also read
The Trouble with Jenny's ear by
Oliver Butterworth. It was just
as good

Yours Truely,
Katherine

*The reading response
journal provides a forum
for exchanging thoughts
and reminiscences.*

Along with written models and patterns to follow, students
need human models who write, express feelings, and edit their
work with the help of an audience. Seeing their teacher participate actively in writer's workshop, having parents at home share
their writing, watching adults write letters all make clear that
writing is not just a school activity done to satisfy the requirements of the teacher or curriculum. Having a published author
visit the class keeps students interested in checking the books
they read for such details as author, illustrator, and publisher.
Students participating in the Challenge Program at South Park

School had the opportunity to meet people involved in the production of books during the time they were working on a major publication of their own. As one of the students describes this visit:

We had an author and a story teller and an artist come. And they were really neat, because they told us what kinds of things they did to make their book, and the illustrator told us what kind of pictures they used . . . umm . . . and ways to do pictures. And then we did a couple more sheets – when we had done our book – about how we felt about our book and what we would change about it if we could do it again.

Sept, 18

Dear Katherine,

How wonderful to know the author of such good books. I like knowing details about writers, composers, and artists (like the bit about Buttesworth having red hair). It makes them very real – as if perhaps they could be your friends (as they were your grandma's)

Still, it is wonderful to have you back, Katherine. I'm so glad you had a good time. I hope Jessica is helping you get used to your new classroom & set-up. Let me know if you need more explaning. Don't be shy!

One thing Jessica may not explain is in writer's workshop, I am asking that you write about subjects that you know something about. Also, write short pieces that are full of details and sensory information. Your farm in New Hampshire would make a beautiful subject for example,

Yours truly,
Marne

The teacher's response goes beyond acknowledging the student's message.

Students also gain from peer modeling and will emulate each other in choice of topic and style of writing. Liz speaks of fads as she describes how students in her class model their writing on each other's work:

I find the students learn by copying one another, and some of their writing has developed according to fads. For instance, after Vicky introduced the 'literary lie' – 'Once upon a time there was a girl named Cinderella who lived in a home with two beautiful stepsisters who were kind and generous . . .' – many children wrote literary lies for weeks after. When Danny became hooked on the Hardy Boys mystery series, he decided to produce a mystery story of his own, and several others followed his example. For some time a group of students wrote comic strips and became quite adept at producing a good sequence of pictures and captions.

WRITERS NEED TEACHERS WHO ARE KNOWLEDGEABLE AND OPEN TO NEW IDEAS

Along with being models of writing and editing, teachers need to bring an understanding of the writing process to their work with students. Nancie Atwell and her group drew, not only on their own experience and observations, but on the work of the foremost researchers in writing. Teachers at South Park School have drawn on the work of Nancie Atwell, other writers, and the local network of whole-language teachers to broaden their perspectives on writing. As a result, they have become learners and researchers in their own classrooms. As they continue to grow and learn, their students are captivated by their teachers' genuine interest in writing and interacting. As you evolve writer's workshop in your classroom, you will find that networking with teachers in your area will spark your interest and enthusiasm. We find that as we respond to our students' work, our own reading and writing take on new life.

How to get started

Supplies needed for writer's workshop are simple. All students will need their own manila folders to gather their daily writing and to note their ideas and progress on the covers. You will need record sheets with the student's names to keep track of who is doing what writing and where in the writing process each student's composition is: brainstorming; first, second, third draft; or finished copy. Once work is underway, you will want to keep special folders on your desk into which students place work that is ready to be discussed in conference with you or to be typed and published, if you decide to take responsibility for that job. With more mature students, you can leave that final job in their hands.

103
*Learning to write –
writing to learn*

Setting the stage for writing

Once writers are on their way, the teacher sets the parameters within which writer's workshop functions. He or she discusses the rules and reasons for having them, then, to remind the students, posts the rules in a prominent spot in the class:

Rules for Writer's Workshop

1. Write every day.
2. Date and label everything: Notes, Draft 1, Draft 2, Draft 3.
3. Save everything you write in your writing folder.
4. Keep your writing folder at school at all times.
5. Talk *only* in the conference corners and in a very soft voice.
6. Write on one side of the paper only so you can cut and paste.
7. Don't erase, just revise and keep.
8. Do your best – and have fun!

Though the steps in writing evolve gradually as the students proceed with their first pieces of writing, it helps to review and post the steps in a prominent location.

Steps in Writing

1. Brainstorm and then select a topic (keep the brainstormed list for ideas for future writing).
2. Begin your first draft – just get the ideas down.
3. Have a conference with a classmate to get response and clarify meaning.
4. Revise and do a second draft.
5. Edit your second draft yourself – start to look at content and spelling more closely.
6. Have a student conference and proofread the writing together with your classmates.
7. After proofreading, put writing in the "ready for final edit" folder.
8. Have a teacher conference.
9. Make final revisions for presentation (perfection!).
10. Publish and share.

In the flexible atmosphere of a whole-language classroom students will follow this guideline roughly, but know that they may skip a step if work is going well. They are also free to abandon a piece of writing that seems to be leading nowhere. Having conferences along the way extends both the content and the mechanics of the writing. Establishing the idea of refining work gradually will eliminate a lot of agonizing for students and a lot of unnecessary work for you in looking over rough drafts.

At the first of the year, Marne tells her students that each day they will have a fixed time for writing anything they choose. As one way to help them find ideas for their writing she tells them of two ideas she has for writing about her summer holidays. She asks for their opinions and suggestions to help her decide which one to start on and how to go about writing it – what to include, where to start, what images to use. Next she asks students to talk to each other about some of their vacation experiences that seemed interesting or memorable and that could yield ideas for writing. As students pair up to talk to each other, the hum of voices swells, and there is no doubt about having much to say. Topics other than vacations surface and are expanded readily.

Students keep a list of the ideas they generate in discussion with their classmates. They keep these in their writing folders and use them as a bank of ideas to fall back on when they have finished a piece of writing and new ideas seem hard to find. Not everyone uses the list; like much of the work in the classroom it is a helpful option but not a requirement.

Once writer's workshop is launched and students write regularly each day, Marne gives her reasons for the need to be especially quiet, for setting aside special corners for conferencing, and for keeping all drafts and notes. It takes a while to establish the routines and have students remember where they may and may not communicate with each other during their writing time. But as their writing gains in depth, they themselves feel the need for quiet or the exchange of ideas to spark their writing. To keep the rules fresh in their minds, Marne posts these rules on a large chart in front of the class. (See "Rules for Writer's Workshop," page 103.)

105
*Learning to write –
writing to learn*

Draft ①

Sept.5   Name Zoe

My Ideas For Writing

1) About my cat Leon catching a babe
mouse and letting it go and chasing and
and catching it in his mouth

Reincarnation
Spirits + Ghosts
Dinosaurs
Herbs
Peace + Hippies
Pyramids

*At the beginning of the
year, students brainstorm
possible writing topics and
keep them in their writing
folders for future
reference.*

Name Morgan

My Ideas For Writing

My first day of School.

When my Mom and Dad
spilt up.

Last night
My trip to Sandiago
Halloise recipy
going back in time
          Mabe rules ernt so
bad

	Tues.	Wed.	Thurs.	Fri.	Mon.	Tues.
Alexis	_ongs.	Draft 2	Polishing	will complete	seq.	strip.
Alison	Lost Cat	Draft 1	Draft 1	Dr. 1	seq.	strip.
Ariel	New Story today	Draft 1	Draft 2	Dr. 2	edited →	recopy.
Benjamin	Bird	Draft 1	Draft 2	Handed in Bird	edited →	published
Brooke	Dream	Draft 1	Draft 1	Dr. 2	edited —→	recopy
Chrissy	New Story	Dr 1	Dr. 1	Dr. 2		
Dylan		Dr 1	Dr. 1	Dr. 1	seq.	strip.
Gillian	Food	Dr. 1	Dr. 2	Dr. 2	edited	recopy.
James	Disney L.	Dr. 2	Dr. 2	Dr. 2	edited	recopy
Jessica	Dream	Dr. 1	Dr. 2	Dr. 2	sequence	strip
Jonathan	1st Day	Dr. 1	Dr. 1	Dr. 1	sequence	strip
Kamil	New Story	Dr. 1	Dr. 1	Dr. 2	edited	published.
Katherine	ab.	ab.	ab.	ab.	ab.	ab.
Katie	New story	Dr. 1	Dr. 2	Dr. 2	edited →	recopy
Kirsten	Halloween	Dr. 2	Dr. 2	Dr. 2	seq. —→	strip.
Kristian	Sandwich	Dr. 1	Dr. 2	handed in	edited	publish.
Lee	Burgerm	Dr. 1	Dr. 1	Dr. 2	seq. —→	strip.
Lisa	Game Show Dragon	Dr. 1	Dr. 2	Dr. 2	edit →	publish.
Luke	ab.	did for dream homework	Dr. 2	Completed	edit →	publish.
Martin	New story	Dr. 2.	Dr. 2	Dr. 1 story 2	seq. —→	strip.
Meg	New story	Dr. 1	Dr. 2	Dr. 2	Words Fair	edited publish
Morgan	Lost Night	Dr. 1	Dr. 2	Dr. 2	seq. - strip	handed in.
Naomi	Mom's Wedding	Dr. 1	Dr. 2	Dr. 2	Dr. 2 seq →	strip.
Rebecca	New story	Dr. 1	Dr. 1	Dr. 1	Dr. 2	seq. strip.
Rhiannon	Gas Turned off	Dr. 1	Dr. 2	ready to hand in	edited —→	published.
Sean	Cat.	Dr. 1	Dr. 2	Dr. 3	seq. strip	handed in.
Shane	New Story	Dr. 1	Dr. 2	Dr. 2	seq. —→	strip.
Shemiya		New story	Dr. 1	Dr. 2		
Zoe						

Marne's status report is modeled after Nancy Atwell's work. While the record itself keeps her informed of students' progress, the daily oral check keeps students up-to-date as well. Hearing about each other's projects reminds them what to do and sets the tone for productive work.

At the beginning of each session, Marne makes an entry for each student to show what he or she is working on that day. As students get out their writing folders and settle down to writing, she calls their names one after another to gather the "status report" for the day. After that, quiet reigns as even visitors are adjured to be considerate of the students, and Marne settles down to her own writing or quiet conferencing with individual students.

Each day Marne takes down information on where students are in their writing.

MARNE: *I really want to see that story published, don't you? It's just great!* [inaudible response] *You're going to hand it in today? Bravo! – Brooke, your goal?*

BROOKE: *I'm working on my first draft of* [inaudible]

MARNE: *O.K. So draft one of . . . Remember, put all your ideas down first. – Chrissy?*

CHRISSY: *I'm on draft two.*

MARNE: *You're working on draft two. So it'll be just about ready for me to read at the end of this session?*

CHRISSY: *Yes.*

MARNE: *Good. Get an editor to look at it to help you polish it up first. You've got an hour. – Dylan? What is your goal for this class period?*

DYLAN: *I don't know. I have to think of an idea for a story.*

MARNE: *You know what I would like you to do?*

DYLAN: *Make a bunch of squiggles to get some ideas.*

MARNE: *Yeah. Squiggle a whole bunch of ideas down. Write down an idea and then a whole bunch of other words about that idea for me – see if you can get a kind of collection of ideas. Dylan, by the end of this session I'd like to see that sheet full of your plans. We'll try to be quiet for you so you can concentrate. – Alexis?*

ALEXIS: *Well, I'm going to complete my story, but I can't find it anywhere. It's gone.*

MARNE: *That makes me very nervous. I think I may have a copy that you can borrow. It ought to be in your red file. Please get that typed up. – Gillian, what's your plan?*

GILLIAN: *I'm not sure yet what I'm going to write.*

MARNE: *You're not sure what you're going to write about, and you need some time to think about it. I'll put down, "Planning."* [Noise in the background] *I'm sorry. It's a little bit too chatty in here. James, please get closer to the person you're talking to. – Yes, Ben?*

BEN: *I don't have any ideas. I don't know what to write next.*

MARNE: *You finished one? O.K. Let's conference on that at your back desk.* [to entire group] *O.K. Writer's workshop now. No talking at your desks at all. If you want to talk you can go to one of the conference corners.*

CONFERENCES ARE IMPORTANT TO THE WRITING PROCESS

To establish a positive climate for conferences, Marne begins the year by modeling positive ways of discussing students' writing. With a student's permission she will ask the class for feedback on a draft that a student has completed. Students quickly take their cues from her, and during peer conferences they focus their full attention on the reader and then offer comments or suggestions in quiet, positive ways. At times the act of reading a piece of writing aloud becomes feedback in itself. But questions about the content can also be invaluable in helping the writer flesh out a first or second draft.

Students confer with each other about good titles for their writing. Together they try to find the right rhyming words or pore over the thesaurus to enliven their writing. Talking things over quietly makes writing sociable, and at times two students will huddle together, trying to keep down their chuckles as they share the humor of their latest writing. Discussions of the vagaries of spelling lead them to consult *SPELLEX* or a dictionary, and research for non-fiction writing includes the exchange of books and articles as students support each other's efforts.

Unless a student wants special input or help, conferences with the teacher are reserved for writing that has moved beyond the first draft. If spelling and punctuation are still quite rough, the teacher may say to the author, "After you have done all your checking for the things you want to say in draft two or three, I want you to check all the periods and capitals and paragraphs, so that I can read it really easily. When that's done, put your writing into my conference folder and we'll get together."

When they do meet, Marne will usually ask the author to read his or her work aloud to capture the real feel of the writing. While the student is reading, Marne will tolerate no interruptions from anyone, and she keeps her attention riveted on the author's reading. To keep track of the story and her thoughts about it, she will take notes, which more often than not take the form of doodles or a type of pictorial mind map. She then goes over the story making comments and suggestions designed to help the author expand or clarify the writing. If, as in Ben's story, revisions are needed, she confines her comments to the content and leaves corrections of punctuation and capitalization until the writing is closer to being published. Focusing on the mechanics of writing at too early a point catches writers at a time when they feel vulnerable. This kind of detailed criticism may

109
*Learning to write –
writing to learn*

*While conferencing with
students, Marne gives them
her individed attention.*

stop their flow of ideas altogether. During the planning and composing stages, drafts may be rough both in appearance and in accuracy. But by the third draft, when it is time for a teacher conference, peer editing and careful checking should have minimized mechanical errors.

MARNE: *Boy, that's some adventure, isn't it? You've got the "now" fairly well established. You've got the nice weather; you've got them on a picnic . . .*
BEN: *Yeah.*

MARNE: *A picnic with the family and the dog. So you've got a really good start to the story. And then you go into the past and tell a silly thing that this dog did, that is so crazy* [laughs] *– he dives forty feet down, Ben? – that I question whether we are in reality or fantasy. Which is it?*

BEN: *This is fantasy here.*

MARNE: *Sure! I guess it is, isn't it? There's no way that funny sheepdog would be able to survive that. So you've got a fantasy there where silly things are starting to happen. But I was wondering . . . you switched there from having a crazy dog to kind of a nice ordinary dog, the kind that you throw sticks in the water and have a good time with – that's a nice warm image. So as the reader – or the listener, actually – I'm a little bit confused as to whether you should follow this fantasy line or the sweet friend line. You give me both, and it would be possible to do both, but you need to tie them together somehow. Right now more information is required, I guess.*

BEN: *Yeah.*

MARNE: *Would it be possible for you to give more examples of craziness?* [pause] *Is that interesting to you, or is the relationship that Christopher has with Mifle* [the dog] *more important to you? This feeling of having a kind, warm companion and playmate.* [pause] *Which one would you like to elaborate on? I'm not saying you can't have both of them; I'm just saying you have to make it clearer for me.*

BEN: *Hmm.* [pause]

MARNE: *Think about other experiences Mifle and Christopher might have. Do you have a dog, Ben?*

BEN: *Yeah.*

MARNE: *What's his name?*

BEN: *It's a her. Tessa.*

MARNE: *Tessa. So you are aware of the crazy things dogs can do and also of the warm beautiful things they can do. I'd like you to write down some of those things about Tessa. Put down words that you may be able to use for these episodes.*

BEN: *O.K.*

MARNE: *Thanks.*

In her conference, Marne may encourage a student to complete a piece of writing and bring it to publishable state, but she does not insist that all writing is either completed or published.

If the author does not like his or her Haiku poem enough to publish it, Marne simply asks the student to save it in the writing folder and leaves it at that. If someone is stuck and unable to move along with a story, it is filed in the writing folder and may never emerge again. Starting a piece of writing does not mean that it must at all costs be carried to the bitter end. Because of that freedom, students will take risks and venture into new topics or ways of presenting them.

Though the students work independently or in pairs or small groups as they begin new writing, you keep in touch with the

Draft

April. 2 missing Mifle the crazy dog

If was a hot sunny day,

Christopher and his family were having a picnic, that includes their dog Mifle. Mifle was a nice dog he was always excited and happy and he loved people, any people no matter who they they were, he was a sheep dog big white and fluffy oh ya he was also crazy and thisiswhy. Right when Mifle moved in with them they took him to the top ofthe byilding to see the veiw and then Mifle high jumped off the top of the 40 floor kbuilding and landed on his feet so thats why mifles crazy. After their picnic christopher and mifle went for a walk on the beach and they came to a big rock so they climbed onto it

and christopher started throwing

sticks into the water for mifle

gradual evolution of everyone's work with the "status-of-work check" at the beginning of each writer's workshop session. As you check on each student's goal for the day, you not only track progress but also find out who needs some help, who needs to be nudged a bit , and who is ready to publish or share some writing. (See page 106.) Individual work with students during writer's workshop will reveal the need for mini-lessons on specific topics.

How to extend and enrich writing

At every opportunity model writing in all its stages
• Write news on the chalkboard.
• Muse aloud about how to pick the right topic.
• Ask students' advice about choice of words/endings/special features.
• Read your own writing to them at various stages of completion.
• Have examples of good student writing available in class.
• Write letters to students.
• Phrase your written responses to their writing with care.

Extend students' reading
• Introduce rich language and interesting story lines.
• Draw attention to particularly striking metaphors or similes.
• Offer students a wide variety of reading materials including legends, fables, allegories, poetry.
• Make students aware of authors' revisions or updating of works.
• Extend students' experience to give them material to write about.
• Go on field trips.
• Bring in materials for interesting science experiments.
• Develop projects and themes for in-depth study.
• Bring in visitors to talk on special subjects.
• Invite journalists and other writers into the classroom.
• Build students' vocabulary
• Read aloud at every opportunity.
• Call attention to interesting words (without disrupting reading too much).
• Encourage the use of dictionaries, thesauri, and phrase finders.

113
*Learning to write –
writing to learn*

- During conferences help students find more accurate descriptive words.
- Invite them to keep a notebook full of special ideas and words.

Create awareness of the usefulness of writing
- Include written tasks in everything you do.
- Show the power of writing through examples of effective letters, appeals.
- Invite students to brainstorm about the many ways they use writing.

Encourage imagination and spontaneity
- Use brainstorming and webbing to get ideas flowing.
- Read fairy tales and similar imaginative writing.
- Discuss the power of myth.
- Encourage students to invent their own fairy tales.

MINI-LESSONS

Following Nancie Atwell's model of providing mini-lessons generally works well. She keeps lessons to no more than ten minutes and draws the topics from the need of the moment. At the beginning of the year, we have found it useful to stay with general topics about getting started – how to get ideas down fast, reviewing rules for writing, presenting students' writings as models, and generally encouraging writers to plunge deeply and quickly into their first drafts.

As writing develops throughout the year, it can be fruitful to get students to refer to their reading to make them aware of differences in style, ways of evoking feelings or building suspense, and of good descriptions or choices of words. Looking at metaphors and similes during reader's workshop can inspire students to add richness to their own writing, and can become a topic of mini-lessons to help students inject more colorful language into their writing.

The mechanics of writing become topics for mini-lessons as students move toward publishing. Marne's lesson on capitals and abbreviations was drawn from material in her "ready for final edit" file. Student's writing that is too general for the reader

Detail

senses

smells
felt like
sight
sounds
taste
+
emotions — how does the writer feel

Draft 1

- read out loud
- "boil down the soup"
  (cross out the watery stuff)
- circle boring words and find better ones in the <u>thesaurus</u>.
- spelling
- re-copy as Draft 2.

Are you stuck?

- read to a friend and ask for ideas
- draw a plan of your story
- find a good book for more information

Report

- GOOD LOOKING COVER.
  - good drawing
  - interesting detail.
  - colourful + bright.
  - clear printing of title + author.

- Introduction — tells (short + concise) about the report. so you don't have to read all the report to find what's in it.

- Text. - typed.
  - short
  - clear

- Illustrations - xeroxes
  - captions. - drawing
  - photos
  - magazine clipping

As she conducts mini-lessons, Marne produces spur-of-the-moment posters that stay up for a while to help students remember the lesson.

115
*Learning to write –
writing to learn*

can trigger a mini-lesson on the need to be specific so that readers can understand the story. Frequently misspelled words may come under review, or the vexing problems of choosing *I* or *me, who* or *whom.*

As long as the lessons are short and are drawn from material that students need to correct at that time, even quite structured lessons on grammar will be carefully attended to. Working with students on material that they need right then builds on their desire to write – and write well – and holds their attention.

GETTING WRITING READY FOR PUBLICATION

"Publishing" ranges all the way from simply typing a page with a poem or brief story to the full-fledged production of bound books. At the upper levels students may do their own typing and use all the technology available in the computer room, but parents and teacher's aides still help a good deal and, as Marne's request slip shows, also do some of the editing.

Dear Publisher for *Alexis*

Please type this wonderful work *Alexis* has produced. It should be well spaced as it needs to be cut up into smaller paragraphs. Please don't make it wider than 20 cm. Feel free to correct any paragraphing or mechanics as you type it. Also, if possible have the author dictate it to you as you go.

Thanks.

M

Marne

Students will take special care with their illustrations, especially if the writing is lengthy – as they are creating something that is more like a real book. They have studied and enjoyed the illustrations in the books they have read and have developed their artistic skills during art sessions. The following exchange during an open house between the teacher, Anne Keay, of the South Park School Challenge Program, and one of her students describes the richness of the artwork that can become part of published books:

ANNE: *How did you and the other kids do the illustrations for your book, Josh? Did you just sit down and draw them?*

JOSH: *No. For each chapter, we had to think of what would be the most exciting part. So we got the most exciting part, and we drew that and we colored it in pastels or whatever and put fixative on it, and then we glued it onto our paper.*

ANNE: *Was that sort of like the writing part where you had to do several drafts of the writing? Did you do the same with the pictures? Did you experiment?*

JOSH: *Yeah. We experimented with chalk and paint, pastels, bamboo pens –* that *was weird! – fountain pens, and turpentine. You could draw with some of these pastels and then use a paintbrush and it would become paint. That was neat.*

ANNE: *How many weeks did this take you?*

JOSH: *Three or four – almost a month.*

ANNE: *So you tried out the illustrations to get a feel for what you wanted to do. You'll notice that all the illustrations are done in different media: some with pencil crayons, some with felts, some with paint, some with chalk pastels. Everyone had to make a choice.*

JOSH: *Yeah. Some people used turpentine over their pastels and some people left them flat. But most of the people used pastels because they're a lot brighter and easier to color with. But sometimes they smudge. After we published our books we had kind of a workshop. That's when we had to write down what each of us thought about our book and what we thought about our finished copy.*

Along with experiments with different media, challenge program students tried a variety of layouts to fit the illustrations to the text in imaginative ways. Several types of bindings held the finished copies together and further added to the eye appeal

117
*Learning to write –
writing to learn*

JOHN EARL HOBBES
AND THE CASTLE OF SMOG

*Cover design and
illustrations become
important parts of
publishing.*

and professional look with which students endowed their work. In the regular classroom, Liz had students paste their finished work into small copy books, and then she provided beautiful wrapping paper to cover the outside bindings.

Although students take a great deal of pride and pleasure in their published work, the real joy of writer's workshop is the planning and writing. Students will readily give away or even lose their work once it is done. The fun of *doing the writing* is the most important part.

Ways of sparking writing

Most of the time you will find that students can generate plenty of their own ideas for writing. But if you need to get writers started, here are some suggestions:

- Ask them to write the text for picture books that have no words.
- Bring in reproductions of famous paintings and discuss why people like them. Then ask students to write their own reactions – positive or negative.
- If they are tired of serious report-writing, ask students to choose a report and then give it an imaginative twist: What happens when a student takes a report on lions and turns them into vegetarians? What if a duck becomes a long-distance runner or a rowboat a means of world travel? Report-writing has been transformed.
- Create new endings for stories or put new characters into familiar tales.
- Create advertisements for garage sales, popcorn sales, hotdog cookouts.
- To give newcomers to class an introduction to their new classroom, suggest that students write descriptions of their school day or what it is like to be in class throughout the week.
- Create a family tree.
- Follow a baby through its first year of life – write a baby book with photographs for illustrations. (In Margaret's class a mother visited regularly before giving birth and then brought her baby in throughout the year.)
- Research UFOs and write a report.
- Write a success story – of a person, a town, a school.
- Write books or stories for younger buddies.
- Write a job description for a new teacher, janitor, babysitter.
- Write about safety – bicycle safety, the importance of seat belts, swimming or boating safety.
- Watch a TV show and then write about the plot, changing the ending.
- Write a play for TV.
- Invite students to write plays for their younger buddies.

Making the reading-writing connection

To move their writing away from simple descriptions or narratives, students begin to adopt the vocabulary, style, and special tech-

119
*Learning to write –
writing to learn*

niques of their favorite authors. Reading a wide variety of materials provides models and inspiration to become more expressive, and, as publishing gets under way, students become quite conscious of title pages, tables of content, and different layouts. Pattern writing is not limited to poetry. Students will emulate mysteries, fairy tales, legends, and the expository prose of their non-fiction research materials. Though much of it may be subconscious, students develop a feel for story development, characterization, and the use of dialogue.

Perceptiveness in reading and writing evolve together. As students do lots of reading (both in class and out), they begin to pay attention to some of the special language and the interesting turns of the plot with thoughts of applications for their own writing. As their writing evolves, they appreciate their reading that much more. It helps to discuss what they think and feel about their reading, but writing *about* these thoughts and feelings is an unfamiliar task. In fact, criticism is a genre of its own. A lot of discussion and modeling is required before students will feel comfortable with it.

WRITING REACTIONS TO LITERATURE

Liz describes her experience when she asked her students to write about literature:

In the late fall, I asked students to write their reactions to literature. We discussed writing about our feelings and what it was about a story that made the reader keep on reading. We also talked about stories that we *didn't* like and how it was all right to express negative feelings too. Since the students seemed enthusiastic I assumed they were ready to write a reaction to literature. I read a story and we discussed our reactions to it. Then I asked the students to write those reactions down. – You would have thought I had asked them to write in a foreign language. As I discovered later, that was just about what I'd done. The students were anxious; they wasted time; some just sat, unable to put pencil to paper. In short, the session was a disaster! Although some of the students wrote something, most of them retold the plot rather than their reaction to it.

As I reflected on the lesson, it became clear to me that I hadn't modeled what I was asking students to do! Though I know all about modeling and use it, I had overlooked the fact that when I introduced a new task, I needed to model what I had in mind. For the next week, whenever I read a story or chapter, I talked to the class as I wrote on the overhead about my reactions to the piece. I talked about how I felt and mused aloud about how I could best express these feelings. As I put my thoughts on the overhead, I commented on the sentence structure, choice of words, and punctuation. At times I asked the students to help me decide the best word to use or to give me suggestions for better ways of expressing an idea. I double-spaced my writing so that I could incorporate the suggestions the students offered and make corrections as I wrote.

After a week of modeling, I asked the students to try a piece on their own. The results confirmed what I already knew. Students need to have lots of modeling before they are ready to try a new task. This time they were much more confident and actually eager to try. Through sharing both their writing and mine, we discovered better ways to express opinions and feelings. Together we learned to talk about the rhythm of the language, the subject matter, the author's choice of conflict and solution, and above all how the words and ideas made them feel. Based on that joint practice, writing about their reading has become an integral part of the day.

Our own observations mirror Liz's conclusion that writing plot summaries is a basic starting point for writing about reading, and is a natural part of the move from concrete to abstract that characterizes natural learning. You may find that some of your students will make the shift from relating the plot to writing down what they think and feel within a week, others will need a lot more time and lots more modeling. If you look at the task, you will recognize that it is really a quite sophisticated examination of the structure of writing, one outside of the experience of young writers who think in concrete terms about stories and events in their daily lives. So allow plenty of time and keep on modeling – both orally and in writing – the kinds of comments you would make about a story or chapter you have just read to your class: "I felt I was looking over the wall of the secret garden. The author's descriptions are so rich that I could make a mental picture of the tangled undergrowth with the flowers peaking through." Or, "I felt confused at the beginning of the chapter, but the flashback gave me the kind of information I needed to make sense of the story. It's a really clever way of giving background information without being boring."

READING LEADS INTO WRITING PLAYS

If a story is dramatic and invites students to act out or mime exciting parts, the production of spontaneous plays eventually leads into scriptwriting. At first students will often simply get together props and costumes and start to rehearse. The physical acting out shapes the scenes, and from there the students will structure their play to fit a fairly standard progression from opening scene through conflict to resolution. There tends to be a good deal of friendly rough and tumble in these productions. The audience loves such action-packed drama, and – within reason – we allow it to unfold. From such concrete work, the creation of plays leads into script writing and, here again, the

121
*Learning to write –
writing to learn*

teacher's help is needed to model the appropriate form and to refer students to printed plays as models.

As students gain experience, you will find that they begin to get together to write the rough outline of a play and may even begin to write scripts as they move into production of the play. If you allow the natural evolution from concrete acting out to abstract discussions and from gross approximations of actions to fine discrimination of dialogue and structure to take their course, students become creative and confident in their dramatic productions. Occasionally a remark that a particular story or book would lend itself to adaptation to a play will spark student interest, but more often students make their own decisions about those novels or stories they wish to turn into a drama project.

Writing for the "real world"

Think back to your university days and recapture the feelings you had about assignments you considered a waste of time. Your students feel the same way about assignments that seem to have no real purpose. But if their writing is connected with real events or genuine needs, they are eager and willing to do their best. They rise to the challenge of responsibility and develop their social skills in the process. So turn over as many writing tasks as possible to your students.

Special events
• Keep notes of plans, jobs, things to be done.
• Take minutes of meetings.
• Prepare and address invitations.
• Prepare and distribute posters to advertise the event.
• Create and illustrate menus, programs, or tables of events.
• Develop scripts for commercials or radio dialogue.

Letter writing
• Write letters to make reservations for field trips.
• Send letters to politicians or government officials about special issues.
• Write to buddies or pen pals.
• Invite authors or people with special knowledge or talent to visit.

- Send thank-you notes.
- Write letters to the editor to voice opinions, praise a performance, make a point.
- Prepare a résumé to get a summer job.

Keep track of what is going on
- Keep a learning log of what is going on in math, science, literature, and so on.
- Keep a private diary of feelings, successes, worries (not for general view).
- Have students do the daily roll call and chart student attendance. (Discuss/predict patterns of absences, highs and lows of attendance.)
- Have interested students set up a weather station and chart meteorological data.

When turning the above jobs over to students, it is important not to make them whole-class projects but to ask for volunteers, offer choices, and consider interests, talents, and special needs. Many of the jobs can be handled individually or in small groups while the rest of the class is concentrating on something else.

Projects generate writing

Meeting curriculum requirements through project work generates a lot of writing. Research notes for dioramas and displays need to be gathered; descriptive labels need to be made for the finished exhibit; and some projects develop into full-scale research reports.

At the end of the school year, Sylvia's class worked in teams to produce newspapers – a marvelous way of drawing all the writing skills together into one final fun project. Planning the content, tone, and extent of each tabloid took a good amount of time. Brainstorming ideas and researching the local papers for suggestions created sensitivity to the overall organization and content of a city newspaper and sparked ideas to fit individual interests and talents. Juliana, with her interest in fashion and drawing, quite naturally became the fashion editor; Jeremy, who still resisted writing whenever possible, built on his enthusiasm for sports and, with the help of his teammates, produced excellent reports on the Stanley Cup hockey play-offs; Amanda, with her interest and wide reading in history and biography, inspired her team to move back into the Middle Ages and to produce a newspaper that sustained the medieval theme throughout. Along with news reports and editorials, there were cartoons, classified ads, political cartoons, horoscopes, and a "Dear Logan" column complete with a photograph of Logan and spirited replies to readers' questions. Sylvia acted as a consultant to the student teams, but let them plan and decide how their newspapers would evolve.

COMPUTERS AID THE WRITING PROCESS

Since South Park School has a computer lab that is open to students on an ongoing basis, the production phase of the newspaper project moved into the lab. Teams of students typed, chose the appropriate typefaces, debated size and style of headlines, and generally collaborated to turn out finished copy. Laughter and excited conferencing at times created something approximating pandemonium, but a warning from Sylvia quickly settled everyone down and production moved along. Being trusted to do the job, to stay on task most of the time, definitely aided the production process. If you think about your own way of working intensely, you will remember the times when you simply needed some time out – a moment to relax, socialize, do something different. Students are no different. Working with computers opens new possibilities for editing and for using creative layout and design, and gives students the opportunity to move out of the classroom. Creating finished copy without the need to retype pages endlessly is a real plus, and students learn to use all of the features of word-processing programs to give their work a polished professional look.

LAYOUT, DESIGN, AND ILLUSTRATIONS ARE PART OF POLISHED WRITING

As a final stage, illustrations and text had to be collated and made to fit the newspaper format. Along with writing, students learned about editing copy to fit not only the topic but a specific space. The discipline of having to fit their writing into an appropriate space and format added a new dimension to the editing and to the design of their finished work. Teamwork definitely helped the process as those with the best graphic skills made suggestions that speeded the trial-and-error process past the frustration point. A school photocopy machine that enlarges or reduces print was a definite help as the project entered its final phase. Last-minute fillers or reductions completed the

The  WASTER

LOONEL 1990

June 8, 1990

A1

Rent Walk

Appearing in small groups on the parliament building lawn were protesting seniors and friends. Apparently to one witness.

"The B.C. goverment allows greedy landlords to starve seniors by raiseing the rent to a point the seniors can't afford."

It's not yet been made clear if this small protest will do any good, but many people think it was a good way to spend a afternoon!

by David B.
Jai K.

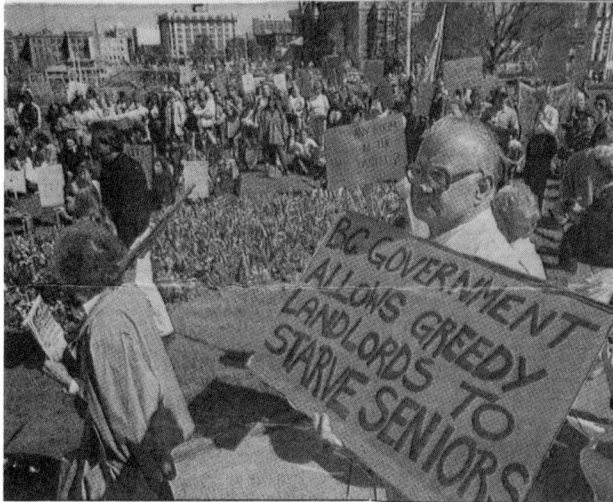

R.P.G.s

R.P.G.s stand for role playing games. In R.P.G.s people role up characters with dice and equipe them with weapons and equipement rangeing from Bo staffs to rifles to time machiens! Since the orginal R.P.G. Dongens and Dragons (the first and arguably the best) R.P.G.s have been played buy many people from old pensioning sinors to six year old kids in grade one, R.P.G.s are a hitwith almost every body who has played them for an amount of time will tell you T.M.N.T., Ninjas and Superspies, Heroes Unlimited, Beond the Supernatral, Robotech and many others are more fun than many people will give them credit for because in the 50's people took D+D to heart and some people got there brains worped and went pychoand some people got kiled. If you are given a chance just try it once.

by David
Brereton

Geraldo Rivera of the wild.

50-50?

You all remember the Carmanah valley, some of you have been there. What do you think of the 50-50 split? Did MacBlow log before they got the word? There are many questions; not enough fitting answers. That's all we know for sure. Log.......... mabey, log near the water shed............... are they nuts? Worse, they want to clear-cut the whole valley! And why did the goverment let them get away with half of what's not theirs in the first place? If took 43 years for the goverment to get around to war crimes (people were killed!), imagine how long it will take them to get around to a logger who cut down a few trees!!??

By David
Brereton

IN NATURAL SURROUNDINGS and on film, whales make a point about the importance of environmental preservation. They're featured in *Island of Whales*, premiering at Environment Festival '90.

ONCE ENDANGERED, the white pelican compelled Canada Life to pursue environmental goals. Saving the bird which graces its company logo was the business's first environmental-protection victory.

As a final project for the year, seventh-graders formed teams to produce newspapers.

The Swift Times

50 cents minimum outside Lower Mainland   Victoria B.C.   50 CENTS

PLANTS, A CURE FOR AIDS?

-TEGUCIGALPA, HONDURAS

David Jessman, 54, a plant collector specializing in the Aratia species has made a cure for the AIDS virus.

David Jessman was experimenting with the Fatsia japonica Aratia plant so he crushed it up into powder. His son Sean Jessman 17, an AIDS victim, swallowed the powder. 2 weeks later, at Sean's doctor's appointment it appeared that Sean did not have AIDS!

After 6 months of research, scientists and doctors have declared the powder a cure for the AIDS virus. The powder is called the "Japonica" AIDS cure. The "Japonica" has made a great relief for AIDS patients.

There is only one problem with "Japonica." The Fatsia japonica plant is very rare and only grows in South America. There are new Aratia plantations are to be started up to make

the "Japonica" cure.

David Jessman started his research on Nov.1, 89 and concluded his research on May 21, 90.

The Fatsia japonica plant is a member of the Aralia family and is a Japanese evergreen shrub that has leathery maple-like dark shiny leaves and it is very attractive.

FATSIA
JAPONICA
LEAF

HOSTAGES TALE OF CAPTIVITY

SYDNEY, AUSTRALIA

U.S. Citizen Lloyd Toicaw - drawn for tweeks as a hostage of African rebels - visited the grave of his wife yesterday died while he was in hostage.

"He's safe! He's safe!" cried Toicaw 43, of Houston Tx. when his brother Tyler met him on his captors washed his clothes, gave him a blanket and coffe "in a bag glass."

Thouever they did beat him. Authorities said ransom was not paid for his release despite the demand that he would be killed unless they receivrd $90,000.

RECYCLE THIS PAPER

release. He brokedown just a few moments after his release when said that his wife, Beshara, had died more than 2 weeks before he was let free.

Lloyd had lost 15 lbs. which had been caused by malnutrition. Lloyd had to have one

toe amputated from the result of being beaten while in hostage. Toicaw said that he and his captors walked sometimes 7 hours a day through the desert to escape military pursuit but said his

BURGLARY IN SNAIL LAND

VICTORIA, B.C.

George Robinson, 39, collects and has a snail farm in Sooke. He collects oriental and exotic snails around the world.

Last friday a burglary took place at Robinsons Snail Farm. 1,029 snails were stolen at the value of $3,359. There is a reward for any information leading to the robbery. IF

you have any information please contact your local police dept.

EIGHT MINERS TRAPPED BY EXPLOSION

ONTARIO, CANADA

On May 23, 90 just 2 days ago, eight miners, trapped by an explosion in the central branch mine of J&J coal company near the outskirts of Ontario are believed to have been killed.

A second blast occurred early yesterday while investigators province inspectors were in the mine. Everyone escaped unin

SNAIL FROM IRAN WORTH $372

Index

International
National
Local

Arts and Entertainment

Weather and Sports

Classified, Dear Abby, Editorial

Sticks and stones may brake my bones but words will never hurt me!

jobs, and all teams were ready to display their finished news-papers to the class.

Field trips spark imagination

Field trips in town can be as effective in sparking the students' imagination as an overnight stay in an ancient forest. As one teacher told us:

> I thought that taking my intermediate students on the same kinds of field trips that my primary students enjoyed wouldn't work. But when I put it to the test, they merely went into greater depth of information gathering and enjoyed the outings immensely. At the local newspaper they inter-viewed layout specialists to get tips for their own work; in the vet's office they gathered information on the care of their pets; and in the local bakery, along with tasting delicious samples, they learned about the ins and outs of running a family business.

Whenever the opportunity presents itself, students at South Park School enjoy the benefits of the local theater scene. Some are whole-class trips, but small-group visits to special shows may be organized by teachers, a parent, or even students. When Shakespeare's *Twelfth Night* was playing at a local theater, one of the seventh-grade students organized a group of classmates to go to see it. When the opera is on, Marne will see to it that everyone who wants to – from kindergarten to grade 7 – has a chance to go to the dress rehearsal, which is offered to students at greatly reduced rates. She makes it a gala event and everyone dresses formally to get into the spirit of attending a truly elegant, adult performance. To help students enjoy the music and acting, plot summaries are discussed in class, and after the performance students at times speculate – in writing – how a sad story might be changed to have a happier ending. (See examples on page 127.)

A trip to the local art gallery became the impetus for continued reading, the production of posters, and research for reports. At the time of the actual visit, students were conducting a scavenger hunt based on Sylvia's suggestions. (See page 31.) Instead of aimlessly wandering around displays, students went in to look for specific information, and with that focus, infor-mation finding moved beyond the required search, because they had a framework for looking at a wealth of material. You will find that setting a framework and kindling interest and enthusiasm before a field trip will spark the purposeful activity that leads to thoughtful information gathering and writing. It is not enough to provide only transportation and supervision on a field trip. As

127
*Learning to write –
writing to learn*

Draft 1

Kate   Jan. 17

The way I would end it is so that Tatyana would move to a diffrent contre with Eugene Onegin and get maired.

And my reson why is that she would probly wanted to mwiry Eugene Onegin insted of Prince Gremin.

And she probley wants to have happnas insted of riches

Attending the dress rehearsal of the local opera production of Eugene Onegin sparked imaginative writing.

Zoë   Draft 1   Jan. 17

I am going to pretend I am Tatyana. If I were the person who wrote the "Opera" I would write the Opera this way.

When they meat I would make Eugene Onegin say 'I love you and I know I have been cruel and I also regret it, I am deeply in love with you please forgive me. I would make Tatyana say no. I would have Eugene Onegin recite a love poem and it would make Tatyana go drousy because the poem was so beautiful and she says I forgive you I would rather have happiness than richness. And they get married and the prince becomes Eugene Onegin's page.

The End

with other activities, you are the one who creates the climate for learning and sets the scene for success.

Imaginative writing is a sure sign of success, and Kristian's "Rights of Dogs Bill" is a delightful example. A trip to the legislative assembly and classroom discussions about rights and responsibilities provided the foundation for his creative writing. Other classmates focused on the rights and responsibilities of students, which brought the ideas to a concrete level for them. Can you imagine a carefully structured lesson on rights and responsibilities inspiring students to the same degree as this field trip-cum-discussion did? The field trip is another instance of the teacher providing a framework for turning an abstract lesson "above the level of understanding of students" into a concrete, absorbing topic for discussion and

Kristian   Rights of Dogs Bill April.3

Introduced by Hon. Kristian Larson, Minister of Animal Welfare Division 6, house of Commons Third reading April. 2

Dogs be allowed access to all parks with the exeptions of parks which are primarily ornamental gardens.

Dog owners should follow These Rules:

① Dog owners should clean up after their dogs. Penalty for not complying will be a $75,00 Fine.

② Dogs should not be allowed to annoy any animal or person in the park. Owners should remove their dog from the park if the dog is being annoying.

③ Dogs should not be allowed to cause any damage to the property. Penalty for not complying will be having the owner pay for the damage.

A trip to the Legislative Assembly had Kristian emulate the work of the members.

129
Learning to write –
writing to learn

writing. Connecting materials to be learned to their own day-to-day experiences and needs never fails to captivate students.

Writing letters is a fine art

Like other forms of writing, letter-writing must be modeled if letters are to be more than scribbled notes. Marne writes letters to her students to inform them of the plans that lie ahead. She sends letters home to inform parents of important events or to ask them for assistance or permission for field trips. She also interacts in letter form with her students in their reading response journals. Here she models – at the students' level – how to inject feelings and thoughtful comments into letter writing to take it beyond the "here is what we did" stage. (See page 131.)

Letters to pen pals can become rich sources of descriptive writing as students exchange information on their interests, family and friends, home town, and special holidays. Making the writers aware that what seems obvious to them may be quite mysterious to someone who lives in another town or country becomes the impetus for thoughtful work and careful detail. For Alexis, who corresponds with a pen pal in Latvia, letter writing became the starting point for research into Latvia and other countries on the Baltic Sea and led to imaginative writing that drew on authentic information about these countries. (See pages 132 and 133.)

If, at the beginning of the year, students have not yet found a pen pal, writing letters to each other can become a fun part of writer's workshop. Liz keeps a mailbox in her classroom and supplies a writing center with letter paper and envelopes. To encourage more formal, correct ways of letter writing, she demonstrates and posts the proper format of letters: information about the sender's name and address, date, proper name and address of the receiver, and appropriate salutations and closings. If students use the classroom mailbox, Liz insists that they adhere to proper format. That request for formality reminds students to check their writing mechanics before placing a letter in the mail. As Liz points out to them, if they were writing to a student in another country, only standard spelling could be found if their pen pal needed to consult a dictionary.

In keeping with the focus on meaningful writing, Sylvia's students send letters to the principal, Trevor, and other teachers for such genuine purposes as formal thank you notes and permission requests. (See examples on pages 134–137.) Similarly, Sylvia had students address letters to politicians at various

Upgrading spelling is part of writing development

levels to voice their concerns about logging practices in ancient timber stands. Their very personal feelings about the topic lent weight to their writing efforts, and no spelling errors slipped by when those letters were finalized for mailing.

Accurate spelling is one of the concerns raised frequently in conversations with intermediate teachers who have heard about invented spelling and the need to let students evolve their own

Sept 6

Dear Marne,

I'm reading Anne of Green Gables I had started it at home and I read all way to chapter 4 and then I stoped and read it today. I read one chapter and one page. I realy like the book very much. I have both movies of Anne of Grean Gabble at home and it's fun to compear Marilla Cuthbert from the movie and the book I'm a big fan of them

Love Lisa

Sept 6

Dear Lisa
I'm a big fan of them too, I think the movie did a great job of following

131
*Learning to write –
writing to learn*

the novels but I always pictured
Marilla as being thinner than the
movie actress. Matthew was just
right. But Anne was just a little
too pretty in the movie. In my
imagination she was more
unusual looking.

I'm glad I'm giving you class time
to finish reading Anne of Green Gables.
You couldn't spend time in a
wiser way! Enjoy it, Lisa!

Love
Marne

spelling. "But when do they finally learn to spell?" is the question we hear most often. Our observations at South Park School in classes that ranged from grade 3 to grade 7 assured us that spelling does evolve gradually to more standard forms, but also showed clearly that even at the upper levels students will still have misspelled words in their drafts if not in their published work. So how *do* we move students toward standard spelling?

Observing primary students on the one hand and adult literacy learners on the other has shown us again and again that

Author's age
Years 11 months 4.

This is E...

TICKET rack
to stamp...
from...

my letter box

I have a penpal in Latvia. Her name is Signe. She is 12 years old. I love getting letters ▓▓▓▓ from her. Her letter always comes in an envelope with a picture on the front the picture is usually of a Latvian girl wearing the Latvian traditonal costume the girl is neeling under a tree.

Asked to produce writing for another teacher within a time constraint cramps Alexis' style.

neither rules nor special exercises make much of an impression on students *unless* they are done in conjunction with writing and/or are given in ways that students relate to and see as important. What *does* make a difference in spelling development is encouraging students to develop spelling patterns gradually in the course of their own writing. As they generate invented spelling they think about the words and their sounds, and they feel a degree of control over their own learning. Just as they are able to gradually evolve and then refine the rules of grammar with their mother tongue, so they are able to evolve and upgrade

133
*Learning to write –
writing to learn*

the rules of spelling if they are given the opportunity to do so in a classroom environment that makes it safe to experiment.

When we have used spelling exercises and drills, we have found that even when students do well on them, they don't transfer their knowledge to their writing. Our finding is poignantly supported by Dr. Richard Gentry who tells of his struggle to become a good speller in his book *SPEL . . . Is a Four-Letter Word* (1987). In his opening letter to his college English professor he speaks of the humiliation of being at university and being called in to hear about his abominable spelling. According to his

> "Boy the parthalon sure was incredable Marika its so um big!" chatterd Alexis "Yes Alexis what do you want to see tommorow?" "um" Alexis was busy trying to wipe humos of her new sun dress she flung up her arms whitch in one way was to mean she had given up with the humos and in a nother way to say she new notheing about Greek buildings "Marika can you decide you seem to be the expert on Greek history" Alexis spoke in a rather xasperated tone of voice "Marika can I have a slovaki Im sort of hungery?" sure Alexis but my mothers going to have to buy a hotol supermarket to feed you!

When free to draft at her leisure, both Alexis' imagination and writing style flourish.

professor, ". . . anyone who is as intelligent as you [Gentry] are and who can't spell is lazy!" But Gentry goes on to show that far from being lazy, he worked hard at his spelling, but never learned to do it well.

Addressing himself to his professor, Gentry writes:

In elementary school I had written two hundred and fifty-two perfect spelling tests. For thirty-six weeks each year, seven years in a row, I memorized the weekly spelling list so I could make 100 on the test. I was my school's expert at figuring out those inane exercises in the spelling

---

May 9

Dear Trevor and Sylvia

In the few weeks of school that are left we (Nathanda and Amanda) would like to start a lunch time running club for girls in Sylvia's class.

We propose that on Thurs. and Tues., the people in the club would be dismissed at 11:45 for lunch. From 11:45 till 12:55 this is what will be happening.

11:45 go to the bathroom to change
11:55 warm up and go for run in the park
12:30 come in and jump in the shower to rinse, sweat off.
12:45 eat lunch
12:55 return to the class as the buzzer goes.

We will suply you with a map of our route so you will always know where we are. We will also get permission slips from our parents. Please respond as soon as possible and we would be happy to arange a time to meat with you

Amanda and Nathanda

Students are in no doubt about the value of effective letter writing.

June

Dear Marg,

Its too bad you have to leave
& we all going to miss you.
I remember when you got us to
make mansions. That was fun. You
have come up with so many original
ideas that I can't remember them
all.

Sincerely,
Jordan

*Marg's departure from
South Park brought forth
students' personal
expressions.*

textbook that required kids to dissect the most obscure properties of
words imaginable – none of them remotely related to learning to spell.
Even my teachers consulted me for help with those exercises. I always
made As in spelling, but I always knew I couldn't spell.

Here is a champion speller telling us he couldn't spell. He
goes on to say that "by the time the write-up appeared in the local
paper praising 'the county's best spellers,' I had forgotten about
a quarter of the words on the list." It seems that memory work,
drills, and special spelling lists don't help us learn to spell for
everyday writing.

> June 24
> South Park School
> 508 Douglas St
> Victoria B. C.
>
> Dear Marg,
>
> I'm sorry about your retirement. You are a good teacher and South Park will miss you alot
>
> I remember when ever we went down to buddies you were always encouraging and you always had some criteria for us or our buddies. You also had creative ideas for each one of our projects
>
> I was sorry to see Elaine go but I was consolled to have you come. I never relly knew you before we had buddies but everybody said you were nice. And you still are.
>
> Sincerely
>
> Eliam

HOW TO FOSTER SPELLING DEVELOPMENT IN THE INTERMEDIATE GRADES

Like Gentry, we have found that "Purposeful writing is a key to learning to spell." If students write to communicate, they are concerned with their readers, and because of this they will take an interest in developing both their vocabulary and their spelling. So fostering that interest in words and language is the first step in moving students toward standard spelling. Drawing students' attention to interesting words whenever the occasion

137
*Learning to write –
writing to learn*

presents itself keeps interest focused on meaning and communication. After reading the story *The Good Giants and the Bad Puckwudgies,* Marne asked students to take a look at the "Yankee language." During read-aloud sessions of poetry she will talk about the beauty of the language and the use of special words to evoke feelings. As a result, students take their cues from her and make a concerted effort to find just the right words for their writing. They have become conscious of the power of language and are excited about experimenting with different ways of saying the same thing.

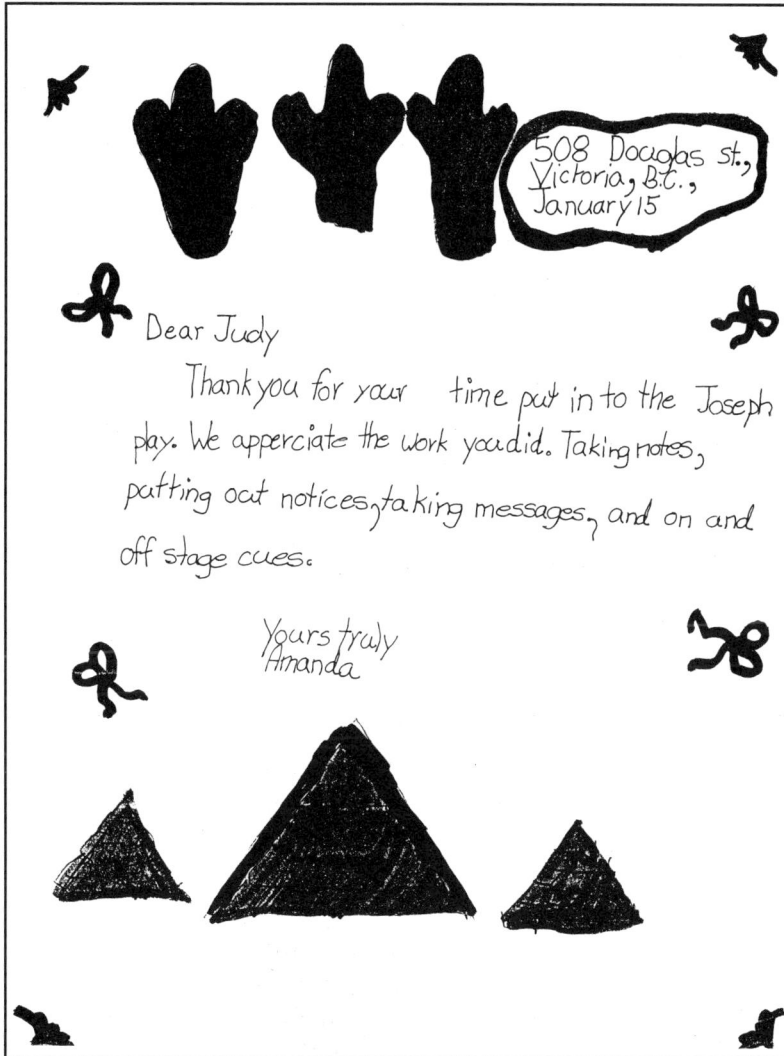

Students share the responsibility of winding up a successful production.

In her class, Liz projects overhead transparencies of pages of writing – printed or produced by students – onto the chalkboard so that students can chalk in changes to express ideas in different ways or to correct words they believe are misspelled. If she uses student writing in this kind of work, then the thought of helping another student with his or her own writing becomes the incentive to learn about spelling. Putting a piece of writing on an overhead and asking students to find any non-standard spelling starts a careful scrutiny and leads to the process of comparing notes. Once everyone has had a chance to write down the words that appear to need spelling revision, the teacher goes over the piece of writing line by line asking students to identify the words that need to be corrected. She then writes down all versions offered and circles the correct one. Once all of the words are on the board, there is a general discussion about the various versions. The teacher asks students to state reasons for spelling a word a particular way. She makes sure to comment on the rationales for all tries so that students come away from the exercise knowing that their way of spelling was reasonable and not just a pure guess: "If you know that *tea* and *leaf* have an *ea,* then it is a good generalization to write *feald.*" "*Beautiful* could be spelled with two *l*'s because *full* is spelled that way." A look at other words ending *ful* may enliven the discussion and is often suggested by students themselves. "The pronunciation of *separate* could suggest that it be spelled with four *e*'s." At this point, if no one suggests it, the teacher might refer to the pronunciation of the word *separation* as a way of getting a clue to at least one of the *a*'s. She would remind students that words come in different forms and sometimes one form is easier to remember correctly.

If you keep these sessions short and lively, students will not only learn about spelling but will be reassured about their ability to think of ways to spell words or to invent spelling when they are unsure. They know they have something to go on. The same exercise can be done by dictating, say, ten words that you have gleaned from students' writing as being in need of review. Once students have given you their various versions and all words are on the board for comparison, you have wonderful opportunities for commenting on spelling patterns, and the students will make their own contributions to enliven the discussion.

Working with spelling in this non-threatening way keeps students interested and willing to look at words in different ways: from the standpoints of how they sound, how they look,

139
*Learning to write –
writing to learn*

what their prefixes and suffixes are, and what their meaning suggests in the way of spelling. Taking the latter, they might find it easier to relate to the spelling of *health* if they think of the verb *heal.* Looking at it that way may also throw light on the difference between *heal* and *heel.* Playing with words in different forms, looking at such homonyms as *heal* and *heel,* can be fun and can also raise consciousness about spelling.

When using the sounds of words as a guide to spelling, it may be more effective to test what the word feels like as one says it. Consonants, at any rate, are easier to spot by noticing "their feel." Paying attention to the lips, tongue, and nose can reveal what consonant is needed. But students will soon learn that in English vowels are rather unpredictable and realize that "taking a mental picture" of a word that causes problems may be a more effective way than sounding it out when trying to commit standard spelling to memory. That approach leads to comparing various forms of a word to decide on the standard spelling. Students' writing will show lists like: *skard, skared, scard, scared* or *aloud, alowd, allowed,* and the right one is not necessarily included in that list. In fact, at times it is hard to give up a well-established sound or spelling pattern. When asking for the spelling of *use,* one student was quite puzzled when the teacher gave him *u s e.* He repeated his request and when the teacher asked him what he thought the correct spelling might be, he put down *youze,* certainly a much better approximation of the sound than *use* and also a fine generalization of what the student knew to be an acceptable spelling pattern. In this case, the student reluctantly agreed to accept the dictionary version, but his teacher acknowledged that his *youze* had the right sound, and thereby affirmed that he was thinking about his spelling in useful ways.

At times, visual depiction of several versions of the same word sound helps a student to identify standard spelling.

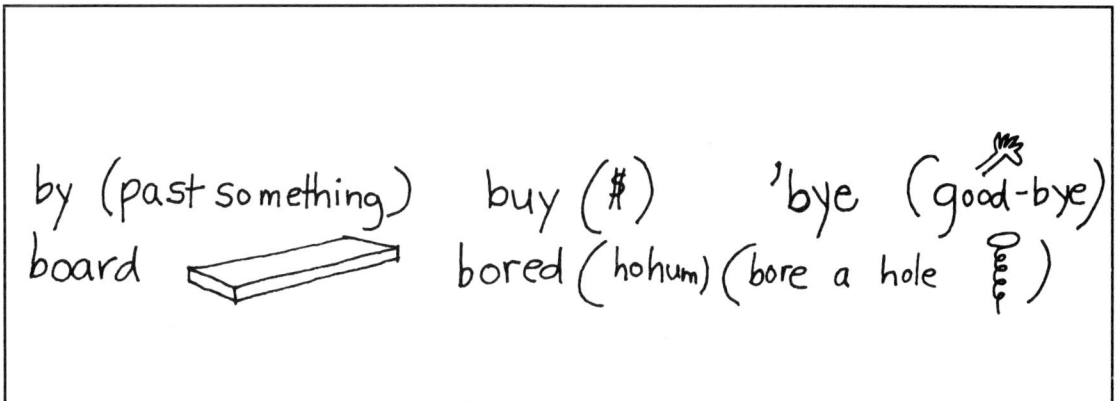

Teaching dictionary and thesaurus skills also helps students to become independent and to take charge of their own spelling development. They soon find that several tries may be needed to locate a word when they are unsure about its spelling. Again, working in teams and comparing notes on the various possibilities can lead to interesting explorations and further growth. If you encourage students to look at the many different versions of words, they can glory in the idea that every time they look up a word successfully, they are learning a number of new words and spellings. Instead of dictionary work being a chore, it becomes akin to a treasure hunt, or as Marne tells her students, "chock-a-block full of learning opportunities."

Communication between pairs of students can be as helpful as a whole-group session and is available at any time during writer's workshop. To encourage careful peer editing (for spelling), Marne asked students to work in pairs after they wrote down the names of their pets, of familiar stores, of rivers, lakes, and streets. Students had done some special work on the use of capital letters and abbreviations and the students' writing was in the nature of a test. Once everyone had finished, Marne gave direction for working together:

Boys and girls, I want you to go through these and correct each other's punctuation, capitalization, spelling. Check with each other. Read your list to your partner and look at it together. Have your partner point out anything that's questionable. Do that with both lists and come up with the best possible results. I don't want to see anything until it is polished, please. Put *both* your names neatly under each exercise that you looked at so that I know who was supposed to be catching those errors.

The subsequent comparison of capitals led to an interesting discussion about the idiosyncracies of spelling names:

MARNE: *I don't think you did this as conscientiously as you did yesterday with Sania. Don't forget that the name of a specific place such as the* Nile River *is proud of itself and warrants a capital* N *for* Nile *and a capital* R *for* River. *The whole business of capitalization is important, there are rules that must be followed.*

CHILD: *e. e. cummings didn't use capitals for his name.*

MARNE: *Right! You can* not *use them, but you've got to be aware that you're not using them. Look at this* [writes "e. e. cummings" on the chalkboard]. *Why do you suppose Mr. Cummings spelled his name like this? (I'm not sure what the* e*'s stand for actually.)*

This is how you are supposed to write it [puts "E. E. Cummings" on the board], *but the great poet didn't write his name that way. He made mistakes on purpose. Why do you suppose he chose to spell his name the wrong way? Shane?*

SHANE: *To make it look good.*

MARNE: *Exactly. I agree with Mr. Cummings that it looks more interesting like that. This is sort of ordinary,* [pointing to the "correct" way] *not as elegant looking as this,* [pointing to the lower-case way] *is it? I like it. Everything is on the same level – e.e. cummings. But he spelled his name that way knowing that he was breaking the rules. O.K. Let's leave the wrong-way spelling of Mr. Cummings and go on to the right way of capitalizing. So if you have a name of a person or the name of a river or the name of a store or business then the rule is that you give it the dignity of a capital letter. If you are leaving a capital out,* know *that you are leaving it out and have a good reason. You have a couple more minutes.*

Building on the discussion about looks of spelling, Marne suggests visual checks.

SHANE: *How will I know if we got it right?*

MARNE: *Write it three different ways and see.*

DYLAN: *We did.*

MARNE: *Did you circle the best way? Shane, can you write it three ways too?*

SHANE: *I do that all the time. I can recognize the right spelling if I see it.*

MARNE: *You do most of the time, but when you're not absolutely sure you could refer to an authority to check your spelling. Jon, how did you know how to spell* Thrifty's? *I'm impressed.*

JON: *I just asked Jessica.*

MARNE: *Aha. Jessica knew. You've got a good resource in her.*

That session built on a more structured lesson showing the importance of rules of capitalization, but the work was neither heavy-handed nor divorced from the students' personal knowledge. Making the learning playful can be a wonderful way to ease anxieties about spelling and make the work interesting. In her capacity as learning assistance teacher at South Park School, Barb Beukema uses many different ways to lighten up the chore of moving toward standard spelling. She describes a session in which she worked with students at broadening their knowledge of words with a silent *k*:

I had fun with my grade 4 spelling group the other day. I came in and gave each of them a card on which to write down their words. First I asked them, 'If a letter starts with a silent *k* what's the next letter?' Then I put *k* on the board and they gave me *n*. Then I told them, 'Now write down every *kn* word that you know.' There was dead silence and then someone blurted out a word. I said, 'Oh, no. I want all of you to write down what's in your head.'

Everybody had at least one word because somebody had blurted it out. Some had two and I said, 'Look at the clock. You're going to feel really good after you have worked for fifteen minutes.' This made them very aware that they were about to learn something. I didn't say another word then, but just passed out the *SPELLEX,* which we had used very little. After these were distributed I said, 'Now listen to my instructions. I want you to write down all the silent *k* words you know.' So they kind of whispered among themselves and one said, 'We can't use copies of the *SPELLEX* can we?' 'You do whatever you need to do to get down all the silent *k* words you know.' So they looked it up and started writing in their notebooks. After most of them were finished writing, I gave them another set of cards and asked them to write down the silent *k* words they still remembered. They wrote down some and then I told them that they could look at their lists for a few more minutes to refresh their memories. Finally I gave them the third set of cards and said again, '*Now* write all the silent *k* words that you know.' Some of them remembered as many as ten.

Considering that these were students who were sent to Barb because they had special needs, that result sounds quite impressive. However, the point of the lesson is not simply a matter of teaching them about silent *k* words, but getting them in the habit of using all resources, including turning to the dictionary or *SPELLEX* for help, and realizing that they *can* learn words in clusters. Again the students are shown that they have ways of finding answers themselves. As Barb puts it, "The more I teach spelling the more I realize I have to teach strategies and create brain empowerment. I try to tap visual memory, thinking, and letting kids figure things out."

Marne's "body spelling"

Marne inserted fun into spelling exercises by having students represent root words, prefixes, and suffixes, lining up side by side to create new word combinations.

143
*Learning to write –
writing to learn*

To start, Marne told them that many words are composed of root words, suffixes, and prefixes. Next she located the root word *move* in the SPELLEX and asked for a volunteer to represent the word, saying, "I am the root word."

MOVE stepped into the center of the circle and waited for volunteers to come up to be prefixes and suffixes. Students vied with each other to find ways of standing in front or behind MOVE to yield:

 re MOVE able
un MOVE ed
im MOVE able
　 MOVE ing

Each time they added a body in the line-up they spelled the word and talked about the need to remove the final *e*, to pay attention to the two *m*'s, to double the final consonant if the root word was a word ending in *t* like *fit* or a word that ended in *p* like *wrap.*

Moving around physically gave students a chance to identify with the word parts "I am a prefix," "I am a suffix," and to look actively for ways of expanding the root word in the center. The fun of lining up together and making the root word into something new, changing its spelling, and altering its meaning created a concrete sense of the structure and flexibility of words.

WHEN ALL ELSE FAILS – USE MNEMONICS

Empowering students and having them think about spelling in creative ways also includes encouraging them to use mnemonic devices to remember words that continue to give them spelling difficulties. Making the difficult part stand out is one way: M*y PAL the princiPAL; tHEIR HEIR.* If you can spell *HERE* you can spell *tHERE* and *wHERE.* When such sayings are written in large print, the elusive part often sticks in their heads. If students are still mixing upper- and lower-case letters in their printing and you don't want to use the capital letters in this way, use a different colored pen instead. Thinking about funny ways of giving emphasis can also help. Marne told one student who was trying to remember the distinction between *dessert* and d*esert,* "This *desert* is arid and dry. There's not much there. But a *dessert* is rich in calories. It needs two *s*'s to show how rich it is."

Wendy Bean and Chrystine Bouffler in their book SPELL *by Writing* (1987) suggest using books with unusual language, such as *The BFG* by Roald Dahl, to have students examine such fanciful words as "cannibully" and "murderful." A book like this gets them to think about imaginative language, and to compare its spellings with standard language. Bean and Bouffler also suggest using puzzles, limericks, jokes, and tongue twisters as ways to interest students in language – and with it, spelling.

All of these playful ways of approaching language and spelling are useful and productive, because they not only invite students to think about and play with language, but they give them the sense that these are workable, fun ways to upgrade their spelling. That attitude takes into account that, "Spelling is a constructive, developmental process" and that "Too much focus on 'correctness' is bad for spelling" (Gentry 1987). If you trust the learners and keep your eyes on steps forward rather than on poorly spelled words, you will see gradual progress in your students' work. The reality is that some students will just naturally become super spellers, others will be fairly good, and some will always have difficulty and need the help of dictionaries. So enjoy all the fun ways of fostering standard spelling and forget about being perfect.

Getting ready for the year-end

Just as you don't end writer's workshop abruptly but give students time to finish up what they are working on, so you don't end the year's work abruptly. You will want to alert students to the need to draw their writing to a finish. Toward the end of the year, Marne decided to give students extra time to complete whatever writing they felt good about. The exchange between her and her students shows the attachment students feel toward their writing.

MARNE: *We've only limited time available and we have to think carefully about how we're going to spend it. We probably have about five writing days left. I'd like to have these last few days as pure uninterrupted writer's workshop so you can get the last piece of the year published, polished, rubbed right down to good writing. Then during the parents' tea you'll read your jewel aloud to share it. – Yes, Jessica?*

JESSICA: *How many things can we do?*

MARNE: *I'd prefer that you did one that you really, really treasured – to focus on one piece that is beautiful writing.*

JESSICA: *I have a couple that I really like.*

MARNE: *So you have a dilemma that you need to solve.*

145
*Learning to write –
writing to learn*

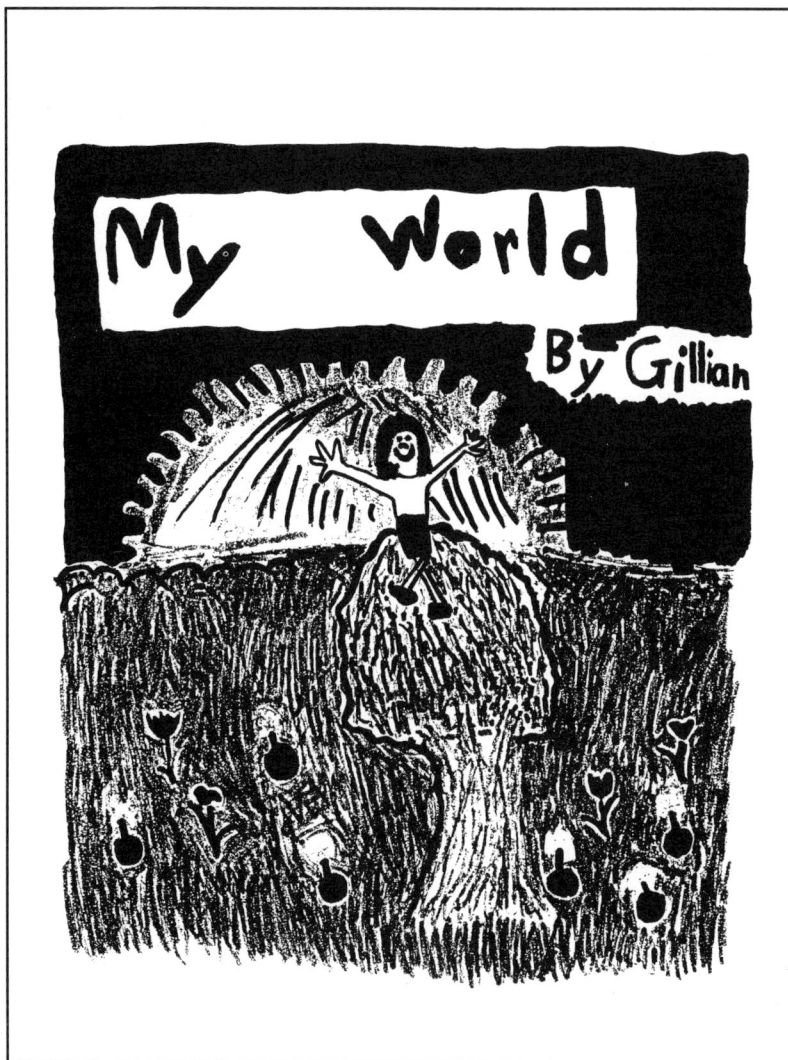

*Year-end anthologies
included the students' own
choices of their best work,
all "published" in a book
that included a cover, table
of contents, and sometimes
illustrations.*

DYLAN: *What if we don't have anything ready?*
MARNE: *I'll guarantee you time during these last five days to
prepare one last triumphant piece.*

Marne's comment about "your jewels" refers to those pieces
of writing students have collected throughout the year for their
anthologies. All students have a regular copybook into which
their favorite writing is copied to make a year's collection.
Covers are lovingly designed and students are free to choose

Table ★ Of ★ Contents

Storys
1. The Day It Rained Weird Stuff 1
2. Hospital Steries 2
3. Teddy 3
4. Banana Spilt --------------------- 6
5. Slime 8
   poems
6. The Garden 9
7. Horses 10

those pieces of writing they wish to include in their anthology. Though some are slim, they are beautiful records of dedicated writing and students' growth throughout the year.

Purposeful writing is the key to learning

Writing pervades the day just as reading does. There are many purposes for writing, and students in a whole-language classroom are not faced with "a writing lesson" or with assignments that have no purpose other than to fulfil a school requirement. When they do mini-lessons or quick checks such as Marne's

147
*Learning to write –
writing to learn*

check on their knowledge of capitalization, the material is tied to their own writing or experience and has relevance to the work *they* want to complete. You will find, as we have, that students, far from shunning writing, will complain and grumble when other activities demand that writer's workshop be curtailed or eliminated for a day. If you have eager writers who are interested in what they want to write, then both mechanics and meeting curriculum requirements will take care of themselves while you and the students enjoy the excitement of being authors.

As you check on the evolution of grammar, style, spelling, idea development, or any other specifics on your list, you will note steps forward and find gaps that need to be filled by means of mini-lessons or special one-to-one conferences with students. Learning to write and writing to learn go hand in hand and are not hit-or-miss propositions. Because you keep track of every student's progress through your status-of-work check (see page 106), you will not only learn exactly where each student is in terms of meeting curriculum requirements, but you will also develop a strong sense of the sequence in which their writing skills evolve. As a researcher in your classroom, you will share the joy of learning with your students.

WHAT STUDENTS GAIN FROM WRITING ACTIVITIES

Writing stands at the heart of independent learning and becomes the core of solid growth in all areas of development. We have prepared lists to record specific gains in a number of areas. No doubt you will be able to think of many more.

Conventions of print
• While writing, students learn about, practice, and expand
• spelling
• sentence structure
• grammar
• punctuation
• style
• formats for various types of writing
• use of dictionaries, thesauri, and other sources
• conventions of publishing

The Process of Writing
Extended practice makes students aware how effective writing flows and evolves. They find out firsthand that writing moves through stages toward greater perfection. They know about
• brainstorming
• information gathering
• note taking
• planning
• drafting
• re-drafting
• editing
• revising

149
Learning to write –
writing to learn

- polishing
- proofreading
- publishing

They also know about the importance of letting ideas flow without censoring and the fact that not all writing comes to full completion. They accept that false starts may be abandoned and simply regarded as interesting forays into new territory. They view writing as a natural and important part of communication.

Thinking
Independent writing requires thought, and students evolve their thinking on all levels and in every conceivable application. In the process of gathering ideas, planning, and writing, they
- analyze
- synthesize
- classify
- hypothesize
- draw inferences
- evaluate
- separate facts from fiction
- integrate facts and ideas
- observe and abstract information
- clarify/consolidate ideas
- make connections between old and new information
- solve problems
- formulate rules
- formulate arguments
- build logic
- use rhetoric to make their points.

Types of Writing
In the open atmosphere of their whole-language classroom students practice and find out about the infinite variety of writing. The useful and enjoyable ways in which they use writing include:
- description
- narrative
- fantasy
- poetry
- drama
- legends
- fairy tales

- short stories
- novels
- letters
- speeches
- resumes
- project reports
- laboratory reports
- sports reports
- science observations
- diaries and journals
- learning logs
- book reviews
- jokes and puzzles
- abstracts and precis messages
- notices and posters
- rules – for games, about conduct
- lists
- dialogues and debates
- records of new learning
- personal expressions of thoughts/feelings
- messages
- reminders
- captions for illustrations
- how to directions

What Writing Can Do
Along with learning about the many different uses of writing, students find out what writing has to offer.

Writing
- has many uses
- communicates
- preserves thoughts and ideas
- opens new pathways of thinking and communicating
- is a way of organizing and recording thoughts
- sorts out and imparts knowledge
- is a way of problem solving
- organizes facts and integrates them
- paints word pictures
- enhances illustrations
- empowers those who use it
- has many different styles
- has predictable patterns that can serve as models

151
*Learning to write –
writing to learn*

- offers many choices
- can elicit responses
- produces a feeling of power

In addition, writing can be
- enjoyable and fun
- adapted to fit different needs and purposes
- refined and polished
- expanded and made more expressive
- shared with others
- private for recording innermost thoughts
- saved to be enjoyed or thought about later

Personal Gains
Writing offers personal as well as academic gains. Writing leads
to and/or provides
- Expanding skills of communication
- Pride in workmanship
- Enjoyment
- Pleasure in process and finished product
- Satisfaction of working with hands
- Feelings of success
- Excitement of being challenged
- Joy of self-expression
- Satisfaction of doing well and completing a task
- Creativity and spontaneity
- Independence and self-reliance
- Self-esteem based on competent work
- Self-assurance in ability to tackle unfamiliar work
- Willingness to try new ways, new genres
- Confidence in effectiveness of personal learning
- Knowledge of writing process
- Stimulation of thought and imagination
- Ways of expressing positive feelings
- Opportunities to vent and defuse negative feelings
- Recording knowledge gained and strides forward
- Ways of sharing thoughts and feelings
- Cooperation and negotiation among peers
- Giving and receiving help and support
- Ways of agreeing and disagreeing without offending others
- Ways of building on the experience of more advanced authors
- Productive social interactions
- Validation of self-expression

- Ability to self-correct
- Building team work and collaboration
- Critiquing own work and that of others constructively
- Fun of sharing and laughter

As you observe your students engage in the many and varied writing activities throughout the day, the year, you will notice many more gains and will know the solid value that comes through writing.

AS READING ADVANCES SO DOES OVERALL LEARNING

5

LIFELONG READING for pleasure and for learning requires more than basic skills, and the intermediate classroom becomes a forum for displaying, sampling, practicing, and discussing the many facets of reading. Thoughtful reading, understanding the subtleties of messages embedded in text, enjoying the riches inherent in literature, the ability to find and to extract information effectively, all need to be carefully nurtured. To become effective readers, students need both classroom time and space for reading, and lively interactions. Though they will usually read silently in class, reading aloud, sharing favorite passages, acting them out, discussing interesting literature, and using reading to learn will be important to expanding their skills, sophistication, and attraction to reading.

Sharing the joys of reading

Though silent reading will be well established by the time students enter intermediate grades, reading aloud and sharing remain enjoyable and important parts of reading development. Delight in listening to an exciting story, a poem, or a chapter of a novel knows no age limit. If you begin the year by spending time reading to your class, you will set the tone for shared reading throughout the year. Select stories full of pathos, excitement, feeling, humor, or special interest. Read materials that you have always loved; your enthusiasm and verve in reading them will be contagious. Ask the students to talk about *their* favorite stories or authors; encourage them to bring in and share books, stories, poems, either with the whole class or with one or more of their classmates. If visitors come to your classroom, encourage them to read to the students too.

As you develop a sense for authors and genres that your students respond to particularly well, select a novel for reading aloud that is sure to hold everyone's interest. Books by Roald Dahl became special favorites in Liz's class, and as she put all her expressive talents into reading, she captivated the entire class with the humor and suspense of *James and the Giant Peach.* Loud groans greeted the recess bell if it forestalled adding just one more chapter to the read-aloud session. Later she read Frances Hodgson Burnett's *Secret Garden* and graduated from there to regale her class with *The Hobbit.* As you read aloud to your students you will find that even your less-than-enthusiastic readers will move to more demanding works once they have experienced the fun and interest inherent in books and reading.

Keeping your eye on the audience is the key to success in oral reading. If a number of students seem bored or restless, stop the reading and either resume at another time or suggest that whoever is interested borrow the book for individual or small-group reading.

To entice readers to sample new authors or topics, simply read a chapter or section of a book aloud and stop at a point when everyone is eagerly waiting to hear more. If you put the book aside saying, "Anyone who wants to know the end of the story can borrow the book," you may actually need to find several more copies or use a sign-up list for eager readers.

Though you may begin with simple, fun books and stories, do not underestimate your students' interest or capacity for "heavier" reading/listening. When Samantha brought in *Folk Tales and Fables of the World,* an adult book given to her for her birthday, her teacher interrupted the Roald Dahl readings and instead built on the excitement stirred by the titles and illustrations of the stories. Reading the legend of "The Hampton Worm" – a monster that could not be killed by being hacked into pieces – sparked a lively discussion of where and how such tales originate and led to students musing on the reality factors in legends. One of them recalled that when you cut a worm in two both parts continue to move.

Read-aloud sharing stimulates both discussion and further reading. But sharing can also become the spark for students' own writing. During a buddy session in which grade 4–5–6 students joined the K–1–2 class, the two teachers took turns

155
*As reading advances
so does overall learning*

reading bits of poetry to the assembled group. The teachers' lively interactions and the poems selected fairly sparkled as Marne and Marg vied with each other to find yet another whimsical or funny verse to add to their reading. Children laughed, marked the rhythm with their hands or feet, inspected pictures, and generally entered into the spirit of the poetry reading. The resulting poetry writing session – done as a collaboration with the older students and their young buddies – buzzed with excitement, and each pair created a poem that captured one or more aspects of the models that had been read aloud. No one was in doubt about what poetry is or how much enjoyment and fun can be derived from using language in imaginative and creative ways. The spirit of collaboration pervaded the session, and the older students took great pride in the contributions their young partners made in words and pictures. With the help of their more knowledgeable buddies, even kindergarten children produced poems, which were then read aloud by their more experienced helpers. Reading aloud took on an extra dimension of caring and sharing as a result of this interaction.

How to draw students to reading

To make reading fun, inviting, interesting, rewarding, and altogether irresistible

- Fill your classroom with books – big books, little books, serious books, funny books, sad books, happy books, mysteries, romances, animal stories, factual books, whimsical books, encyclopedias, the classics, your own favorites, the students' favorites, your children's favorites, children's stories, adult stories, biographies, history books, poetry, how-to books, anything that attracts you. Your students will take their cue from you.
- Do lots of read-alouds – short stories, poems, chapters in books, special reports in newspapers or magazines. Put lots of feeling and expression into those readings.
- Invite others to read to your students – visitors, older buddies, peers.
- Show your enthusiasm for what you read – the feelings you experience, the knowledge you gain, the curiosity raised, the memories evoked.

- Discuss books with individual students, small groups, the whole class. (Be sure these discussions are not quizzes but are genuine exchanges of personal impressions of books and reading.)
- Invite authors into your classroom. Ask them to talk about their work or read from it to students.
- Work with your school librarian to make the school library as accessible as possible to students.
- Plan class trips to the public library and encourage students to use the library to find books of interest to them.
- Learn about the special interests, joys, fears, and concerns of your students, and introduce them to books that mirror their feelings and interests.
- Talk about TV series that are based on books and make the books available.
- Have students create a "favorite author corner" where they collect all the titles or copies of books by Roald Dahl, Robert Munsch, Judy Blume, Kit Pearson, or . . . .
- Encourage the rereading of favorite books or reading a number of books in a series – Hardy Boys, Nancy Drew, Anne of Green Gables.
- Do a lot of wondering – thinking aloud – that requires looking things up or finding more information in books or encyclopedias.
- Encourage students to follow up a question at the moment, when interest is high. Send the student or a small group to the library to find answers or background material right then – not the next day or after school.
- Validate students' interests by assuring them that you would like to know more about their topics, and ask them to find books on these topics for their fellow students.

Transcript excerpt of a buddy session

[Marne's grade 4–5–6 students are visiting Margaret's K–1–2 class. Older students are sitting on the carpet with their young buddies.]

MARNE: [holding up a book] *I love this kind of book. Look at the old pictures and shiny paper they used to use. Brook brought it in, bless her heart.* A Child's Garden of Verses *by Robert Louis Stevenson . . . he wrote this in 1929. It's very old.*

MARG: *Do you know about Robert Louis Stevenson? He was sick all his life, and he lay in his bed and thought of all these poems.*

Marne: And he thought thoughts that were beautiful, like "The world is full of wonderful things. We should all be as happy as kings."

MARG: *He even used the squares on his counterpane to imagine soldiers and battlefields as he was lying in bed.*

NEIL: *What's a counterpane?*

MARG: *It's a bedspread.*

MARNE: [holding up the book to show a picture] *See, here his bedspread is a sail for a boat. "My bed is a little boat. / Nurse helps me in. / She girds me in my sailor's coat / and starts me in the dark." So even though he wasn't able to take full part in play the way we do, he wrote with his imagination. And did he ever write!*

MARG: *Yes, lots and lots of books.*

MARNE: *And he wrote from a child's point of view. "In winter I get up at night / and dress by yellow candlelight. In summer, quite the other way, / I have to go to bed by day." How many of you remember how hard it is to go to sleep when the sun is still shining and the birds are singing? And on a winter morning you get up when it's still dark and you think you should still be sleeping.*

MARG: *And while you are reading some of those beautiful words from a man who wrote ages and ages ago, here is a poem by a current writer, Dennis Lee. You might want to compare this with some of the words that Marne read: "Psychapoo the silly goose / brushed his teeth with apple juice. / Psychapoo the melonhead / rode his bicycle in bed." Now what do you think of what Marne read and what I just read?*

MARNE: *Tova, what's the difference between the two poems and their language?* [pause] *Is there such a thing as a psychapoo?*

TOVA: *No.*

MARNE: *But Dennis Lee wrote that. Can you explain that, Kathy?*

KATHY: *Yeah. He used made-up words.*

MARNE: *Yes, but Robert Louis Stevenson didn't make up words. He used dictionary words. But Dennis Lee feels free to make up words.*

MARG: *Here's a book full of noisy poems where the words make the noises.* [reads "Clickety Clack" from *Noisy Poems*]

MARNE: *Neat. "Clickety clack, clickety clack." Everybody say that four times.*

CHILDREN: *Clickety clack, clickety clack, clickety clack, clickety clack!*

MARNE: *Isn't that satisfying?*

MARG: [reads poem "Scriffely Scraffely"]

MARNE: *Great. Say scriffely scraffely four times!*

CHILDREN: *Scriffely scraffely . . .* [bobbing up and down as they do so]

MARG: [reads "Spaghetti" Poem]

MARNE: *So we can have food poems . . .*

NEIL: *. . . and animal poems.*

MARG: *Right. Those can be wonderful poems. There's "Mary had a Little Lamb." That's one you are really familiar with. Here's one about a snail.* [reads it]

MARNE: *That poet has gone nose to nose with the snail, I promise you. He has gone right down and made himself imagine what it would be like to be a snail. And if you can use your imaginations like that, I guarantee you that you will find some interesting things to write when you go nose to nose with something.*

MARG: *This one I always loved when I was a little girl. It's called "Fog." "The fog comes in on little cat feet. / It sits looking over harbour and city on silent haunches and then moves on." – Did you notice the fog this morning, Marne?*

MARNE: *No!*

MARG: *Well I must have been up a little earlier than you, and the fog was rolling in over the water.*

MARNE: *Why is it a good image to compare fog to cats? What do cats and fog have in common?*

JESSICA: *They are both very silent.*

MARNE: *Very silent!*

JESSICA: *They creep.*

MARNE: *They creep. Good!*

MARG: *Here are some limericks I brought in for today.* [reads] *"There was a young lady whose chin / Was as sharp as a point of a pin . . ."*

MARNE: *Can you say that? "There was a young lady whose chin . . ."* [everyone repeats]

MARG: *"Resembled the point of a pin . . ."* [everyone repeats]

159
*As reading advances
so does overall learning*

MARG: *"So she had it made sharp and purchased a harp . . ."*
[everyone repeats]

MARG: *"And played several tunes with her chin."* [everyone repeats and laughs] – *Do you have a Jonathan in your room, Marne?*

MARNE: *Yes.* [points to Jonathan]

MARG: [reads limerick about Jonathan – everyone laughs]

MARNE: *Were you listening when Marg read that, Tova? Katy, it's your job to keep Tova on task, to help her to focus. Turn your body around, Tova.*

MARG: *That helps you to focus.*

MARNE: *Did you notice that Marg bobbed her head as she was reading? There is a real beat to some poems. They are very rhythmic. Do it again – the cow poem.*

MARG: *"Jonathan Guy went out with his cow. / He climbed up a tree and sat on a bough. / He sat on a bough that broke in half / And Jonathan's cow did nothing but laugh."* [everyone laughs]

MARG: *What do you think you kids are going to do today?*

CHILD: *We're going to write our own poems and draw pictures.*

MARNE: *Let's get some paper.*

[lots of excited noise as children get settled with their buddies – see examples of buddy poems on pages 160 and 161.]

Expanding sustained reading into "reader's workshop"

Inspired by new authors and the introduction of novels, "book time" or "sustained reading" practiced during primary years takes on greater depth. Following the example of Nancie Atwell's *In the Middle,* teachers create a reader's workshop that bears similarities to writer's workshop in its focus on sustained practice, having the students work with material that has meaning, and keeping track of progress over a period of time.

At the beginning of the year students may quietly read one or more books of their choice for a period of fifteen to twenty minutes. As they settle into the routine of the classroom, the books without words, cartoons about Garfield, or toy catalogs that some students select at the beginning of the year give way to novels and short stories. Liz starts her day with a reading session and sets the tone by playing a tape of soft classical music. As students come in, they select their books and sit down to read. The quiet reading practice expands to half an hour (or more) as the year progresses. At intervals – once a week or more

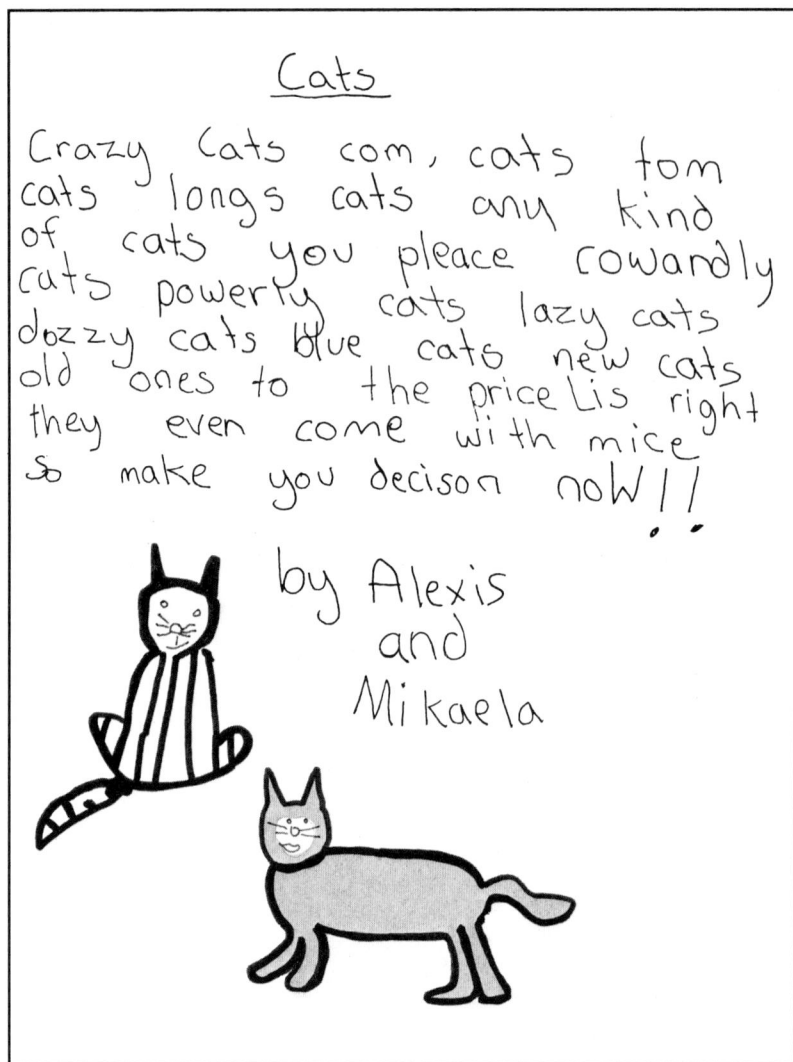

<u>Cats</u>

Crazy Cats com, cats tom cats longs cats any kind of cats you pleace cowardly cats powerty cats lazy cats dozzy cats blue cats new cats old ones to the price Lis right they even come with mice so make you decison noW!!

by Alexis and Mikaela

An example of the poems written by grade 4–5–6 students and their K–1–2 buddies.

if children are eager – the students write down their reactions to what they have read. To model making comments about reading, the teacher talks about the stories and novels everyone has been reading: the beautiful descriptions; how all of the senses are involved as the author makes you see, smell, and hear, the waves crashing against the rocks; the interesting characters; the opening that draws you right into the story; the suspense and excitement; the satisfying ending.

Students keep a "reading response journal" in which they keep track of the books they have read. This journal also serves

161
*As reading advances
so does overall learning*

as an ongoing personal dialogue between the students and teacher. Though the teacher has modeled the kinds of reactions he or she wants to elicit from the students – what they like or do not like, how the book makes them feel, what may be special about it, what aspects disturb or repel them – students at first simply retell what they have read. We find that before they are ready to move to any kind of analytical thinking *about* what they have read, they need to practice writing about the story *per se.* Nancie Atwell writes of her attempts to move students away from plot summaries by telling them that if she already knows

There once was a girl named
Taigen who got a wagan for
her friend Megen. But the wagen
was to small for ~~Taigen~~ Megen
So she gave it to Taigen.
And thats how Taigen got her
wagen.

By Morgan and Taigen

TAIGEN

Another buddy poem.

the book, the summary becomes boring, and if she does not, the summary might spoil her fun when reading the book. But it is important to realize that summarizing plots is a natural phase that students will eventually leave behind. We have observed this first step time and again. Audrey McMillan (1989), a teacher who used *In the Middle* as her inspiration, speaks of having to wait until December for the breakthrough to more insightful, exciting writing that moved beyond a simple retelling of the plot.

Sept 6/89

Dear Katherine

Here we are, beginning the '89-'90 school year together. I'm really excited about these next ten months. It looks as if there will be some wonderful discoveries made by all of us.

I want each of you to make some discoveries about reading I am going to give you daily reading time. Because I can't keep track of each book you choose to read, could you write to me in this journal, tell me what book you are reading and some of your ideas about it. I am very interested in what you think and I will write you back!

Marne

This is the letter Marne wrote in each students' reading response journal at the beginning of the year.

*As reading advances
so does overall learning*

Date	Title	Author
Sept	1. MAD QUEEN OF MORDRA	Elwy Post
Sept 20	2. Bunnicula	Deborah+ Jamest
Sept 29	3. Jacobs Little Giant	Barbra Smucke
Oct, 5	4 Quincey Rumpel,	Betty Warter
Oct. 30	5. Dawn and The, Impossible mue Ann M Mar	
Nov. 7	6. Danny Champign of the World R. Dole	
Nov.	7, Pasport to West Germeny	
Dec.	8 Isrel	
	9. Turkey	
	10. Forties and Fittys	

*Students use their reading
response journals to keep
track of the books they
have read and to reflect on
their reactions to their
reading.*

DTE	Books I Have Read Title	Aathor
Spt 14	Differrt Dagons	Jean little
St.20.	Best friends,	
Spt20	So Long grandpa	
Oct 15	little hause in the Big woods	Wilede
Oct. 28	Anne of green Gabbeles	
Oct. 31	One my antter Honour	
	Doubledare O'TOOLE	LongTanc
	Cyble wor Best, Ru	E.C. Green.
Nov.12	Reptiles do the Strangest Leonand	
Jan.1	Floners	HaroLDOLDRays
" 1	The Parnet Game Besty Hydns	
" 1	The Turth About Stacy Ann M. Martin	
" 8	Kristy and the walking disaster	

Reader's workshop – whether held first thing in the morning or later in the day – provides students with the quiet time they need to practice and then expand their reading. Their written dialogues with the teacher (through their reading response journals), discussions with other students, and the stimulus of the read-aloud sessions provide the incentive to shift to more demanding reading. As the book lists on page 163 show, some students read a great many books during the year, while others manage only a few. Records may not always be quite accurate, but the teacher continues to encourage those who still find it difficult to advance in their reading. By the end of the year each student will have read at least two novels and, as the written commentary in the example on page 165 shows, even though a less mature reader may not have read as much as more advanced classmates, he or she will nevertheless have made great strides in writing commentaries.

The availability of books in the classroom, easy access to the library, encouragement to bring books from home, and "book talk" in class all combine to challenge students to move from Hardy Boys and Nancy Drew mysteries to classics like *The Diary of Anne Frank* or *Lord of The Rings*. At the grade 6 and 7 levels, students may read biographies or such works as *The Mists of Avalon.* As their reading material becomes more sophisticated, their reactions expand in length, specific detail, and sensitivity. (See page 166.)

The teacher's input through his or her own reading and written comments in the reading response journals act as catalysts to the children's reading, but like catalysts in a chemical reaction, they are not readily visible. Children may not respond directly to the teacher's comments, questions, or suggestions, but look for them eagerly, and in the long run, the comments make a great deal of difference. Audrey McMillan (1989) made the same observation. Her mini-lessons on writing styles, characterization, and points of view were listened to intently by her students, but they did not discuss their reading in these terms in their response journals. It was not until they integrated what they heard in reader's workshop with their own work in writer's workshop that they fully understood and applied what they had been learning. Once they read as writers and wrote for their readers, the information made sense and became theirs.

We will return again and again to this need for students to apply and actually "regenerate" knowledge their own way. As teachers we so easily get caught in the need to *teach* specific

165
*As reading advances
so does overall learning*

> Sept. 6
>
> Dear Marne I am reading the Book
> SIDE WAYS StōrIES.
> From WAYSIDE School.
> written By LOUIS SACHAR.
> Illustrated by JULIE BRINCKLO.
>
>
> I like this book because it makes you
> laugh. It is a funny book. The other thing
> I want to say is you ever get that book
> you should read it.
>
>   Sept 6
>   Dear Shane
>   I can tell that you're really
> enjoying it by watching you read it
> will keep my eyes open to see if
> can find any other books by Louis Sachar
>
>   Marne
>
> P.S I will try to get a copy to read to my son

Shane's artistic abilities enhance his first attempt at written commentary.

knowledge because it seems important or is part of the curriculum, when, in fact, we should be remembering that *all meaningful learning is generated by the learners themselves.* What the students generate may not be new to us but is a wonderful discovery to them. And because *they* found answers or made new connections, they will remember the information and build upon it. If this seems strange, think back to your university days and to those occasions when you could understand what was being said in a lecture, but the information made little impact on you. However, once you were teaching, you were suddenly able kate   Dec 1

Dear Marne,

The books I am reading is called: The diary
of a young girl ~~Anne~~ Frank.
It is the saddest book I have ever
read, because I really start to feel like I
am with her on her adventures, I really think
she had a right to live and grow up to be what
she wanted to be. I feel that it is really
unfair how she has to get pushed ~~out of~~ out
of her home and into a secret hiding place,
they call a secret annexe, all because of
fear of ~~they~~ being shot and killed.

                                    Dec 1

Dear Luke,

        I hope that your sadness
at the horrible unfairness of her life
gives your strength to act against
the possibilities of that happening
to other people

        People come to Canada to live
(refugees) because they are afraid to
live in freedom in their own countries.
        There is much sadness in other places,
Luke, We are trying to change that. Marne

Luke writes a thoughtful commentary in his reading response journal. Marne responds with her usual sensitivity.

to see – to reconstruct – that information because you were connecting it to your own work. So when you pour forth your knowledge about literature and reading, simply accept that the children are receiving that information at one level, but will need to regenerate it and apply it in their own ways before it makes sense to them. What they will learn from you in that exchange of information is that reading is truly important to you and that you are enthusiastic, curious, and involved in your own reading – and that is the best lesson of all.

167
*As reading advances
so does overall learning*

Involvement certainly is a key to success. Teachers often tell us that they have little opportunity to read adult books because they are so busy reading books the children are interested in, books that are on the recommended list for their district or that come their way from librarians, conferences, and from interested colleagues. To comment knowledgeably on the children's favorites, it is important for you to have read most of them, but it is also important to show yourself to be a learner and listener who is genuinely interested in the students' accounts of their reading. If there is to be shared learning in your classroom, then the students need to have the sense that they are information givers as well as information receivers.

If you take the attitude that you now have a wonderful opportunity to recapture the joys of your childhood reading, to indulge yourself by spending time on your favorite classics and many of the fine new additions to children's literature, your delight will be evident to the students. Never hesitate to share your most cherished books, stories, and poems with your class. Students are never too old or too young to appreciate your obvious pleasure. One mother recalled having her fifth-grade teacher read *Winnie the Pooh* with such wonderful expression and liveliness that the class could hardly wait for each instalment. Some people might think that fifth-graders are well beyond enjoying such childish tales and might also consider them quite unsuitable for school reading, yet years later this woman was still savoring the fun and looked upon the teacher who provided it as a pivotal figure in her reading development.

How to fill your classroom with books

- Cooperate closely with your school librarian and seek help with selecting books for all occasions. Take out as many at a time as library rules allow and have a library table in your room.
- Work with the librarian at your public library, and check out as many books as possible at one time. Rotate your supply regularly.
- Ask your students to bring in books.
- Ask parents to send in books on topics of interest.
- Bring in books of your own.
- Become a garage sale fan and buy books for pennies.

- Check with the resource center for your school district to see which books you can obtain there.
- Encourage your students to join book clubs that offer book dividends.
- Ask your principal to give you the money that would traditionally have been spent on worksheets and spirit masters, and spend the money on books instead.
- Have your students organize a fund-raising event to buy books.
- Ask local businesspeople to donate books or funds for books.
- Ask local service clubs to give books or funds for books to your class.

STARTING AND MAINTAINING READER'S WORKSHOP

If you have begun your year with lots of read-aloud sessions and sharing of favorite books and stories, students will readily settle down to fifteen or twenty minutes of silent reading with materials they have chosen themselves. Present the time as one in which they can choose freely and read the books that interest and delight them most. Allow them to find comfortable spots to settle into – a corner filled with cushions, the class sofa (if you have one), the floor, a secret spot behind the coat rack. But tell them that being comfortable does not mean that they can disturb others, that truly becoming absorbed in a story requires a degree of privacy and quiet. Wandering around the classroom, talking, or fidgeting unduly are not conducive to establishing the friendly warmth of shared pleasure in reading. But enjoyment is not just solitary; it is enhanced by sharing with others. So assure your students that – later – they will have the opportunity to share the laughter and excitement that bubbles up as they become immersed in their stories.

To underscore the importance of being fully involved in reading, sit down yourself and read a book, professional journal, or any other solid reading material that will be sure to absorb you fully. Give yourself over to the pleasure of an undisturbed reading session with material of your choice. When it comes to sharing, you may feel like telling children – in their terms – about the latest theory about reading development or the feelings that have emanated from the novel you are currently reading. In short, model the kind of involved, eager reading that you hope to foster in the students.

As you read, keep your sensors open to restlessness and don't make the session a test of endurance that must at all costs run a prescribed length of time. At the beginning of the year, on warm, sunny days, or just before a holiday, when students' minds stray into channels other than reading, end the session early or go outside to read. On the other hand, if everyone is totally involved in reading, take that as your cue to extend the session to thirty or even forty minutes or more.

Do not end the session abruptly by suddenly saying, "That's it. Shut your books." Instead, tell students a minute or two before you intend to close the session that time is almost up, and ask them to find a good place to stop reading. Occasionally, if someone is totally enthralled, allow the student to continue to read while the others are sharing. In short, be flexible within reason and always keep in mind that your main goal is to help students build the love of reading that can only arise from being immersed in books and stories of their choice.

MARNE'S RULES FOR READER'S WORKSHOP

1. Students must read for the entire period.
2. They cannot do homework or reading from another course.
3. They must read a book (not a magazine, newspaper, comics, or books where print competes with pictures.)
4. They must have a book ready to read *before* reader's workshop. (Students who need help finding a book or who finish a book during the workshop are exceptions.)
5. They must not talk or disturb others.
6. They may sit or recline wherever they'd like as long as feet don't go up onto furniture and rule #5 is maintained.
7. They must sign out to go to the washroom – emergencies only!
8. They must work hard.

SHARING WHAT HAS BEEN READ

Though some teachers establish the reading response journal at the beginning of the year, you may find that it is easier to interest students in oral sharing to begin with. Oral sharing also gives you many opportunities to ask leading questions about the reading to entice the students away from simple plot summaries. Sharing can be a whole-group activity during which you invite volunteers to say something to the group about the books or stories they are reading and to compare notes on favorite authors and topics – mysteries, ghosts, humor – that may attract your emerging reading enthusiastics.

Sometimes buddy sharing is more effective than whole-group sessions. As small groups of two or three students cluster around, the hum of animated talk is a clear indication of on-task talking, and the students are more deeply involved than they are when in a whole-group session. To get such sharing off to a good start, Hanne MacKay asks some of her most advanced readers to get together with her in front of the class to model a

Marne and her students share thoughts about their latest reading.

Another class shares a book that they have written and illustrated with Marne's students.

group discussion that focuses on whatever has been read and on reasons why the author's writing is effective. Students respond well to such modeling.

Once students begin to use their reading response journals, you will have many opportunities to reinforce their reactions to reading. If you show genuine interest in their concerns and pleasures, they will be ready to "write letters to you" about their reading. If you are open and honest with them about your likes, dislikes, and personal tastes, they will feel free to let you know what they like and don't like. If you assure them that they are under no obligation to hang in there to the bitter end, whether they like a book or not, they will be on their way to developing their personal tastes and will be open to sampling all kinds of reading materials.

Look upon the exchanges in the response journals as friendly correspondence and focus strictly on the content of the messages. Although you might make note of specific spelling and grammatical errors for future mini-lessons, do not turn the correspondence into exercises in composition or spelling. Simply enjoy and respond to the messages just as you would respond to the letter from a friend. As students become comfortable with the exchange of messages, they may share personal anecdotes about their lives. If you respond in kind, the response journals will help you establish a closeness with your students that will enhance the climate of delight you are striving to establish and maintain.

FINDING TIME TO WRITE YOUR RESPONSES

Though a stack of reading response journals waiting for your reading and response may not look like a stack of letters, try to capture that spirit of happy anticipation as you delve in. It is not that formidable a task. As you can see by the examples, Marne's responses are not lengthy. Set definite minimum requirements – at least three entries a week, a set number of lines, x number of comments about a novel or chapter – and give students time once a week to write in their journals. But give students the clear choice to respond more often, and to do so during writer's workshop time. If you find yourself overwhelmed with writing responses you, too, may occasionally want to use writer's workshop to work on students' reading response journals. Marne snatches time during breaks, recess, when someone else has taken the class to a special phys. ed. session, or while the students are particularly busy with projects.

Sept.19   To Sylvia,

This book (KWAIDEN) is by far the best book that I have ever read. It's the kind of book where you cant wait until you forget about it so you can read it again. This book has manny stories and so far, I like all of them. Theyre Japanese strainge tales. I like the way the wrighters make the storries vivid and well discribed. I can really get a picture in my mind of whats going on in the storries.

I have no bad comments about Kwaiden.

Sept /9

Dear Alex

don't it wonderful to have a book that you really enjoy reading? Are Japanese strange tales peculiar to Japan do you think? By that I mean, do you think that the content is different because it is Japanese? Have you read

Alex and his teacher, Sylvia, use his reading response journal for a dialogue about Alex's latest reading. His enthusiasm shines through.

If you remember how long it used to take you to mark worksheets and skill paks, writing responses takes on a different perspective. Don't think of your responses as additions to your paper work, but as ways of replacing a tedious chore by a far more rewarding and interesting task.

Working with literature

While reader's workshop introduces children to literature at an individual level, from time to time teachers obtain class sets of

173
*As reading advances
so does overall learning*

a novel to have everyone participate in reading and discussing the same book. Read-aloud sessions, reading during reader's workshop, homework reading, and reading during choosing time help children move through the novels at approximately the same pace. But the divergence in students' proficiency in reading does present a problem with whole-class reading. It is best to limit this kind of reading to special books that lend themselves well to discussion and that are relatively easy for everyone to read. Enjoyable books, like E. B. White's *Charlotte's*

other Japanese books and, if so, do you feel that the Japanese have a different style of writing from other countries?
Sylvie   Sept. 26

Response— To Sylvia,

I abselutly think that Japanese storries have different style than the writing style were use to. I prefer the Japanese style because I have seen alot of Japanese movies such as: Ran, Hoïchi O-Te, the seven Samurias, Akura ext. And the books are just the same as the movies because they'er so well written.
                    Sept 26

Dear alex
    I am now very curious! Can you describe how the style is different. Some North American books are well written too so what makes Japanese ones superior in your view?
          Sylvia .

*Alex is now obviously aware
of different writing styles.*

Web, which add suspense to the fun of reading, keep everyone moving along. Discussions about the plot, the animal and human characters and their traits, introduce children to ways of thinking about the story as well as about other books they have read on their own.

Though class sets of the same book give children the opportunity to work together on specific tasks and to look back over chapters, discussions can readily be based on the teacher reading a chapter of a book to the class. Building on the children's personal reading and accumulated experience enlivens discussions and gives meaning to such abstract terms as "protagonist" and "antagonist." Marne selected a gripping New England legend, *The Good Giants and the Bad Puckwudgies,* for her mini-lesson in literary analysis. She started the session with an expressive reading of the legend, which held the entire class spellbound and captured the feelings of playfulness, fear, rage, and mystery that pervade the story. She used this story to

Drawing on their own store of reading experience, students readily followed Marne's example in debating which story characters fell into which role. Building on their store of reading imbued the lesson with personal meaning, and assured that the students made the abstract concepts of the mini-lesson their own.

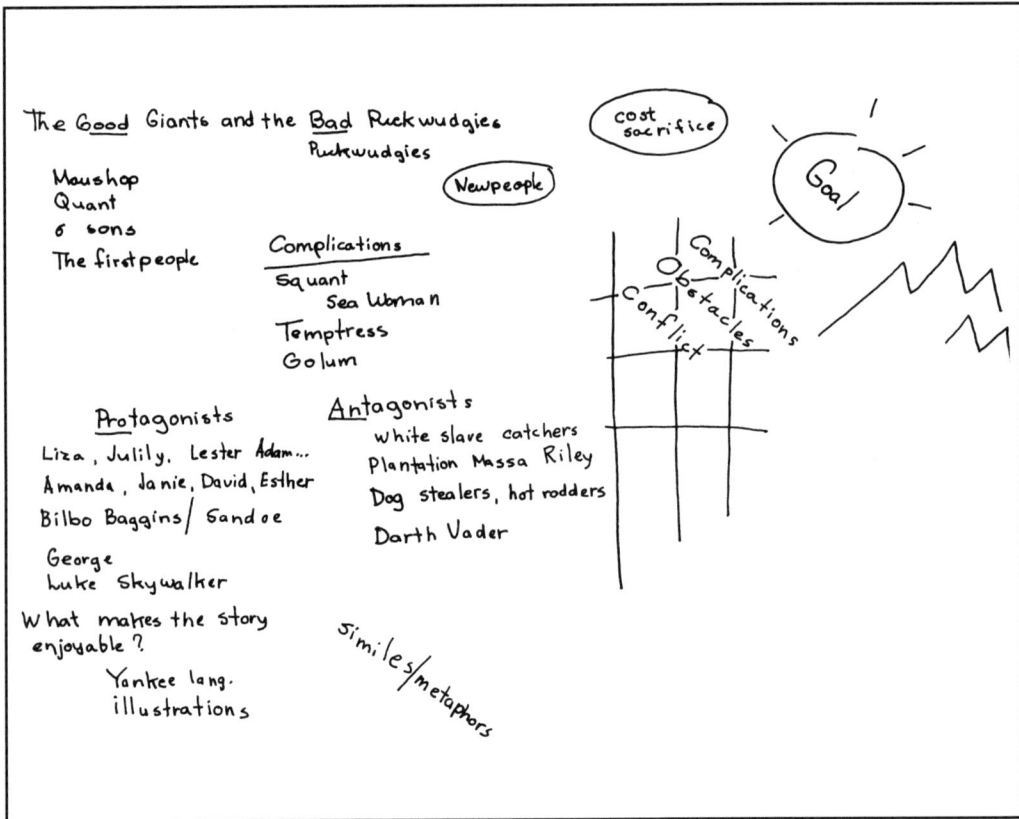

175
*As reading advances
so does overall learning*

initiate a discussion about the concepts of good and evil, and then asked the students about the use of these concepts in their own reading. To keep the abstract concepts as concrete as possible, Marne produced an overview on a large sheet of paper as the discussion moved along (see page 174). She had selected a story that illustrated the points she wanted to make, but she also drew on the children's own knowledge to emphasize that the concepts she was discussing – good and evil – are universal and are frequently elements in stories and novels.

From discussions of protagonists and antagonists, Marne moved to goals and complications or conflict to elucidate how stories are structured. Throughout, she kept the discussion lively by referring to the students' own lives, to the reality factor in legends, to the pictures that added extra zest to the story, and to the feelings the story evoked. Audible groans greeted the recess bell and Marne closed the session with a comment about rarely getting *everything* you want in real life or in stories.

The success of this mini-lesson and the students' interest and eagerness to participate derived from the extensive reading experience of the students and the personal involvement that Marne injected. From the powerful reading of the story to her comments about being naughty at times, she modeled passionate absorption in her topic. She had chosen a story that appealed not only to the students but to herself, and so she sustained a very real interest as she elicited input from her students that rested solidly on their own experience with stories and novels.

Think back to your own experiences in English classes. When did literature and reading come alive for you? What captivated you more, abstract considerations of style, theme, and character, or the enthusiasm of a teacher who obviously loved the work being discussed? Covering the curriculum is a laudable aim, but if the topics have no life or feeling for you or your students, your lessons will soon be forgotten, however carefully you may have prepared and presented them.

With the renewed emphasis on reading in school, you have the opportunity to build upon students' strong feelings and needs. Along with the cherished classics of your own childhood, a wealth of new literature has emerged that truly captures children's concerns and feelings. The sadness, worry and despair of split families, of having to move, of battling with drugs are addressed forthrightly, and the tenderness of budding romance is presented in modern settings and terms. Children need to have their feelings acknowledged. They need to experience the comfort of sharing with others. If you allow your own passionate involvement with life and with interesting reading to shine forth, your literature lessons will be a joy both to you and to your students.

What you can do for late bloomers and reluctant readers

Interest, practice, fun, and stress-free involvement with reading will do more for your late bloomers and reluctant readers than the very best phonic drills of old. Here are some ways we have found helpful in drawing students to reading.

- Students who are not yet good readers can nevertheless listen. So make reading aloud a big priority. Read to them yourself and ask peers, visitors, classroom aides, parents to read to them too.
- Keep reading materials of many levels in your classroom and encourage students to use whatever they find interesting or enjoyable. Don't deter students from using books that are "too easy" or "too advanced" for them. They will draw whatever they need or want from books of their choice.
- Have listening centers with books on tape where students can listen while following along with their eyes.
- Bring in magazines of all descriptions – children's nature magazines, magazines about cars, sports, pets, travel.
- Invite students to read to younger reading buddies. (Working with non-readers will give your students a sense of confidence and enjoyment.)
- Ask them to help you with catalog reading: "We have money to spend. What do you think we should buy?"
- Play cloze games with them.
- Invite them to read their own writing to you, a classmate, their buddies, the whole class.
- Ask them to help you with jobs around the classroom that require reading – taking roll call, following directions, reading out recipes, or . . .
- Bring in books that will interest the students, and invite them to look at the pictures and their captions.

177
*As reading advances
so does overall learning*

- Ask them to look things up for you in reference books or magazines.
- Encourage them to help with library work – checking books in and out, setting up displays, selecting topics or books.

The wonderful world of non-fiction

Excitement and passionate involvement with reading are not limited to fiction. In fact, fiction can be a solid bridge to the exploration of any number of topics based on interest stirred by reference to famous people, places described in the stories, animals and their habitats, or historical events – the possibilities are endless. Here, as in all other teaching, let the students lead the way and make choices. You will make your input by showing curiosity, sparking interest, and helping to find materials. Avoid that all too predictable prompt, "Now that we have read about _____, let's study _____." Instead, muse aloud and say, "I wonder . . ." or "I sure would like to know . . ." or "What puzzles me . . . ." Children will eagerly respond to your genuine desire to find out more about subjects that interest them.

Books like *Charlotte's Web, Julie of the Wolves,* and *Owls in the Family* readily open discussions that lead to serious study about spiders, wolves, and owls. To avoid everyone trying to use the same books, Liz suggested that students think about other animals that were featured in stories or books they had read. When some of the boys opted for snakes, even though they had not read anything about them beforehand, that, too, was acceptable. After all, the aim was simply to generate interest in non-fiction reading and research. Snakes continue to have a special fascination, and source books like those in the Nature's Children series provide not only basic facts but include interesting sidelights. Students love to pass these tidbits along, and teachers learn from the work as well.

Making books readily available and displaying them prominently both in the classroom and in the school library is certain to attract readers. In collaboration with the school librarian, Marne put together a collection of non-fiction books and placed them strategically around her classroom. Topics included biography, computers, the human body, history, natural science, art appreciation, and inventions – anything except how-to books. If you need extra help finding interesting books on a whole range of topics, use Beverly Kobrin's book *Eyeopeners* as a reference.

She not only provides a guide to over 500 children's non-fiction books on such diverse topics as boats, children on their own, endangered species, grandparents, lasers, medieval days, and space, but also offers excellent advice on how to judge books and "give your kids TLC – "The Total Literature Connection."

Having interesting background reading material available makes it easy and stimulating to draw students into specific topics that form part of the curriculum. Projects, contract work, and science or social science work need the support of non-fiction reading to enrich textbook material. The teacher may open a special topic by reading one or more articles or chapters about the subject – a country they are studying, special holiday traditions, the life of an artist or inventor. If the teacher involves the students in the ensuing discussion and makes the topics relevant to their interests and lives they will go on from that initial reading. If several books and articles are available on the topic being studied, teams of students may decide to use them as their research base for dioramas, special reports, or dramatization. Discussions and information sharing enliven the reading and draw everyone into the excitement of discovery. Students not only acquire facts and information, but learn about information gathering, collating facts, and working with a diversity of sources. Here, again, choice becomes a strong catalyst. If students are allowed a wide range of topics and methods of presentation, they never question, "How much do we have to do?" They simply move along and find as much information as they possibly can, often continuing their research at home.

COLLABORATING WITH
THE SCHOOL LIBRARIAN

Working closely with the school librarian adds further depth to reading in your classroom. Plan on having your students visit the library regularly, either as a class or in small groups. Schedule these meetings with the librarian and discuss your students' special needs before you make your library visit so that he or she has a chance to set out a selection of appropriate books. If the students have not had library work in the primary grades, begin with an orientation that focuses on a specific topic; in other words, don't give general comments on how the library works, but arrange with the librarian to have the students come in to find books on a specific range of topics, and make that concrete task the vehicle for introducing how the library organizes books, keeps track of its holdings, and makes books available to teachers and students. Include a brief session on some of the reference works, but don't overdo that first visit. Make it an enjoyable, relaxed, and tantalizing event to give students a sampling of the wealth of interesting material to be found in a library.

South Park School Librarian, Barbara Beukema describes an example of the kind of special projects that librarians develop:

Last week I put a whole bunch of the Nature's Children series books out in a circle. Then I asked all the children to sit down by a book of their choice. I let them look at their books for a few minutes, then I asked them

Barbara Beukema and the South Park staff developed this effective planning form.

to close their books because I wanted them to concentrate. After that we talked about the difference between the index and the table of contents, and then used the index to look up something interesting. Next we went around and each one read one entry from the index. Of course by that time they wanted to hear about the interesting findings.

Excitement of discovery and interest in unusual information will draw in even your most reluctant readers. The task given by Barbara Beukema was easy, yet it taught children in a concrete way how to look for specific facts. More advanced students may draw the same benefits from being introduced to special readers' indexes that help them locate information. Liaison with your local public library may be the necessary next step. In this instance, too, the work will be most effective if you give the librarian the students' specific needs before you visit and use an actual search as the means of introducing the use of, say, a guide to periodical literature. Lecturing students about the indexing system merely results in foot shuffling and covert side conversations. An actual search for information they want to know keeps the introduction relevant and interesting.

Close liaison with the school librarian also avoids the frustration of students choosing a project topic for which there is little or no information at all, or information that is overused. You will also do well to find out if other classes or schools are working on similar projects. If so, do some rescheduling to give your students a chance to obtain the resources they need.

A visit to the main library to meet with the children's and/or reference librarian will also alert you to special resources offered by your public library. Many libraries have newspaper and magazine collections, clipping files on a wide variety of topics, special reference encyclopedias beyond the usual standard works, and perhaps a special index to science fair projects.

Your most important contact person will always be your school librarian, who not only serves your students but acts as a liaison between your school and the public library.

If you want students to become lifelong readers who see books and reference works as part of their quest for knowledge, then the library must be a focal point in the school. Knowing how to find information and being familiar with methods of locating specific sources and facts become the foundation for thoughtful, enjoyable reading and study. As the whole-language ways of learning expand, the role of the librarian in your school will grow in scope and importance. Once students see the library as their first line of information gathering, they are on their way to becoming effective readers and researchers.

*Students at South Park
School make full use of
their library.*

Fostering the development of specific reading skills

Good comprehension, speed, and information retrieval need fostering and special practice. A few of your avid readers will build speed and comprehension simply by reading voraciously, but help with their reading development will be useful to most of your students. Taking a look at how effective reading functions helps to build practical ways of guiding students.

USING PATTERNS OF LANGUAGE TO BUILD COMPREHENSION AND SPEED

Reading is more than simply recognizing and saying words. Unless the words are put into phrases and sentences, they make little sense. Our early research with beginning readers revealed that even though the teacher focused on sounds and the particles of speech, children actively tried to find patterns of familiar language to make sense of what they were looking at. Reading carefully, word for word for word, did not help the students gain fluency. Once we shifted from controlled basal readers to familiar stories and nursery rhymes, children used those patterns of language to develop their fluency and comprehension. Knowing the material and the style of writing allowed the children's brains to take over as their eyes followed the lines of print. Instead of the eyes marking every single word, sending it to the brain for recognition, the children watched for familiar patterns and phrases. Knowledge of our language and its structure helped the children construct meaning and develop fluency of reading.

The same process continues with more mature readers. If they are still too concerned with seeing and understanding every single word, encourage them to read familiar and easy stories, poems, songs, or descriptions. When you are reading aloud to them in your whole-class work with literature, have them follow your oral reading with their eyes in their personal copies of the book. Tape-record the story reading you do in class, or keep taped books in a listening center. Invite some of your slower readers to use the listening center during reader's workshop. Welcome the provision of series of books by familiar authors and encourage students to read as many of their favorites as they like. (Children will expand their choices at some point.) Provide song sheets or make large charts of songs and keep them in view even after students have memorized the lyrics. Because melodies demand proper phrasing, the brain will signal the eyes to take in chunks of meaning and get the readers accustomed to moving beyond word-by-word reading.

All of these suggestions will help students practice appropriate eye movements that speed up their reading and build good comprehension – without tedious worksheets or anxiety-producing speed drills. If the reading material is both familiar (in

language and general content) and exciting or full of suspense, *As reading advances*
your slow readers will move right along. As their eyes become *so does overall learning*
accustomed to taking in larger chunks of print at a time,
comprehension increases along with speed.

BUILDING FLUENCY BY
ANTICIPATING WHAT COMES NEXT

Proper eye movements that are guided by the brain are crucial to
fluent oral (and silent) reading. Experienced readers move their
eyes ahead of their voices. Their fluency and expression come
from an ability to anticipate what comes next. Their eyes are
ahead of their voices as they read aloud, and the readers' minds
are engaged in conveying *meaning* – not simply in reading
words. Inexperienced readers need training in looking ahead.
Cloze exercises with familiar texts can be a fun way of teaching
students to use the context to help them read more fluently. With
slower readers, you could begin by blanking out the most
obvious or familiar words on a page. As a game for the entire
class you could move from there to putting a series of dashes on
the board to see if they can "read" your message. ("_ _ _   _ _ _
_ _ _ _   _ _ _ _ ?") ("Can you read this?") may be a fun beginning.
On the second of April, even first-graders (who had experience
with this game) could figure out: ("_ _ _ _ _ _ _ _ _   _ _ _
_ _ _ _ _   _ _ _ _ _ '   _ _ _ .") ("Yesterday was April Fools' Day.") You
may have to begin by providing first letters ("Y _ _ _ _ _ _ _ _
W _ _   A _ _ _ _   F _ _ _ _ '   D _ _"), but soon your students
will become proficient at scanning those blanks and finding the
words that fit. Like cloze exercises, these games give students
practice drawing on their knowledge of language and English
phrase structure to reconstruct the message. Don't use such
games as tests, but simply offer them as fun, as challenging
riddles and interesting ways of playing with language. Students
learn to project their knowledge of language into their reading,
and fluency grows when they aren't faced with anxiety and
abstract lessons.

For some of your more needy readers a bit of one-to-one echo
reading (reading aloud to a student while he or she reads along
with you, saying the words as you read them) will help you
discover where a student's difficulties lie. As you sit together
and read, you will note when and why the reader hesitates. If he
or she is stumbling over long words or clinging to word-for-word
reading, a bit of practice with a highly familiar piece of writing
may help to build that student's confidence. You may also find

that if you demonstrate – as though by accident – that fluent readers don't necessarily read every word exactly as it is shown in print but are more concerned with making meaning, your student will relax enough to let go of a too strict adherence to the exact wording. (Next time you read aloud to someone, keep your eyes and ears open for the minor changes you make in the text as you read aloud.) If you assure your students that this is not a sloppy way of proceeding but a natural part of fluent, meaningful reading, they will get the message that meaning is more important than anything else, and they may just relax enough to take the next step forward in their reading.

BUILDING VOCABULARY
AND FIGURATIVE LANGUAGE

If your students read widely during reading workshop, their knowledge of both book language and figurative language will grow. To help the process along, Liz used a form of cloze exercise to create awareness of the rich language used in the literature being read in class. Making an overhead slide of a page in a book familiar to most students, she would stick Post-it Notes over interesting words and invite students to offer suggestions as to what the words might be. Before peeling off the paper to reveal one of the printed words, she would encourage students to offer as many choices as possible, writing these on the chalkboard (onto which she had projected her overhead slide) so that there was a record of all the different words that might fit. A spirited discussion of the merits of the various suggestions enlivened the process and provided a good bridge to the students' editing work during writer's workshop.

Better than lists or specific vocabulary exercises, these games alerted students to the wide choice of expressive language that is available. The discussion made them more conscious of the value of picking just the right words for their writing and had them rolling interesting words like *tremulous, sweet-tempered,* or *edifice* off their tongues. At various times throughout the day we would hear students repeat a particularly delicious word under their breaths, and they could be counted upon to use it at every opportunity to test its beauty and fit.

If a story you read is rich in figurative language, stop occasionally and ask the students if they know what it means when the author says, "His white-haired father was sinking into the grave," or "She was thirsting for knowledge." Here again, the

185
*As reading advances
so does overall learning*

Kristian

Simile or Metaphor

She breezed along the highway

The rectangles and ovals shimmered like jewels

His eyes were hard and sharp like pale-blue icicle

You're growing like a weed

The sun made bright scales on the water.

The leash was as slim as the tip of my fishing rod

His muzzle pointed upstream on a bough.

Long after, there we still would be swimming across the night sky together.

I imprisoned him like an animal in the zoo

A ram charged the fence, moving like a locomotive

And when he stood stock-still on the flor and moved both fet sounded like some sort of a Leather orchestra.

It's like having birds between your toes.

*Kristian adds his own
similes to the list provided
by his teacher.*

reading-writing connection helps to provide meaningful practice. Ask students to watch for interesting phrasing such as "journeying through time," "glowing with pride" and to incorporate them in their own writing. As students become aware that language lends itself to expressing feelings richly and beautifully, they become interested in using such figures of speech in their own writing. Naturally, their reading is also enhanced by their awareness of imagery and figurative language.

**IT'S NOT TOO EARLY
TO INTRODUCE STUDY SKILLS**

Since your students are beginning to do content-area reading in both textbooks and trade books, they are ready to develop the special skills needed for extracting information effectively. As with all other learning, you will find your job of imparting information far easier if you wait for your students to build an experience base first. Make available lots of non-fiction books and, if possible, several different textbooks for their use for specific projects. Then begin to model the kinds of behaviors you would use to locate information in a text.

As students look over source material to extract the information they need, do some think-aloud talking about how well the pictures show what is described in the text and how the headings let you know just where specific information can be found. In short, make them aware of advance organizers – without calling them that – and of ways of extracting specific information without reading every single word. If they have participated in the library exercise in which they used the index to find specific facts, your students will be able to use it to help them locate what they want to know. If they are using the index, you can show them an efficient scanning technique to locate the information

Students at University Hill Elementary are hard at work in the library doing research for their latest projects.

they want if there is a lot of print: tell them to keep the word they are looking for, for example, *parachute* clearly in mind, and when they turn to the page given in the index, run their hands with spread fingers from the bottom of the page to the top scanning for the word *parachute* as they go. It may be fun to give them a little practice in that kind of scanning. Once they know it, a lot of time and frustration in locating information on a page will be eliminated. Explain that you scan from the bottom of the page to the top in order to resist the temptation to read every single word.

If you are working with textbooks and more extensive descriptions, show students how the first sentences of a paragraph can provide a good idea of what they can expect to find in that section. Here again, you will need to wait until students have had independent experience working with textbooks. Once they feel the need for a more organized approach that will help them think about the material without reading every word, they will be open to your demonstration about first sentences. Make sure you stress that this is just a way of getting a good overview of what is there, not a substitute for reading with care.

Depending on the age and experience of your students, it may be a good idea to have a brainstorming session during which you record both the problems they have encountered with textbook reading so far and the methods they have found helpful. You can then add a few of your own: underlining (or using a highlighter) to note key words (only if the book is their own), taking notes from textbooks, rephrasing difficult sentences, summarizing paragraphs, or anything else you feel will be helpful. End the session by inviting students to experiment and share ways that help their search for information. A group mind map or list on the chalkboard will draw together all the information you and your students can generate. (See page 188.)

As reading advances so does learning

Whether your students are confining themselves largely to novel reading or are branching out more fully into non-fiction reading, there can be no question that the extensive reading time each day builds not only thinking and reading skills but knowledge as well. Throughout this book we continue to refer to the need to develop a knowledge base before new skills can be meaningful. There is no sense talking to students about writing styles, about good openings or closings, about using interesting words, if they do not have a vast stock of stories, books, and some favorite

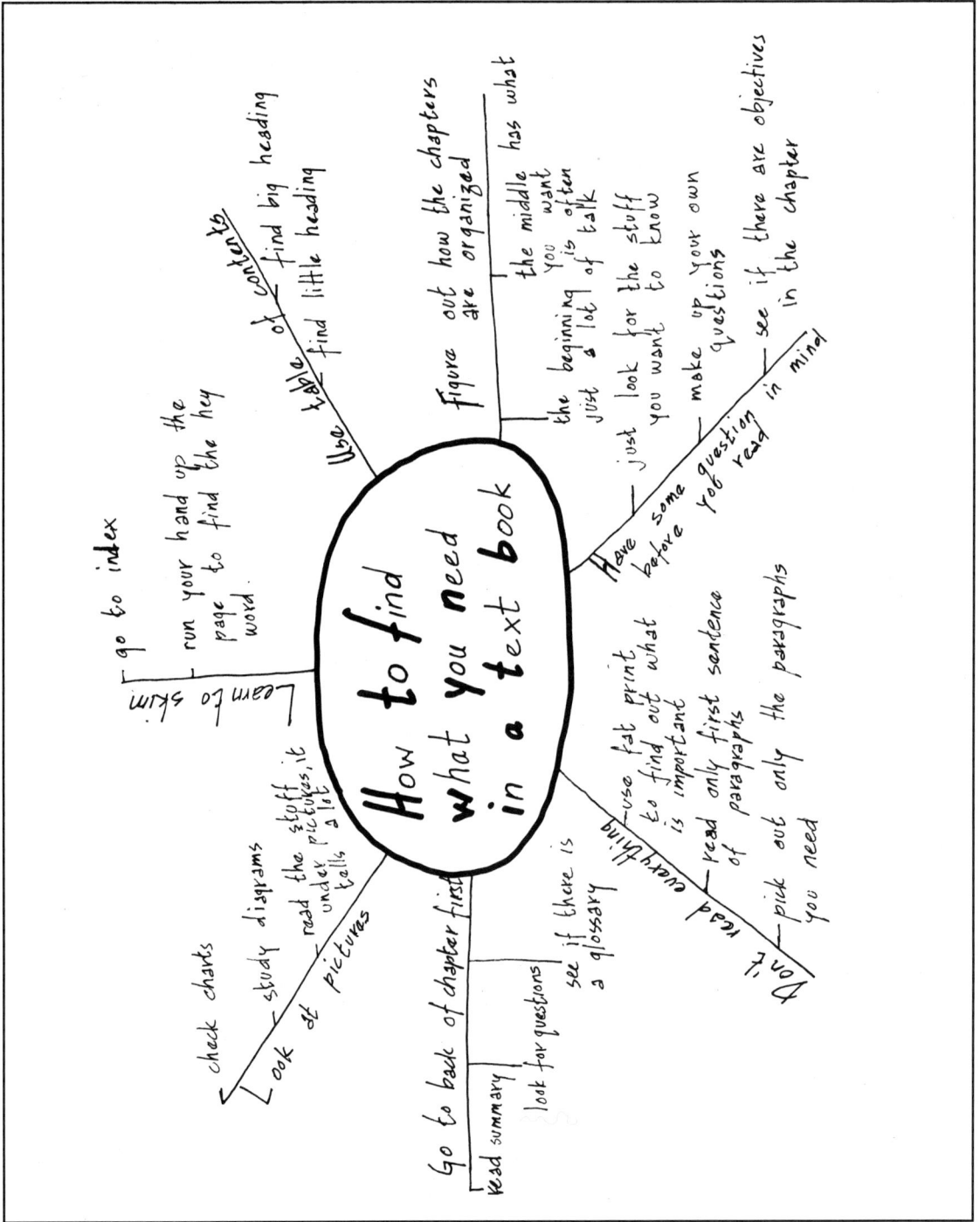

How to find
what you need
in a text book

Use table of contents
— find big heading
— find little heading

Figure out how the chapters are organized
— the beginning is often you want a lot of talk
— the middle has what
— just look for the stuff you want to know
— make up your own questions
— see if there are objectives in the chapter

Have some question read before you read in mind

go to index
— run your hand up the page to find the key word

Learn to skim

Look at pictures
— read the stuff under pictures, it tells a lot
— study diagrams
— check charts

Go to back of chapter first
— see if there is a glossary
— look for questions
— read summary

Don't read everything
— use fat print to find out what is important
— read only first sentence of paragraphs
— pick out only the paragraphs you need

Students helped their teacher develop this mind map.

189
*As reading advances
so does overall learning*

authors to draw upon as a knowledge base. Any kind of writing they do – poetry, mystery stories, reports – builds upon models students have internalized from their reading or from listening to others read to them.

As we have suggested elsewhere, reading fiction can also enhance the scope and breadth of subject area studies. Absorbing literature will help to build both a knowledge base and interest to draw students into the study of social studies or science. And such reading will lead quite naturally into comparisons, contrasts, and fact checking. In short, students' thinking and critical judgment are stimulated by extensive reading. And when their interest and excitement have been aroused, students are motivated to read. They will be sure to ask you, "Will we have time for reading?" – not once but several times – if they are worried that their reading session may be taken up by something else.

So look upon building reading interest and skills as one of your primary goals as an intermediate teacher. If your students become avid and competent readers, they will be prepared for studies of all kinds. More important, they will become lifelong learners because they have become imbued with the benefits they can derive from reading. No amount of textbook study in isolation can stimulate individual students' drive to search for knowledge, nor can it link that knowledge to the learners' personal lives. But when students are encouraged to pursue their own interests through reading, they will continue to read both in school and out.

What students gain from reader's workshop

If you are used to structured teaching, spending an hour or more on silent reading may seem too long, but students gain immeasurably from their reading. Here are some of the skills and benefits they gain. No doubt you will be able to think of others.

Students learn that
• reading is interesting and enjoyable
• they can gather information from reading
• reading helps generate ideas and formats for their writing
• they can identify with characters in books
• reading can satisfy emotional needs
• reading can be fun

Students also gain from their reading because they
- acquire facility with understanding and using book language
- improve their reading speed and comprehension
- learn to judge reading material and become discriminating readers
- develop personal preferences and find favorite authors
- cherish their reading
- develop their powers of oral expression
- become storytellers and descriptive writers
- expand their vocabulary
- learn about the conventions of print
- build their spelling skills
- pick up research skills
- build an information base on many topics
- learn about different cultures, ideas, and outlooks
- develop their imagination
- sharpen their analytic and critical thinking skills
- gather ideas for their future
- become inspired by some of the writing
- keep up with current events, learn about history, geography, our heritage, or . . .
- become familiar with the different genres of literature
- learn to distinguish fact from fiction
- find ways of solving problems or facing difficulties
- become familiar with the structure of stories
- build lifelong habits of using print for enjoyment and learning
- model their writing on the materials they have read
- develop confidence and self-esteem

MEETING CURRICULUM REQUIREMENTS IN SOCIAL STUDIES, SCIENCE, AND THE ARTS

6

"WITH THE EMPHASIS ON FLEXIBLE PLANNING and with large time blocks being taken up by reader's workshop and writer's workshop, how can I meet the curriculum requirements? How can I make sure that the students will acquire the knowledge they need? How can the students know what they should learn without specific instructions from me?" These are some of the questions raised by conscientious intermediate teachers who worry that they will not be able to do as thorough a job if they switch to whole-language ways of teaching. At first look, the need to convey a specific body of information and learning skills may seem incompatible with the kind of classroom management in which students have input and often determine the direction of the learning. But as their teacher you will continue to be in charge of the content and direction of learning in your classroom, although the students will set the scope and sequence to fit their interests and needs. As a result, both you and the students will engage in more solid, satisfying learning than structured lessons and worksheets have delivered in the past.

In this chapter we will offer suggestions for meeting curriculum requirements in ways that are compatible with the kind of classroom management we described in chapter 3. However, we also want to discuss the shift that is now taking place in curriculum planning, not only in British Columbia but elsewhere in North America and further afield.

Your knowledge of the curriculum becomes a starting point

Focusing on the process of learning and giving students wide choice still allow you to present topics for study to fulfil the curriculum requirements of your district. Your knowledge and experience will suggest ways of drawing students into the topics; and then you will give them the freedom to explore the material in many different ways. You will enliven and broaden the work by making interesting resource materials available, following up on special student interests that may not be part of the "regular" curriculum, connecting what is learned with issues you know to be of interest to the students, and encouraging them to discuss and present the material in their own ways. The key to letting ideas and information flow is to be flexible in planning your day and to be ready to shift your timetable to fit the needs of the learners in your class.

As one experienced intermediate teacher put it:

When I write my long-range plans, I go through the relevant curriculum and I group topics into several chunks to be covered during the course of the year. I also list all the things that I know the children will need help with, or that I will need to check for. After learning about the kinds of activities they want to do and which subjects they're interested in, I go to my list and build the projects. Last year, for example, we did a Halley's comet project as the children were eager to learn more about it. They had lots of newspaper articles and books on the subject, and I used their interest to help them fulfil their need to learn about note-taking, building rough drafts, forming paragraphs, and producing a final copy. We practiced all those skills while learning about Halley's comet. *(Davies 1989)*

Using the content that interested the students not only produced solid science knowledge but also fulfilled language arts curriculum requirements.

FOCUSING ON PROCESS
BUILDS KNOWLEDGE AS WELL AS SKILLS

Advocates of writer's workshop assert that the process of writing is more important than the product of writing. The realization that a focus on the *how* of writing and composing is more productive than a focus on the *what* has led to widespread adoption of writer's workshop as the most effective way of fostering writing at all levels. Now there is a strong move to extend that focus on process to all areas of schooling. Because we are in an information age, it has become clear that acquiring knowledge is a never-ending process and that the *how* of learning is the most important factor in preparing students to become lifelong learners. In science, students need to develop expertise in ways of enquiry, in finding, collating, and synthesizing information. They need to test hypotheses and solve problems, and they need to be highly proficient readers who can extract information effectively from all kinds of sources. In the humanities, too, reading skills are essential, and effective communication enhances information sharing. Social studies requires many of the skills needed in scientific enquiry and also demands unbiased judgment and good observation skills.

The draft of the new British Columbia Intermediate Curriculum Guide speaks of "learning for living," and the personal involvement and reality-based learning that are integral parts of whole-language learning exemplify that concept. Under such a process-oriented curriculum, students actively search for answers to questions that engage them and that are important to them. They learn for the real world, not simply for an academic purpose or a test, and they remember the knowledge that they have acquired.

The kind of learning for living that engaged students in many classes we observed had a strong focus on environmental issues. As the year unfolded, students continued to raise issues of interest to them and to integrate what had already been learned. Activities surrounding recycling, pollution control, and environmental safety gave students a feeling of having definite means to influence their world in positive ways. They not only engaged in learning at school but extended their work to their homes. Their learning moved far beyond the temporary acquisition of bits of information.

Think back to your own school days and try to remember items in the curriculum that made a strong impact on you. How much do you remember of the history, social studies, science, and math you studied? In contrast, think of activities you engaged in then that had personal interest to you. Can you remember working feverishly to learn about the mysteries of a computer, to master a hobby or craft? Do you remember the elation you felt when you made a new breakthrough?

Teaching the learners' way engenders the same kind of excitement and commitment in students because they are personally involved. When asked about meeting specific curriculum requirements, one teacher commented: "I do not choose which aspects of the curriculum we'll learn about; the kids do. If I did the choosing I wouldn't have their learning as intensely engaged. They choose what they want to know." Anne Davies' comments about responding to the children's interest in Halley's

**Ways of making
sure students
learn what they
need to know**

comet is a case in point. But teachers do not abdicate their responsibility for making sure that students learn both the skills and concepts they need and the factual information that will become a foundation for more advanced work.

Just as students have choices, so the teacher can choose which materials will best address the topics students are expected to cover. Choosing books, field trips, guest speakers, audio-visual presentations on specific topics will draw students into the orbit of the curriculum you need to convey. Reader's workshop, writer's workshop, and research projects offer wonderful ways of exploring topics in depth and making learning more personal than textbook study has done in the past.

USING READER'S WORKSHOP
TO GATHER INFORMATION AND ENTHUSIASM

Librarians, your school library, the public library, and private book collections – yours and your students' – are your most valuable resources in your students' quest for knowledge. Textbooks generally present the essence or facts of a topic, but to capture students' enthusiasm and interest, you will need much more than facts. You will know which topics are to be covered during the year, and if you discuss your needs well in advance, your librarian will be your staunchest ally in providing materials to attract your students' interest.

The Study of Ancient Civilization

Faced with the need to include ancient civilizations in her classroom studies of the year, Sylvia obtained novels on ancient Rome and Greece, travel literature on the Mediterranean, books on sculpture and architecture, collections of legends and myths, scaled-down versions of classics like the *Iliad* and *Odyssey,* and information on Greek drama. Displaying these materials around the classroom, reading aloud to students, inviting guest speakers who had traveled to Greece or had a strong interest in ancient cultures all combined to invite students to read not only the background materials but the textbooks as well. Including books with lots of photographs, drawings, and maps attracted the slower readers or less mature students who felt overwhelmed by the reading materials. No matter what their interests or levels of reading, students had ample opportunity to gather information and to link it to their knowledge of present-day cultures. Adding material of their own drew the teacher into their studies, and learning about antiquity became a shared experience that had depth and personal commitment.

Geography

Margaret's daughter, Anne Peterson, used the study of Canadian children's literature to fulfil the requirement to study Canadian geography. Her librarian not only delivered two large boxes of books for the project but became an enthusiastic collaborator who added her own special knowledge to the work. As children read books by and about Canadian authors and illustrators, they marked the locale of the stories and the authors' places of residence and/or birth on their maps of Canada, and collected additional detail about those regions for their writing. Illustrations and gripping stories conveyed a greater sense of place than the most exacting textbook description. Voluntary reading both in school and at home extended the study far beyond the expectations of the curriculum. At the same time, Anne had the opportunity to introduce children to her favorite authors, and the children had time and incentive to learn about Canada in a personal and pleasurable way. No amount of map study could have achieved as much.

Science – The Study of Animals

Science study is enhanced and expanded by extensive reading. If your classroom is well-stocked with non-fiction works – especially those that are well illustrated – students will gravitate toward such material during reader's workshop. Several students in Liz's class spent days poring over a guide to rocks and minerals. Fiction reading led to non-fiction study of animals described in the stories; information on owls, wolves, spiders, dogs, and horses went well beyond the descriptions gleaned from the stories, and novels involved reading that was invested with personal interest. Here again voluntary reading continued after school, and personal engagement ensured that the material became part of the students' long-term memory store.

Literature

Learning about literature is the obvious outcome of reader's workshop. Marne makes it a requirement that her grade 4–5 students read novels – not comics or magazines – during reader's workshop. To spark interest in the classics that are on the "suggested reading" or the "required" list, Marne will read particularly appealing or suspenseful segments to the class and then place the books on display with the suggestion that students may want to find out more. Hanne McKay brings large stocks of books into her class and will do a brief book talk to introduce five or ten books at a time: "This is a book about a boy who lost his dog." "This story takes you back to the days when the first settlers came to the prairies." Along with such cryptic comments, she may show pictures, read a page, or ask an intriguing question that can only be answered by reading on. She then places the books on the chalkboard tray and often finds that by the end of the day all have been claimed by students who want to know more. No amount of drill or questioning about characters, plot, or setting can inspire students to read as prodigiously as these inviting ways of offering literature. And extensive reading opens students minds to those very aspects they are supposed to learn. With this approach, questions and comparisons about literature arise from a solid stock of experience, not simply from worksheets or exercises assigned by the teacher.

Student Research

Reader's workshop adds the crucial component of personal research and commitment to students' learning. Thinking back to your university days, you will no doubt remember that your best learning and most exciting discoveries arose from the reading and research that you had initiated. Chances are that "discovery learning" not only opened new knowledge for you but also helped you to integrate information presented in class or in some of your more daunting textbooks. As you watch your students during reader's workshop and see them choose materials for study, you will discover the same solid learning and excitement. And you will find that the need to spark their interest in ancient civilizations, geography, animal anatomy, or literary analysis will draw you into new and intriguing ways of approaching those topics. Be sure to build on your own special preferences and interests – be they history, literature, or any other topics – to inject that personal commitment and enthusiasm into your discussions or presentations. If sports are your forte, looking into the origins of the Olympic games may offer some novel ways to introduce the study of ancient Greece that will keep you intrigued and will also captivate the sports enthusiasts in your class. As you keep track of discoveries your students make in the course of their explorations, your own knowledge will grow and deepen, often in quite unexpected ways. At the same time, showing yourself to be a learner will forge a close bond between you and your students. As you acknowledge them to be dedicated, curious learners, you will find yourself becoming a "co-creative teacher" who cooperates in the students' learning and gains from the work. Instead of trying to "pour the curriculum" into your students, you collaborate with them in learning more about the topics they need to cover during the year.

WRITER'S WORKSHOP EXPANDS AND RECORDS LEARNING

Keeping track of new learning often becomes part of writer's workshop. Just as students draw upon fiction to help them develop their creative writing, so they look to non-fiction to expand their report writing. Making notes, drafting findings in anecdotal or tabular form, listing questions, and brainstorming or information sharing are all integral parts of writer's workshop. Research and writing become ways of doing in-depth thinking about the topics under study, and writing enhances knowledge gathering and describing.

Writing also becomes a way to formulate and express opinions that are based on more than personal feelings. As a sequel to their Carmanah field trip, students collected information on the effects of logging on the Carmanah Valley and collated that information to serve as background information for letters to legislators. Similarly, a student presentation on driftnet fishing led to animated discussion and then to writing letters to protest the practice.

If you model the process of gathering, tabulating, sifting, and then drafting material for a report, you will lay the foundation for systematic study habits in all the topics to be studied. And if you ask the students for their input as you move along, they will take an interest in the topic, feel ownership in the final product, and be far more likely to remember the material than if you had simply asked them to study the textbook and make a summary. Here, as in reader's workshop, the personal involvement and affective components of the work will make learning meaningful and lasting. The environmental concerns coming out of the Carmanah field trip engendered strong feelings and a great deal of dedicated work. Social issues close to the students'

Jessica

Tebet

In the show about Tebet they had human skulls, made into drums and tepots. There was also a human thigh bone made into a trampet. I felt very odd being around these bones. The reson they did that is because it is part of their religion.

There was some really neat sculptures made out of wax and very hot metal. They decribe the different stages of life. There was one big one of a person who was very rich. But when he saw all the poor people who lived by him he gave them all of his money and went to pray under a tree. He took an arms bowl with him, People gave him money and food in the arms bowl even though that wasn't what he prayed for.
There was also a tea block. But I can't remember much about it.

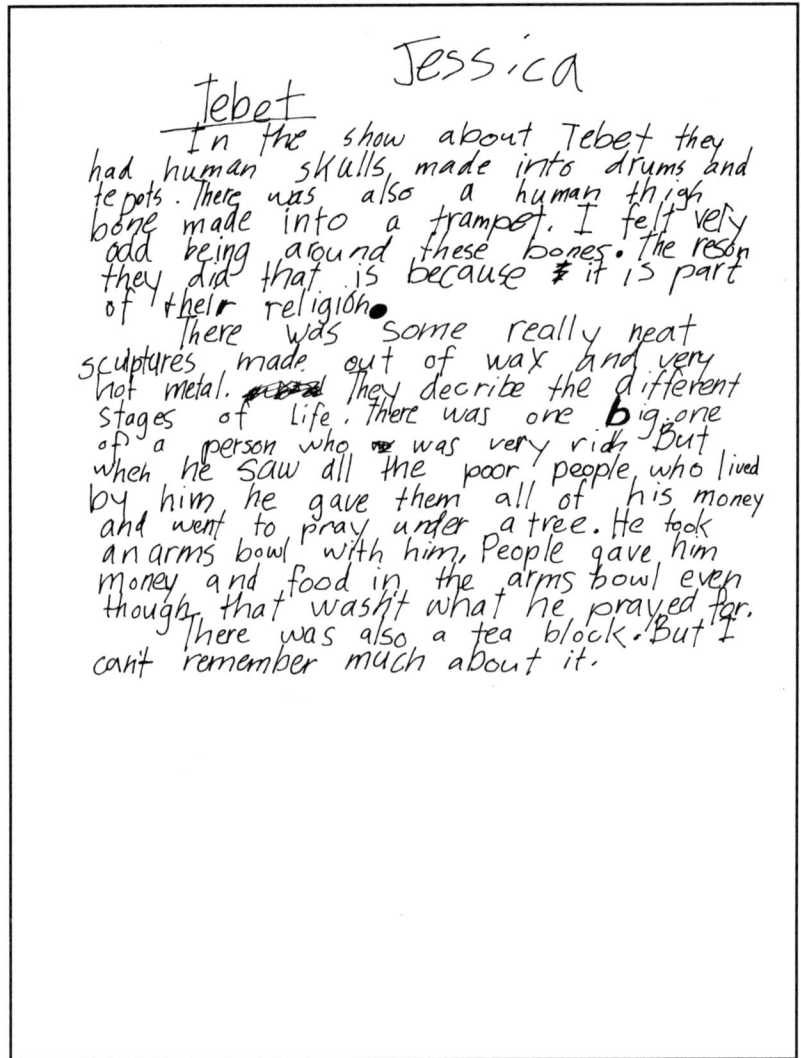

Writing develops along with knowledge.

lives, history that connects them solidly with their antecedents, or science that captivates their interest in nature or in technology will produce the same kind of dedicated study and writing.

PROJECTS ARE IDEAL WAYS TO INTEGRATE TOPICAL KNOWLEDGE AND SKILL DEVELOPMENT

Projects add further scope to knowledge building. In the research phase, field trips, audio-visual presentations, hands-on experiments, and interviews enhance library research and written information gathering. Cooperative learning, partner work, and small groups enliven and expand the research. When consolidating their findings, students are not limited to unidimensional reporting but have the option to build dioramas, create science displays, tape-record interviews, and put on plays or pantomimes to represent their new-found knowledge. Not surprisingly, the level of activity always seems highest and most purposeful when we observe classes in the midst of project work.

Nov.27

Dear Reader,

Driftnet fishing is a verry wastefull method of fishing going on in the center of the Pacific Ocean. Driftnetting is killing thousands of sea birds and mammles a year. Some people call the nets curtins of death, because they are stretched right across the gray whale's migration route so that it makes it almost impossible for them to migrate without getting caught in the nets

Many of the animals get caught in the nets and then they are thrown back in the water when they are half dead!

Concern for the environment was a major focus for students' work throughout the year.

To satisfy the need to include studies about industrial and less-developed nations, Sylvia invited guest speakers who had visited or lived in countries around the globe. A Fijian topped his description of his homeland by demonstrating an ancient war chant and having the students try it out; a German visitor engaged them in making Christmas ornaments; and Sylvia's daughters enlivened their travelogues by recounting personal experiences from their travels to Japan, China, and Europe. The class used these brief encounters as a stimulus for further research and chose two countries to study in greater detail. Japan became the major focus for study of an industrialized nation. Students had a choice in the method of presenting their findings and the specific focus of their project. In addition to basic information about geography, population, and industry, students looked at art, religion, and history. Trips to the local art gallery and information on Shinto shrines formed the bases for some reports; dioramas of Japanese homes portrayed the life style of present-day Japan; and the preparation of a Japanese feast served by students in traditional Japanese kimonos was the centerpiece of one group's work.

Study of African nations built on the Japan project, and here, too, both the method of study and the manner of representing the knowledge that students had gained varied widely. Physical involvement in creating masks and dioramas ranked high as ways of showing information. Students thrive on involving all of their senses in their learning. Even at the upper levels, concrete

Preparing a meal and serving it in traditional kimonos was one form of reporting on the study of Japan. It enhanced the students' written reports.

manipulations continue to be important parts of learning and are excellent ways of reinforcing academic learning.

To consolidate knowledge gained from the visits and projects, Sylvia presented brief synopses of relevant chapters in the social studies textbook and invited students to use it as a further reference to draw together what they had learned through their independent work. Those who were ready to engage in more abstract reading acted on her invitation. Others contented themselves with the summaries. But students at all levels of maturity gained quite personal impressions of the countries they studied, and the curriculum requirement was fulfilled in an effective, non-threatening way.

A whole-class cooperative project in Liz's class had different groups of students draw together information on the culture and way of life of the natives of the West Coast. Here again, a wide range of choices in topic, method of information gathering, and manner of representing knowledge culminated in meeting curriculum requirements in a very dramatic way – the construction of a miniature native village, complete with totem poles, long houses, and impressive backdrop. Written and oral commentary combined to elucidate the display, and *all* students took part, in their own ways, to recreate the past.

Toward the end of the project, an entire day was given over to completing the village. Different teams added their work to the finished display, and there was much information sharing on transportation, housing, food supplies, and native traditions. Students who are normally quiet and not very forthcoming developed leadership skills in guiding their teams and became eloquent in explaining the extent and import of their teams' parts in the project. Along with information on native culture, these village builders had built enough confidence in their knowledge that they felt free to speak up, not only among their peers but among adult visitors to the class. The project fulfilled curriculum requirements, built confidence, skills, and knowledge without constraining students to follow a prescribed route to reach the goal.

STUDENTS SHARE RESPONSIBILITY
FOR THEIR OWN LEARNING

Projects give full scope to students' ingenuity and natural curiosity. Beverly Schreiber, the grade 6–7 teacher at Strawberry Vale School near Victoria describes the work her students do:

I try to turn the power over to the kids. I just tell them, 'Here is what you are expected to do.' And then they have the choice of how to go about it. Last year a number of them got quite excited about the Romans. Others did Neanderthal man, and when that became intriguing, some of the students would say, 'Can we work with them on that?' So you can see that they pool their efforts. At the end of each project they give some kind of report. They've got to learn from each other as it would be impossible to have everyone do everything.

Actually, I give the students very few directions; I do very little teaching. They do the research themselves. Last year one kid did a whole unit on sign language and then taught sign language to the class. That kind of learning is very exciting to students, and they get hooked on the research and on finding things out. In short, they get hooked on learning. The same thing happened with the presentations. We did a lot of creative drama, which they enjoyed, and that got them into using drama for the presentations. Everybody participated. Now that they have had lots of experience in gathering information and dramatizing their knowledge, I can also connect their drama work with their writing and reading and talk about characterization, plot, and overall development.

Here again we have evidence of the benefits of learning by doing, of giving full scope to the students' needs and interests, and of letting learning emerge from the wealth of experience. Learning about specific topics leads, of necessity, to the acquisition of skills. But more important, it inspires students to learn.

Integrating the different areas of learning yields solid benefits

The concept of "learning for living – living for learning" best exemplifies the benefits of integrating skill-building with content teaching. In the world outside of school we learn by doing and neither compartmentalize our learning activities nor set specific time limits on them. Learning a new task extends over days, weeks, or months and is embedded in meaningful work. Though we forget at times to give or take full credit for that prodigious out-of-school learning, we nevertheless grow from day to day without experiencing many of the problems and strains that can attend learning in school. Yet the knowledge gained is solid and lasting. Learning for living works equally well in the classroom once we find ways of connecting the lessons we want to convey to the students' experience and concerns.

Grade Seven Research Project

1. Choose a controversial subject. BE SURE TO READ THIS ENTIRE SHEET BEFORE YOU CHOOSE.

   Here are some examples...

abortion	saving the Walbron	air pollution
euthanasia	sewage disposal	capitol punishment
water pollution	land pollution	Indian land claims
oil pollution	value of military	preservation of heritage
bilingualism	immigrants and refugees	

2. Begin a media file. Cut out articles from newspapers, magazines, etc. Videotape appropriate TV news broadcasts. Audio tape appropriate radio broadcasts. Copy out information from television and radio.

3. Research your topic. Go to the library. Talk to concerned people on the phone. Send letters to politicians, loggers, whomever makes sense in terms of your topic. LETTER WRITING MUST BE DONE IMMEDIATELY AS IT SOMETIMES TAKES A LONG TIME TO GET AN ANSWER. This part of your project must be done by Christmas—so get busy!

   NOTE—be sure that you are getting both sides of the topic!!!!!!

4. Prepare a questionnaire. You must make the following decisions:

   – what questions are you going to ask?
   – why are you asking them?
   – whom are you asking and why did you choose this population?
   – how many people are you going to survey?
   – are they going to remain anonymous and how are you going to ensure that?
   – how are you going to make sure that people are going to answer your questionnaire?
   – how are you going to show your information in graphs and tables?

   NOTE—you may not begin your questionnaire until you have completed your background research chapter. You need this information in order to ask intelligent questions.

5. You will prepare a report. I suggest that you use the following format:

   Chapter One
     Introduction—reason you chose this topic

   Chapter Two
     Background research chapter—synthesize the information that you collected from your research, letters, phone calls, media file, etc.

   Chapter Three
     Methodology—describe your questionnaire, population, etc. Report on your findings and display them in a graph and/or table.

   Chapter Four
     Results—combine what you learned from Chapters Two and Three and write about what you discovered and what you have decided about this topic. Please give your reasons for your decision.

   Chapter Five
     Conclusions—a brief summary statement and some ideas for further research.

*Bev Schreiber's guidelines
for her research project
show that whole-language
teaching does not mean the
abandonment of specific
guidelines for students.*

A LESSON IN MATH
TURNS INTO DESIGN OF A DREAM HOUSE

Knowing that her students want something practical in their work, Judy Woodward of St. Patrick's School in Victoria decided that the math curriculum requirement to produce a scale drawing of a house would do little to inspire them. Why do a drawing of someone else's house? So she asked her students to produce a scale drawing of their own bedrooms down to the finest detail including the location of electric sockets. From that initial drawing, the idea of designing a dream house emerged, and the simple math task evolved into the centerpiece of the last part of the year's unit – "Back to the Future."

By listening to her students talk to each other about the initial project, Judy allowed the dream home project to emerge. Letting go of control, of the need to say, "Here is the way this should be," she gave them freedom to work their way. As she puts it, "I have to stop myself from barging in to tell them what to do, but when I give them the freedom to work their way, they usually come out with far more than I ever started out giving them or expecting from them." In this case, the scale drawings evolved into considerations of building styles, architecture, interior design, color schemes, questions of layout, and ways of best meeting personal needs. The math work extended to cost estimating, mortgages, financing, and budget planning. As Judy's outline shows (see page 205), by building on the simple math drawing task, students worked on all areas of the curriculum. She merely provided the initial impetus and then the encouragement to carry on from there.

Work on the project extended well beyond the classroom and involved parents, relatives, librarians, and knowledgeable professionals, who supplied all the information that enriched the project. Students conferred with each other outside of class as well as in. They brought in books, designs, color samples, and architectural magazines, built scale models at home, and worked on interior design. They gathered information on building codes and zoning regulations and discussed their relative merits and fairness. In short, they did everything a thoughtful adult would do in planning a home. Students knew they were solving real problems, and they acted accordingly. The excitement generated by the project energized them, their families, and their teacher.

Back to the Future

Social Studies

- analysis of land prices in last 100 years (survey of landowners) and prediction of where to purchase in Victoria (population district analysis)
- family size poll: grandparents, parents, self in twenty years
- influence of electricity on modern life: home survey

Art

- visits to art galleries to determine preferences for art to put in rooms
- coloring and interior design/decorating considerations (guest speaker)
- analysis of common architectural designs (guest speaker)

Science

- general study of electricity (ongoing project) and energy
- technological advances: new appliances, gadgets, systems to meet needs in house
- examination of building code restrictions
- ethical issues surrounding technological advances (such as pollution)

Dream House

Math

- measurement: area, volume, perimeter, length; square footage of rooms for purchasing carpet, wallpaper, trim, paint; square footage of outdoor area for fencing in yard; grass seed, roofing materials; volume in pool, concrete for base
- calculations of costs; sales tax, discounts
- mortgages: interest calculations (simple and compound)
- scale drawing of house plans
- land price analysis over last 100 years

Language Arts

- real estate advertisement for house (written and for TV channel)
- survey of homeowners for practical criteria in planning house
- oral presentation to describe the house
- analysis of "Jetson's" cartoon for 'modern house' idea
- names for new gadgets: how are new words formed in English? Invent words for gadgets,

*Reflecting on the work
of her students, Judy
Woodward found that
designing a dream house
involved all areas of the
curriculum.*

SCIENCE THAT CONNECTS TO THE STUDENTS' EXPERIENCE MAKES ABSTRACT CONCEPTS CONCRETE

Physics, chemistry, and, to a lesser extent, biology can be abstract and – if the teacher is inexperienced – textbook driven. While some students enjoy the challenge of relating to new vocabulary, to formulas and theoretical considerations, the majority think and learn very concretely. They need physical involvement in learning and, in order to move learning beyond rote memorization, they need to understand the abstract concepts involved through hands-on work and physical examples that have meaning and relevance to them.

Here, again, projects that extend over time lend themselves well to making students aware of science in their everyday lives. As Malcolm Sneddan, a science consultant with the Victoria School Board, puts it, "Science is an integral part of life. It is a way of knowing. There is no part of science for which you couldn't find a personal connection." Malcolm has been teaching science for years, and his suggestions for moving beyond textbook descriptions moves science learning into the sphere of the students' own lives: growing things, observing the real world, and making thoughtful connections between what they see and what they think and know.

Biology for me focuses on the processes of biology, on growth and development. It doesn't matter whether we're looking at organisms or ecosystems, they all involve processes, and that's what I would tend to focus on, trying to find similarities and comparisons and asking, 'What does that mean for you? If that's true of this little fishbowl as a system, what does that mean for the earth and for you? If it has this effect on a little organism, what would the effect be on a larger scale?' So I would make constant comparisons and have students look for themselves.

Math and science projects to make learning concrete and relevant

Concepts that need to be learned in math and science can be abstract and difficult to internalize. If you embed them in projects or jobs that are meaningful to students, these concepts become part of the overall learning and are far easier for students to understand and internalize.

Money management will teach a lot
- Have students keep track of money for lunch, milk, field trips, special events.
- Set up a company (produce and sell T-shirts, publish students' writing) – sell stock, estimate production costs, call for bids, do bookkeeping, balance the bank account, calculate interest, calculate profit/loss.
- Do fund raising – have a bake sale, white elephant sale, service auction. Have students keep track of cash intake, petty cash for change, making change for customers.

- Plan field trips – include cost estimating, buying of supplies, keeping contingency funds.
- Organize a concession stand for field day – estimate how many hot dogs, buns, drinks to buy, how much money is needed. Do purchasing, selling, and accounting.

Cooking teaches more than how to make cookies
Students
- Work with fractions in recipes.
- Learn about volume and weight.
- Convert cooking temperatures from Fahrenheit to Celsius.
- Learn about nutrition – food groups, balanced diets.
- Follow directions.
- Find out about customs (eating preferences) of different cultures.

Gardening offers many lessons
- Use drafting and trigonometry for layout and planning.
- Study seasonal planning, regional climates, micro-climates.
- Set up a weather station to track rainfall, sun, and wind.
- Keep track of expenses and yield.
- Graph growth and yield of plants.
- Compare soil nutrients and their effect on plant growth.
- Study organic gardening, organic pest control.
- Learn about the chemistry of composting.
- Study Darwin's theory of heredity.
- Find out about plants (varieties) that are suitable for the local climate.
- Learn about climatic zones.

Sports
- Plan field day events and do all the necessary measurement and layout work.
- Study physiology and anatomy as they relate to peak performance.
- Chart performance of athletes in training, teams, competing schools.
- Examine the effect of nutrition on performance.
- Do comparison study of various forms of exercise and their effects on fitness.
- Study the trajectory of the ball in various games.
- Use physics to explain force and direction of bodies (including human bodies) in motion.

The minute we talk about something real, the students are bright-eyed. They sit up and they pay attention. I've always asked myself, 'Can I relate this – whatever it is – in some way to their lives?' And if I can't, then I don't teach it. And I have rarely found something that I can't relate to their lives. You know, the problem isn't the science curriculum – there's been a lot of thought put into it – it's just poorly taught. Now lately there has been a trend to remove things that people find difficult and often the decision has been made for the wrong reason. For example, one of the things I like to focus on has to do with forces and inertia and the way in which objects interact. This topic was actually dropped from the junior high curriculum because it was said to be too difficult. And yet, these children are going to be riding bikes and taking responsibility for vehicles, and they will have to know exactly what happens when a vehicle has to stop. Where does the energy go? And this concept can be made very concrete. You can give kids opportunities to observe the interaction of rolling carts, marbles, or billiard balls to show how things gain or lose energy, to show that when something stops it loses the energy it contains – and that's not hard to demonstrate. And then you can talk about why you need a seatbelt and why you need a headrest. So I have always continued to teach this unit even though it has been removed from the textbook.

You need that knowledge because it leads to an understanding of simple machines. Now I like simple machines too, but they're not simple; they're abstract. With simple machines we are talking about forces acting through levers acting through planes, and so on, and if students didn't understand forces in the first place they would simply memorize: 'There are six types of machines and three kinds of levers . . .'

So when I teach simple machines I tend to focus on: 'How do they give us an advantage? What are we able to do with a simple machine that we couldn't have done better by ourselves?' This is the exciting part for me. I tell them, 'You can't push a nail in backwards, you know, because the sharp end has to go down. Go ahead and try it.' It's not that we are beating nature; it's that we are using nature – and that would be the aspect of

Malcolm Sneddan and Liz share the students' interest in examining life in their jar of pond water.

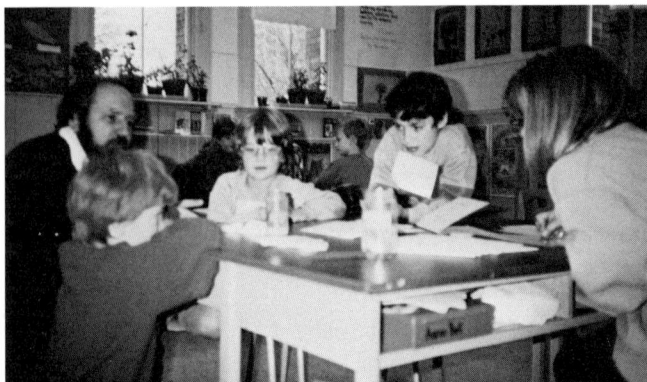

simple machines that I would use to teach kids. It's the old story of 'Give me a lever and I can move the earth.' That is the essence of simple machines. And what you're looking for is the advantage. So I would probably use this kind of intellectual activity to reach kids. And in elementary school that would be really exciting, because kids would say, 'Gee, if I only do this, then I can . . .'

Making that kind of connection becomes the lever that moves learning. And teachers as well as students would enjoy this way of teaching/learning far more than dragging students through a textbook. Relating material to the students' lives at every turn would certainly help science teachers to come into their own. They would be offering much more than empty concepts. The great thing is that learning about those connections would open new vistas for them as well as their students and infuse excitement and wonder into their teaching.

**Inexperienced
teachers
now have models
to build upon**

If science and math have not been areas of strength, here is your chance to make exciting new discoveries in the same safe ways as the students in your class. If you don't have a colleague to call upon to exchange ideas, draw upon TV series like James Burke's *Connections* or Jacob Bronowski's *The Ascent of Man.* Programs like these will provide you with good background knowledge. Then there are books. One of the many excellent books available, *Teaching Elementary Science – Who's Afraid of Spiders?* (Selma Wassermann and J. W. George Ivany 1988) will turn you, along with your students, into thoughtful science explorers. Wassermann and Ivany talk of "sciencing" as a process and offer the "play-debrief-replay" instructional model as a way of involving learners in finding out about the world around them. Like Malcolm Sneddan, the authors remind us that science is all around us in everything we have contact with, and they suggest that teachers foster enquiry behavior as a vital part of sciencing.

Hands-on work, small-group interactions, lots of discussion of what learners have observed become the starting points for describing, predicting, testing hypotheses, and then retesting. Their comparisons between the usual lessons about things to be learned and "sciencing" activities that allow learners to discover information capture the excitement and viability of scientific enquiry in the classroom. Along with detailed descriptions about how to get started, they offer many practical examples for classroom work that will give you and your students lots to think about.

Make science come alive

Science will come alive for you and your students if you fill your classroom with interesting materials – living plants; live animals; specimens of rocks, minerals, fossils – anything you or the students find interesting. Your regular science curriculum will introduce students to the ways of observing, measuring, recording, and interpreting data. To expand their work and give them ample opportunities to work independently, keep a science corner with simple supplies and invite the students to add to your own stocks. Making them responsible for keeping the center safe as well as neat and tidy sets the tone for working with the materials and equipment provided.

Provide a science corner (near the sink if you have one)

A chemistry lab
- Provide simple kitchen chemicals – soda, salt, borax, vinegar.
- Encourage interesting projects such as building a volcano.
- Include scales, measuring equipment, and a pan or trough for
  wet work.
- Invite students to bring in their own experiments or supplies.

A biology table
- Provide microscopes or magnifying glasses borrowed from your resource center.
- Observe effects of light on plant growth and pigmentation.
- Display students' collections of biological specimens.
- Keep track of the transformation of caterpillar to chrysalis to moth.

A weather station
- Include a thermometer, rain gauge, wind gauge, or weather vane.
- Chart information, note patterns, and prepare weather forecasts.

Grow a garden in the schoolground

- Do planning and layout.
- Decide on proper crops for your area.
- Look into needs for fertilizer and soil enrichment.

- Make and use compost.
- Learn about the differing needs of plants – sun, water, type of fertilizer.
- Observe growth with proper watering and tending.
- Use organic pest control methods.
- Harvest and enjoy.
- Advertise and market produce.

The more independence you give the students, the more their interest in science will flourish. As Jerome Bruner puts it, "messing about" teaches a lot. So do not deprecate the playful ways in which students will from time to time use the science materials. If you encourage them to report to the class on any interesting findings they have made during their science "work," they will rise to the challenge. Trust and have fun!

ENQUIRY AND THINKING SKILLS
BECOME INTEGRAL PARTS OF EVERYDAY LEARNING

Far from denigrating subject-area teaching as some teachers have feared, shifting to sciencing and encouraging active exploration in your classroom will bring enquiry and thinking skills into all of your classroom work. Here it is a case of science enriching the classroom climate rather than being submerged in a sea of general skill-building activities. Malcolm Sneddan provides a number of examples of integrating the enquiry attitude of science into other realms.

I often use historical approaches and relate the material to the reality of that time. What always annoys me is that children think that old ideas are bad ideas. They'll say, 'How can anybody ever have thought that?' And I come back and say, 'Well let's think about some of the things they truly believed at that time and see how much sense they make.' And in the biology area one of the things that people believed was that meat turned into flies. And I'll say, 'But this was a perfectly rational thing for them to think. Meat did appear to turn into flies.' The question to be asked is, 'What were the people then missing?' And then the focus becomes, 'And what are you missing today?' That's the way life is – you miss the connections. You make a judgment based on what you see, and if there now are a bunch of flies and there is less meat, where did the flies come from?

In electricity I talk about the dancing frog leg of Galvani – an electrical reflex reaction – and I'll say, "A dozen years after Galvani's discovery, a woman called Mary Wollstonecraft Shelley wrote a novel called *Frankenstein* – the first horror story. And what was it based on? It was based on the fact that people thought they'd finally discovered the factor that made living things different. Scientists had looked at the differences between a dead body and a live one. As there was no weight difference, they thought electricity was the difference. And then I tell the kids that this greatest horror story of all times was written because the author had read about science – 'so who says poets don't read science, guys?' It's my way of giving kids the idea that science does not happen in isolation. It's a whole part of life. So I do that sort of background talk whether I deal with simple machines now or in the time of the pyramids. That to me is true integration, because the science – wherever it occurred – was integral to life.

Making such connections and capturing teachable moments whenever and wherever they arise is yet another benefit of integrated teaching, teaching that is unhampered by time constraints or the requirement to follow preset lesson plans.

FLEXIBILITY OF PLANNING MAKES ROOM FOR SPONTANEOUS TEACHING

When planning is open to change at a moment's notice, teachers have the opportunity to capitalize on teachable moments that present themselves, and there is no requirement that the teacher must know the answers in advance. In fact, if you, too, are a curious, engaged learner, the enquiry process will be that much more viable for the whole group – including you. With that focus, following up on spontaneous questions, remarks, or requests often produces wonderful on-the-spot lessons, individual projects, and at times entire units:

• Picking up on a boy's comment that for him the ideal bedroom would have a bathroom built in launched the entire class on the dream house unit.
• Boat building done in conjunction with a pirate unit produced questions about stability and an impromptu lesson on ballast, the role of the center of gravity and its importance in boat design.
• Using the tuning fork to start singers on key turned into a lesson in physics when the teacher placed the fork against the chalkboard to amplify its sound. Comments about sound waves and how they travel expanded to a lesson in states of matter, and the molecular structure of air, liquids, and solids.
• Producing individual descriptions of Greek deities for the benefit of children in lower grades seemed to call for the construction of a family tree of the gods to show their relationships. Dubbing their unit "The gods must be crazy,"

Judy Woodward's students voiced their revulsion at the mating of brother and sister and gave her the opening to launch into a discussion on heredity, DNA, and the undesirable aspects of such unions. By acknowledging comments about "gross stuff," Judy built on the strong feelings of the moment to teach an abstract topic in a down-to-earth way.

- Leafing through an atlas and finding a page that showed the routes followed by various explorers opened the door to questions and then to reading about the lives and adventures of these men, first for one boy and then for a group.

The excitement of the moment, intense curiosity, desire to know, and fascination with the unknown or mysterious are sparks that ignite learning. They can be fanned into passionate involvement and total absorption or just as easily snuffed out if ignored or put on hold "till another time/class period." Going with the moment acknowledges the inner drive to find out and tells your students that their thoughts and feelings are valid and important. You affirm them as learners when you respond fully to a question of physics right in the middle of a music lesson, send a boy to the library when it's geography time, expand a simple math task into an entire unit that spans all parts of the curriculum.

Natural-science projects and units

The possibilities for natural-science projects and units are infinite. If you have curiosity and are ready to explore, your students will join right in. Here are some examples from Val Carter's years of exploring science.

Insects and spiders
- collecting and observing large specimens
- visiting museums and displays
- doing library research

Geology
- collecting, identifying, and classifying rocks
- classifying and dating fossils
- running simple tests to identify minerals
- building models of crystal shapes
- studying volcanoes

Reproduction
- looking at body systems – human, animal, bird
- comparing embryology of different organisms
- making models and drawings of stages of development
- tracing chick embryology complete with "autobiography of a chick"

Adaptation of animals
- camouflage, feeding habits, changes in fur and plumage
- observing classroom animals

Classifying plants
- studying mosses, seeds, moulds
- examining parts of plants
- dissecting flowers

Classifying animals
- dissecting fish, frogs, worms
- comparing human anatomy to animal anatomy
- studying birds and their nests

Interdependence of living organisms
- studying diets
- examining owl pellets
- comparing teeth
- making drawings of life chains – who feeds on what

Microscope club
- examining pond water
- making hay infusions
- looking at cells of plant and animal tissue
- studying cell reproduction
- growing cultures of microscopic organisms

When students engage in genuine research, their energy and persistence are boundless. The excitement of discovery, the eagerness to find out yet more, and the satisfaction of interacting with the real world – as opposed to worksheets – carry them along and extend their work beyond school. Reading, writing, drawing, thinking, discussing, hypotheses testing, and experimenting become natural parts of research. Imaginative work, poetry, fantasy, and creative problem solving add extra fun as students build creativity and spontaneity along with knowledge.

Flexibility of planning works *for* the subject specialist

Just as your students thrive on the flexible planning that acknowledges their desire to learn, so your professional work will blossom when you are free to develop ideas and lessons fully. When you are no longer bound by the thought that "if this is Tuesday, this must be chapter 2," then you can recapture the excitement you felt when you built your professional background in the field that had captivated your interest.

Whether you work in your home room or work with other classes for designated periods of time, you have the freedom to extend, alter, or shift work on a unit. You have the opportunity to get students physically involved in experimenting, discovering, building, exploring, drafting, and then refining the work they do. Extending work over time builds in-depth understanding, commitment, and a lot of peripheral learning that is the essence of what students need as lifelong learners.

USING NATURAL HISTORY AS THE "HOOK" TO LEARNING

Val Carter, who has taught grade 5 in Yellowknife, N.W.T., for over fifteen years, has brought her collection of curios and her enthusiasm for natural history into her classroom – alternately known as "the jungle" or "the museum" – to build interest and joy in learning. She talks of using natural history as the "hook" that generates curiosity and the desire to learn.

When I was a little girl, my grandfather collected all kinds of things that I was interested in, and so I became 'Hector the Collector.' When I first started teaching and took these things to school, I noticed that the kids were really interested in them too, so I began to build on that interest and on their love for animals. Instead of having them memorize facts from a textbook, I had them use plants, animals, the environment, minerals, fossils, all kinds of hands-on material to have them find out about nature. (See page 216.)

Hector Collector's "Goodies to Entice" Curiosity Shelf

Val Carter, alias Hector the Collector, was drawn to science by her grandfather's collection of natural science objects. In turn, she attracts her students to science by sharing her ever-growing collection and encouraging them to add to it.

Touching, sorting, inspecting, comparing, and just simply enjoying the large array entice students to become junior scientists. Most of the items are the accumulation of years of picking things up and keeping them. Becoming known as a collector of curios is sure to generate donations to make the collection grow.

Here are examples from the curiosity shelf:

- Shells of all sizes and types from large conches and giant clams to tiny exotics
- Sand dollars – mini to large
- Dried fish – blow fish or puffer, porcupine fish, piranha
- Eggs – robin, seagull, ostrich
- Teeth of all kinds – canine; molars of herbivores, carnivores, insectivores
- Bones of many sizes and descriptions (great for comparative anatomy)
- a caribou leg with hoof, skin, and bone
- Whalebone (known as baleen)
- Turtle shells
- Butterflies
- Animals preserved in formaldehyde – octopus, tarantula, pig embyo
- Room-sized python skin and skins of smaller snakes
- Rocks, minerals, and fossils

If botany is your interest, a collection of leaves, flowers, seeds, cones grasses, anything else that can be preserved, could add to your curiosity shelf.

Live Animals / Jungle Pets (over the years)

Val Carter's classroom "jungle" includes not only live pets and growing plants, but a cast-iron bathtub filled with pond water and a stand of bullrushes.

- crayfish
- land crabs, hermit crabs
- water crabs
- ferret
- snakes, worms (invertebrates)
- aquariums galore (tropical fish)
- frogs, elephant fish, piranha
- gerbils
- hamsters
- salamanders, newts
- guinea pigs
- turtles
- pond water
- birds
- iguana
- rabbits (lop-eared, angora)
- chickens
- brine shrimp

I stretch that eagerness to learn into all areas. We read poems about sea monsters and sharks, and then the kids write poems about their own animals. As they make observations of the living things in class, they write reflective logs or an evaluation of jobs such as dissecting fish and frogs. From there they move into presentations, in which they give research reports to the entire class, so their communication skills grow along with their fact finding, which also involves a lot of reading and research. All along they know that they are doing science and genuine research, but I know all the skills that they are learning too. Thinking and problem solving certainly move right to the top of Bloom's taxonomy. The kids are observing, analyzing, classifying, inferring, testing hypotheses, and synthesizing information. (See page 218.)

Along with the learning, the contact with living things fills emotional needs for the students, particularly for the special needs kids. Animals are the recipients of their love. Kids who may have been abused at home relate deeply to the animals and develop great responsibility in caring for them. So they develop their social skills and a sense of responsibility as well as academic knowledge.

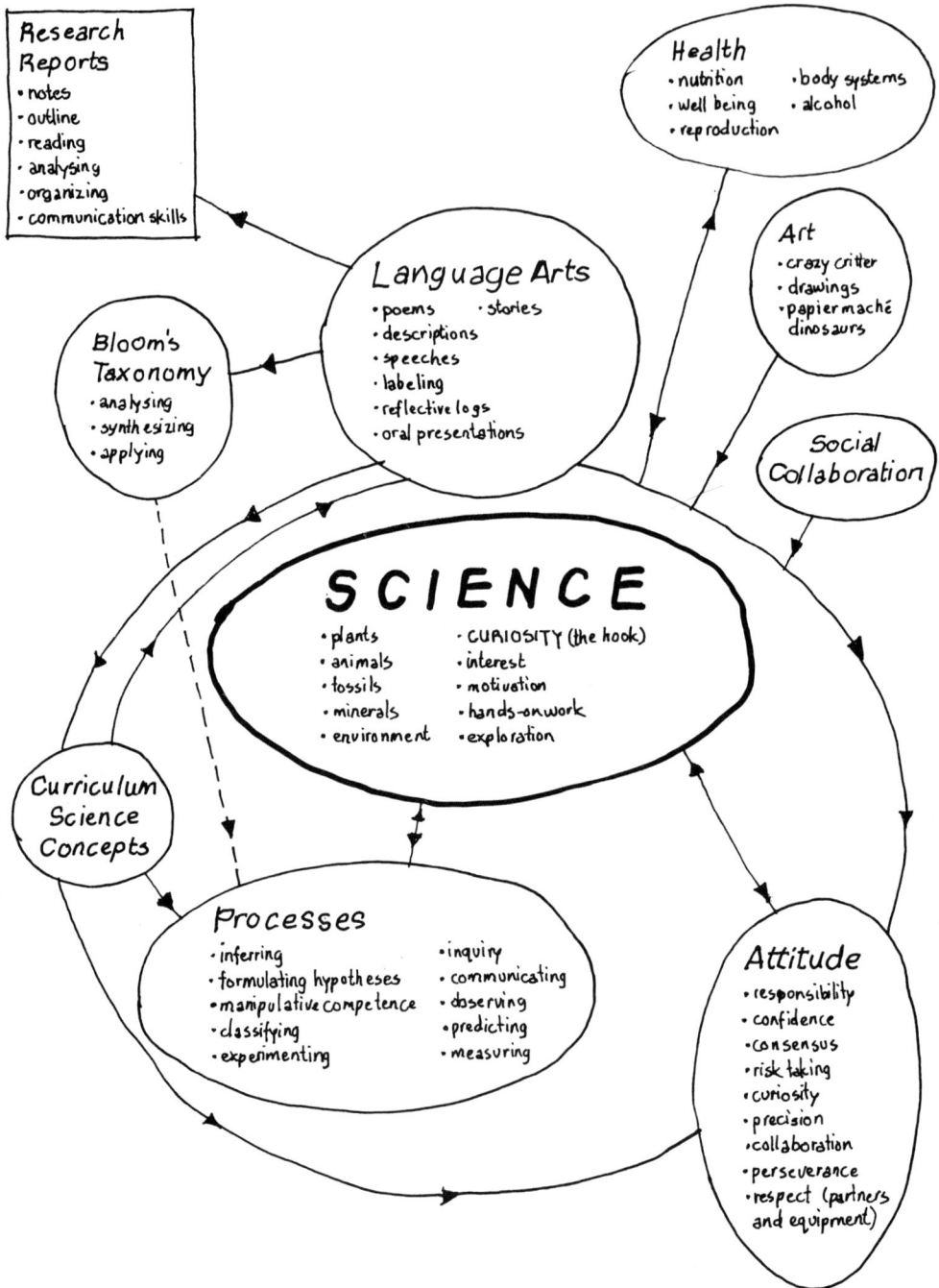

Research Reports
- notes
- outline
- reading
- analysing
- organizing
- communication skills

Health
- nutrition
- well being
- reproduction
- body systems
- alcohol

Art
- crazy critter drawings
- papier maché dinosaurs

Language Arts
- poems
- stories
- descriptions
- speeches
- labeling
- reflective logs
- oral presentations

Bloom's Taxonomy
- analysing
- synthesizing
- applying

Social Collaboration

SCIENCE
- plants
- animals
- fossils
- minerals
- environment
- CURIOSITY (the hook)
- interest
- motivation
- hands-on work
- exploration

Curriculum Science Concepts

Processes
- inferring
- formulating hypotheses
- manipulative competence
- classifying
- experimenting
- inquiry
- communicating
- observing
- predicting
- measuring

Attitude
- responsibility
- confidence
- consensus
- risk taking
- curiosity
- precision
- collaboration
- perseverance
- respect (partners and equipment)

Val Carter sees her way of teaching science as a recurring cycle that involves all aspects of learning and the curriculum.

My own academic background in natural history is limited to a grade 12 biology course. I simply built on my curiosity and the interest that my grandfather kindled. My collections of natural history items continue to grow and expand and my students share my interests. I find I need not be an 'expert.'

GEOGRAPHY BECOMES
A LESSON IN THINKING AND PLANNING

When Liz had students make Thai masks, she began with a travelogue on her trip to Thailand and moved from there to the design and creation of individual masks. As students progressed from simple paper cutouts, to cutouts with intricately crayoned decorations, to the final, elaborate masks, they were:

- experimenting/creating
- thinking about their work
- working physically – making mind/body connections
- talking about what they were doing
- solving problems
- trying many different ways of approaching the task
- using materials creatively
- building on mistakes
- sharing/comparing/collaborating
- building vocabulary
- studying design
- considering cultural patterns
- creating combinations
- keeping their workplace clean

The production of Thai masks produced wonderfully imaginative results.

Val Carter's students keep in close touch with their animals.

Far from being "just a cut-and-paste job" as it may have appeared on the surface, the two days spent on mask-making generated intense interest in Thailand, other Asian nations, and their cultures. The classroom hummed with positive energy, and even reluctant participants – who usually affect a superior attitude toward such lowly jobs – were drawn into the excitement and produced beautiful masks to their own intense and obvious satisfaction. For the teacher, such absorption and involvement cannot help but create a warm glow of joy and an affirmation of the productivity of open, flexible ways of teaching/learning.

FROM SINGING TO CREATING LYRICS

A student's suggestion to develop lyrics for Pachelbel's Canon resulted in two full days of creative work. Building on the music teacher's professional way of bringing singing to beautiful clarity and precision by the consideration of major and minor keys, voice exercises, and practice gave students the confidence to become creators of songs. To make their lyrics work the writers had to consider phrasing, rhythm, mood, melody, and overall effect. They worked in teams, used tape recorders, practiced both with and without a piano accompanist during their trial runs. To culminate their production, they performed their version for the entire class after first transcribing it into their music notebook.

Their work cut across regular reading/writing periods and gave everyone a chance to complete their lyrics and then practice their songs. Music, professionalism in teaching/learning, and the internalization of abstract concepts of composing were on a high plane. Music and specialty teaching, far from being submerged, blossomed.

SPANNING TOPIC AREA AND TIME
LIFTS ARTWORK TO A NEW LEVEL

As one of the projects designed to save the environment and cut back on waste, Marne's class decided to produce reusable cloth gift-wrap. Following a general discussion about recycling and the reduction of throwaway goods, the work of printing designs onto cloth got under way. Marne demonstrated the necessary steps of making printing stamps, selecting colors, spreading on just the right amount of paint, and then stamping the cloth. Her detailed instructions included cautions about trying not to fingerprint or smudge the cloth, and by the time the production crew got under way, everyone was filled to the brim with the mechanics of cloth gift-wrap production. But despite the desire to help save the environment, there was no inspiration or creativity in the mechanical proficiency of "doing the job right." Peace symbols, yin/yan designs, and similar clichés showed up, though the creative spirit of the class normally brought forth a wide range of imaginative and individual artwork.

To spark creativity, students needed a fresh start, one that began with their intense feeling for the trees and the environment that are in jeopardy. Once Marne led a session in which she and the students shared feelings about being in beautiful surroundings, looking at the trees, and at the beauty in the environment, the design work of students took on new life. The images and sentiments that emerged generated the spontaneity and inspiration lacking when mechanics of production were used as the starting point of the project. By making time, affirming the importance of strong personal involvement in art and the need to make drafts and to experiment, the designs that the students produced moved through a number of stages to a high point of accomplishment. From simple, cute clichés they moved to beautifully executed drawings that were imbued with a sense of nature and the desire to preserve it. Multicolor prints, special layouts, and careful printing completed the job, which took up a block of time each day over an entire week. Both instruction and production time provided ample scope to allow the students' work to blossom.

Teamwork enhances professional work in all areas

Integration works in the staff room as well as the classroom. Teamwork, networking, and whole-school collaboration are integral parts of whole-language teaching. Instead of being isolated in their classrooms, teachers reach out to each other to team-teach, to share information and planning, and to participate in joint projects. As for the students, the increased interaction sparks new ideas and greater creativity. Anne Petersen speaks of the support she and her colleagues gave each other as they worked on their whole-school "Year 2000 project." At University Hill Elementary School in Vancouver, teachers combine classes and team-teach in a large open area that makes room for special projects and easy movement. On a larger scale, national and even international networks are being formed to share ideas, resources, and conferences.

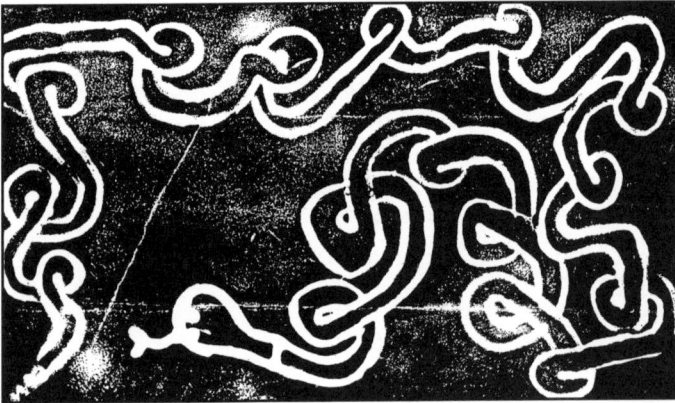

*Producing re-wrap,
cloth giftwrap that can be
recycled, tapped students'
creative talents and
organizational skills as
they worked in teams
over a period of time.*

The energy generated by such cooperation is reflected in Margaret's description of South Park's all-school astronomy unit.

At our staff meeting in June we discussed our goals for the following year and planned an astronomy unit to create a focus on science. As we brainstormed ideas the full creative power of the staff came to the fore. We fairly tripped over ourselves to get our ideas out. Malcolm Sneddan, the Science Helping Teacher, was amazed at our energy and the wealth of ideas that poured forth. Here we were at year's end with low energy levels, yet the whole place became energized as we generated and sifted ideas faster than we could record them. Malcolm helped us pull our ideas together, and later we worked with art experts, representatives of the Royal Astronomy Society, and other knowledgeable people from the community who came into the school to share their knowledge and enthusiasm with us.

When we started the unit in September, each class worked at the children's own levels and with their ideas. My class made lunar landscapes of papier maché, read books about astronomy, and had a visitor who brought in a meteorite, which absolutely delighted the children. Here they could actually feel and hold a piece of space. All over school students were reading about the universe, and books, magazine articles, and newspaper clippings filled classroom shelves. Students brought in books from home, from the library, from the university, and slides and videos augmented the printed information. We truly became a learning community as teachers, students, parents, and support staff joined to take in information about planets and galaxies. Teachers were as involved and enthusiastic as the students and modeled learning and enquiry behavior all along the way.

Later in the year we had a 'planet walk' with planet stations set up along the waterfront at the correct relative distances and in such a way that at the end of the walk you could look back and see 'the sun' where you started. The older students set up the planet stations, manned them, gave out information to space visitors, and stamped the passports that each child presented upon arriving at the planet. While there, each child was weighed and given his or her relative weight for that planet. CHEK TV, the local television station, was suitably impressed, and after filming events at each station, included the planet walk on that evening's news.

The unit ended with a 'star night' at which students from each class presented what they had learned to parents and visitors to the school. The presentations were followed by potluck suppers in each classroom, and even though the main attraction of the evening had to be canceled, the gathering was a resounding success. We had planned to go to lookout hill in Beacon Hill Park to watch the stars through telescopes. There were to have been four stations, all manned by experts, but poor weather forced us to abandon that part of our study.

We are already planning for next year and will set a star-gazing night for the spring when we can hope for clear nights and warmer weather. In the meantime, all of us have learned. Parents entered right in and probably learned as much as their children. All of the teachers gained new information and excitement, and the entire school, including the parents, became a community of learners.

And what about the curriculum?

In all of the examples we have given in this chapter, students acquired a certain body of knowledge. They learned about Greece and Rome, about Canadian geography, about making scale drawings, about astronomy . . . . They also learned about

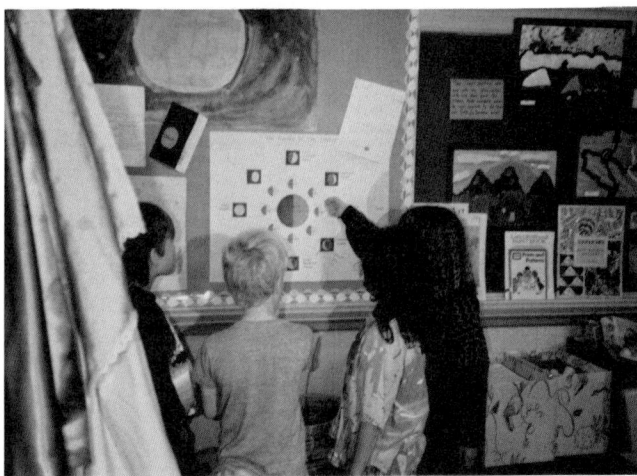

A whole-school astronomy unit produced learning not only for students, but for teachers and parents too.

research, writing, doing artwork, and creating in the realm of music. But perhaps most important, they acquired attitudes towards learning, towards working cooperatively, and towards being independent observers and thinkers. As our star diagram shows (see pages 226 and 227), these attitudes are now part of the British Columbia intermediate curriculum. So on this score, too, the integrative, open approaches of whole-language have fulfilled curriculum requirements. Instead of simply accumulating "facts," students have developed a broad understanding of the subjects they studied and have made the knowledge their own. Speaking of her grade 7 students, Judy Woodward comments:

> The interesting thing is that students don't come out with a common body of knowledge; they come out with an *area* of knowledge. In a unit they will develop a general feel for the Olympics and a general feel for the democratic process, which we also looked at, and a general feel for the way in which a belief in "the gods" gradually became a belief in one god, which led the way for the Christian faith – and other faiths – which then shaped the world as we know it. So although they don't all know the name of every god and can't tell you the exact steps of moral development, they do have some understanding of moral development and the democratic process. So an area of knowledge is there as opposed to a specific body of knowledge that might be laid down in a curriculum guide. But somebody has to give them some parameters to start with. Without them, my students would never have studied antiquity.

And so we have come full circle. You, the teacher, are still in charge of seeing that curriculum requirements are met, be they process components or factual components. But the whole-language ways offer you far greater scope to present and develop material for learning. As a professional you are trusted to draw your students into your sphere of learning and to open the field to them in ways that will make you a co-learner in the classroom. Though the change may seem difficult at first and at times it may be hard to relinquish control, the learning, excitement and joy in your classroom will be ample rewards.

Astronomy unit

• *adapt and change*
• *respect and care for the environment*
• *learn cooperation*
• *become responsible membe of society*
• *accept and demonstrate empathy*
• *value, respect, and appreciate cultural values, and respect individual contributions*

Social responsibility

Social / e

• **discuss pros and cons of space exploration**
• **examine collaboration aboard spaceships**
• **speculate about life in space**
• **discuss the effects of air travel on the environment**
• **develop concerns about cleaning up the environment**

• *develop social skills in conjunction with physical activity*
• *develop motor skills*
• *learn about good nutrition*
• *care and learn about respect for the body*
• *learn and practice safety*

Physical development

• **be spacepeople**
• **use parachutes**
• **act out the landing of spaceships**
• **do the "planet walk"**
• **move as though weightless**
• **create artwork**

• *foster enthusias for the art*
• *imagine ar visualize*
• *respond through art*
• *create and interpret*
• *manipulate new media to develop new skills*

A comparison between the new B.C. Curriculum Guide and the school-wide astronomy study reveals a close match.

- encourage parents and community
  to learn along with kids
- invite guest speakers (amateur and professional)
- hold potluck supper before stargazing
- work with buddies (children of other ages)
- invite parents to stargazing night
- visit senior citizens' home to show models and
  presentations of space research
- work in groups
- work in pairs
- be flexible enough to change school day
  (for example, 4 P.M. to 10 P.M. for stargazing)

**Students developed wonder and
curiosity and learned about**
- **stars and planets**
- **history of astronomy**
- **moon calendar**
- **scale (relative distance between planets)**
- **physics (evaporation and condensation)**
- **math (relative weight and age of planets)**
- **astronauts**

• develop a positive self-concept
• develop independence
• cope with change
• share and cooperate
• develop friendships
• learn from others

They participated in
- **reading information and stories about space**
- **writing about the solar system**
- **sharing stories and presentations**
- **writing poems about space**
- **listening to presentations by experts
  (Royal Astronomical Society)**
- **doing science experiments (making a comet
  with dry ice, clouds in a bottle)**
- **doing research**
- **going on the "planet walk"**

Intellectual development

Artistic / aesthetic development

• sustain and extend curiosity
• develop thinking skills
• use language to think and learn
• use language to communicate
• develop and integrate attitudes, skills

- **make a space ship with night sky
  using a refrigerator box**
- **draw murals of sky**
- **make lunar landscape**
- **build a space city**
- **cut out and paste up solar system
  as a mural**
- **make moon buggies**
- **make models of the universe**
- **make kaleidoscope (stars) out of tubes**
- **make space suits**
- **design flag for a planet**
- **make a big book**
- **use star charts**
- **use view finders**
- **make model of red star (death of star)**

To plan or not to plan

If you're going to teach, you've got to have a plan. How else would you know what to do? How would you set goals, follow the curriculum, set deadlines, or keep students busy? You've got to look ahead to get everything ready . . . or do you? Lesson plans, day books, and annual overviews have been around for so long that we sometimes forget to question their value and usefulness. Talking to hundreds of teachers throughout her travels, Marg has raised the issue: to plan or not to plan.

As I attend teachers' conferences and ask teachers about the previews or overviews they have to prepare each year, they seem to be resentful. I ask them how long it takes to draw up these plans and am told 'considerable time.' I then ask the teachers what they do with these plans, and they look kind of startled. 'Give them to the principal, of course.' 'Well, what does your principal do with them?' 'I guess he [or she] files them or gives them to the superintendent.' 'Are the plans useful to you?' 'No. I never look at them again!'

It seems to me that planning would be a lot more useful to everyone if it were done differently. Why not wait till you have met your students and have information on their talents, interests, needs, and backgrounds. A plan that takes all these factors *and* the curriculum into account would be of far greater use to you and your students, and at the same time would satisfy the principal.

A brainstorming session is valuable. If you and your students jointly consider all the things they want or need to do, you have a great reservoir of ideas to draw upon the rest of the year. Asking teachers at the beginning of a workshop what they hope to derive from the session never fails to generate lots of input and personal involvement. Students are no different. When they know that you are genuinely interested in hearing about their personal interests and needs, they will give you their ideas. If you take their suggestions seriously and incorporate as many as possible into your plan, they will readily agree to work on tasks you are adding so that curriculum requirements will be met.

If you outline the overall curriculum goals for the year and work with students to find enjoyable ways to fulfil those goals, your planning will change from being an energy sink to an energy generator. Here again, flexibility is the watchword. Chart your path as one way to go, but realize that your plans may self-destruct at any time as the students bring in more ideas, as teachable moments present themselves, as resource people become available, or as some noteworthy event in the community or the world demands everyone's attention.

If you can assure your principal that you are keeping your eye on the curriculum and are setting definite goals throughout the year, you may find that demands for elaborate plans disappear. Yes, you are planning, but the process is far more ongoing and fitted to the students' needs and the opportunities of the moment. Instead of draining your energy, you will find this kind of ongoing planning both stimulating and productive for you and your students.

An experienced teacher talks about the role of the curriculum

Dr. Anne Davies is now working for the School Board of Greater Victoria, but prior to her doctoral studies and administrative work she taught intermediate classes in Whitehorse, Yukon, and was among the first to apply what are now known as whole-language ways in her classroom. As she shifted to more open ways of teaching, she made certain that curriculum require-ments were met in her classroom. Her reminiscences offer much to teachers who are just embarking on the shift to whole-language teaching. She points out that in many cases teachers were not so much guided by the curriculum of their district but by the program or programs available to them. Usually, adminis-trators look over commercially available programs and check them to see how closely they meet the requirements of the curriculum. Teachers then use these programs and their guides and worksheets as a way to plan their course of instruction. Levels tests and books designed to meet the special require-ments of the various grades more or less prescribe the activities in the classrooms. Now that teachers are asked to take over the responsibility for fitting the learning at each level more closely to the needs of individual students, they still have to meet specific curriculum requirements, but they are often unaccus-tomed to doing their own planning while also taking into account the needs of their students. Anne Davies described for us how she used to approach the job of planning for the year.

PLANNING FOR THE YEAR

Around May of each year I used to draw together all the curriculum guides for the grade I was going to teach the following year to look for the main themes they included. I would look at the areas of overlap in the various parts – such as creative problem solving, writing, and the like, then I would make two lists. One would show the big topics for each area and the other all the little things that I was sure to forget. In language arts it might be that I was supposed to cover things like *there, their,* and *they're* or *lie* and *lay* or quotation marks or dangling modifiers. In science the guides addressed more of the large concepts, and in math I had a good sense of what students needed through using the sequel to Mary Baretta-Lorton's *Math Their Way*.

Then throughout the summer I simply let the ideas come and gathered books and other reference materials. I did no further work on planning.

When the kids arrived in September I would spend a month working with them just to find out what interested them, what they knew, what they wanted to learn that year, what was important to them. I also sent notes home to parents to find out what they knew was important to their kids and what they felt their kids needed. Finally I would look at what the next grade's class was doing and what program my kids would move into the following year so that they would be ready for that class after their year with me.

At that point I would finalize my overview, which would include about half the things that we were going to do in the big projects – the things that the kids had come up with on their own that I would never have thought of, like the unit on Halley's comet. Then there would be things that I really liked and that I knew, that because *I* liked them, the kids would like too. So we would plan the topics together and get ready to begin – the kids were always eager to get going. But when kids are interested in a topic, they just want to know about the big ideas and concepts. They are not interested in skill-building. So I would build the skill development into those topics and units, and they would learn all those things on my detailed lists while they were working on the topics that interested them.

GIVING STUDENTS A CHANCE TO TAKE ON RESPONSIBILITY FOR LEARNING

I used to talk about planning as if there was a monkey sitting on my shoulder. When you first leave the programs behind, you take that monkey with you and he's always talking to you: 'You're not doing your job.' 'You're going to forget something.' So to quiet him down I had those lists. Initially I carried them with me and looked at what I had accomplished each day or week, but that got to be too much work, and then I gave that chore to the kids and they did it for me. That way they knew that they were supposed to learn that stuff, and they could keep track of things when they learned them.

I know that my best teaching strategies have emerged when I have thought, 'I can't do all this. It's too much work!' If I acted on that thought and turned responsibility over to the kids, they did a fine job and learned even more than the curriculum specified. So in this instance the kids developed their own criteria, and they wrote their own report cards. We put that list we had negotiated at the beginning of the year on the board,

Dear Parents,

Welcome to the new year! I am looking forward to an enjoyable time.

I would like to have a parent meeting on Wednesday, September 10 at 7:30. I wish to do this early in the year as there are decisions that have to be made now (camp and awards). I would also like to explain to you the program for the class and answer any questions you may have concerning the direction of education in these days of change. I do hope that this time is convenient for all of you. We will hold the meeting in the grade 6-7 annex.

In the meantime, though, I think it would be helpful for you to know that beginning tomorrow your child will be expected to do homework. Work is assigned to the children in such a manner that they will need to do 45 minutes a night in order to get it done. If your child needs to do more than 45 minutes please let me know. It means that I am expecting too much and that adjustments will have to be made. If your child consistently claims that there is no homework I also need to know as I may not be giving your child enough of a challenge. HOWEVER, it is just possible that your children have yet to learn how to organize time and without our help may find themselves unable to complete work on time. If your child says that there is no homework I would appreciate it if you would try one of the following strategies:

1. Have you child read a book for 45 minutes.

2. Ask your child to read to you for 45 minutes (or to a younger sibling).

3. Ask your child to watch the news and write a brief summary of all the items and a brief comment on each one in the form of a report to the class.

4. Give your child a commercial sales flyer and ask him or her to design ten math problems using the sale items as focus points.

5. Ask your child to rewrite the front page of the newspaper in his or her own words in the form of a report for the class.

In most cases the children generally figure out it is probably better use of their time to get their regular school work done! If not, we can meet and figure out another solution.

Sincerely,

Anne Davis

*Close contact with parents
is an essential part of
whole-language teaching.*

and we talked about it, and then I told them, 'Now write your report card as I would write it.' So they wrote it in my voice – which always tells me a lot about myself. They worked on their report cards for a couple of hours, and the next week I took their drafts in to my principal along with the drafts I – by that time – had roughed out. Two days later together with the report cards a note appeared in my box, 'I think your kids' report cards are better, why don't you send those home?' So I did, together with notes saying, 'Your child has written this report card. I have read it and I agree with it.' Some of the parents could hardly believe that their children wrote the cards themselves.

Skills I Must Master During Grade Five

Capitalize correctly

Use possessive form of singular nouns (the cat's collar)

Use possessive form of plural nouns (the horses' hooves)

Use 'its' and 'it's' properly

Use commas correctly

Use quotation marks correctly

Use colons and semi-colons properly

Use correct verb tenses

Use 'number' consistently

Identify nouns, verbs, prepositions, conjunctions, adjectives, and adverbs

Identify phrases and clauses

Use a variety of sentence forms: compound and complex

Write a three or four sentence paragraph attending to introduction, body, and conclusion

Write paragraphs using first, second, and third person viewpoints

Write a three paragraph composition organizing its contents as follows: introduction, body and conclusion

Organize and write on selected topics

Anne Davies continues to work with skills lists to make certain that students fulfill curriculum requirements.

AS THE YEAR PROGRESSES, SO DO THE PLANS

The intriguing part about planning was that it changed and shifted so much that it just wasn't possible to replay any one year – not through paper documentation anyway. But I never wanted to repeat a year anyway, because the units had become so much the kids' that I couldn't use them with another bunch. They just wouldn't work, and of course they would be boring. So I would pull out the structures, the neat things that really worked that kids loved, such as writing a novel. But whether the novel the next year would be a detective novel or some other form depended on the kids. And as I gained experience and trust, the structures became looser. For instance, the first time around we all wrote the same kind of novel within a framework I had provided. But by the time I worked it through I realized that the next year we could write five different kinds of novels because I felt so much more comfortable with the framework. So I could enlarge it and still know I was safe within it.

Teachers suggest – students make choices

Working in open ways gives teachers as much choice as students. Keeping both the curriculum and students' interests in mind, teachers lead the way and then stand back to give students lots of room to work in their own ways. The result is harmony and productivity in the classroom. Here two teachers give their descriptions of working cooperatively with students while keeping within curriculum guidelines.

Vicki Green:

Defining a topic for kids when you first start out helps them find their ground. You certainly elicit topics from them, but you wouldn't say, 'Choose whatever you want.' Who can make a choice when it's unlimited. So there have to be boundaries to confine that choice. And those boundaries make it much easier for negotiated learning to take place. If the sky is the limit and I don't know the sky, then I become unsure. But if you say to the kids, 'Here's the way I think this should happen,' or 'Here's something you can try,' they can say, 'Can we change that?' They have a choice and the work comes from some kind of negotiation to alter or the decision to go with what's offered.

Judy Woodward:

When we decided to design the dream house, I probably had a list of thirty things that I hoped we would touch on. For instance I wanted them to learn something about building codes, and I wanted each of them to survey someone to find out how a grownup would design a house. 'What would your parents think would be part of their perfect house?' Things like a laundry bin right next to their bedroom or whatever. So I listed all kinds of the things that are involved in building a house, and if we could have got to them all it would have been great. But we got to about half of them in really good depth, as they brought them up.

Sometimes you do have to push students a bit to get into a new area. For instance, aside from the fact that it's part of the grade 7 curriculum, I feel that students should know how Greece and Rome have influenced our culture. I know none of my kids would have picked these topics if they got some sort of free floating do-anything-you-want message. At some point you've got to say, this is the topic. You have lots of flexibility about how you want to approach it, lots of ways to express yourself. Let's look at it together.

So as the year progressed the planning and goals changed from a more visible structure to less visible structure. The kids took on more and more control. I never knew how much control they would be able to take. That depended a lot on the group and the group dynamics. But I would start out the year with this great overview, and when I looked back, most of it was done in their way. What it comes down to is that planning for the year has to include the willingness to let go and the admission that although there *is* an overall plan you will inevitably deviate from it. Plans are not carved in stone. But the teacher's role is to be the gatekeeper for the long-range goals. For me it was a matter of knowing what my long-range goals were and my administrator having confidence that I knew where I was going. Then it didn't matter if I took quite a different route to get there.

Now there are two ways of thinking about this sharing of planning and taking responsibility. One way is the kids choosing their own path through the materials; the other is working with your kids so that you are both going down the path that's partly your path and partly their path. And that's difficult, especially for beginning teachers but for more experienced ones too. It's that monkey on my shoulder that tells me that as a professional I have to guarantee that they stay close by. And with some kids it's easy and they buy right in and take your path because it's the right path for them, but for other kids it's not. And you can't imagine what their path is going to be, and you have to go with them. But sometimes you have to give them a tug or a gentle nudge, and the balance is different for every child you work with and for every curriculum.

WITH FLEXIBLE PLANNING
FIXED ROUTINES ADD STABILITY

One other thing I want to talk about with regard to planning is establishing a routine that carries the kids through the day. You read about rituals and how important they are, and routines *are* important to the students. But there is also flexibility, and when you leave the routine you all know that you are leaving it, and when you come back it is obviously a conscious decision.

Doing things routinely offers a chance to mark growth over time. I remember one year we did that time-honored thing of listening to the news on the radio each day. We would listen to CBC news for five minutes at 1:00 o'clock and sometimes we talked for an hour afterwards. I started this listening-to-the-news routine because I wanted them to learn to listen and then record two items that were important. But I found that they couldn't do that; they couldn't listen for five minutes and retain it – and these were grade 5 kids. So they started taking notes. Well, you have to take notes pretty quickly – nice and short and just the main ideas. And then we would talk about the news. The whole activity was very simple. It got the kids so interested in the places in the news that we got maps out to locate the places we talked about and they put pins in the maps to keep track of the places. I found out afterwards that one of the boys who used to go home at lunch would turn on the TV news while he ate because he could remember the news better if he saw it as well as heard it. So he'd watch the news and then he'd come back and listen to the radio. He learned a lot about current affairs that year, and yet this work was language arts. It all had to do with language and listening and communication and interpretation, and that routine was really valuable to those kids. They knew what to expect, and they blossomed in the safety of this framework, a framework that was flexible enough to be open to conscious choices but that also helped kids fulfil the curriculum requirements.

FITTING REQUIREMENTS
TO THE NEEDS OF THE STUDENTS

Teachers take the responsibility for meeting curriculum requirements seriously, and while on the surface it may seem that whole-language teachers "are not doing much," they observe carefully how their students are progressing and time their input to fit the needs and readiness of the students. When we asked her about the fit between students' ways and prescribed ways, Beverly Schreiber, the grade 6–7 teacher at Strawberry Vale School near Victoria described her observations in these terms:

All the time I work with the kids I have my scope and sequence chart at the back of my mind. I used to go over it with them and they liked it, but it became too time consuming to do that. The interesting thing is that if I go where the kids are going, the sequence in which they learn is quite different from that on the chart. In fact, it's amazing what they will do. They'll go on to something huge that I wouldn't expect them to do. Math is where I find it particularly pronounced. These kids are solving quite complicated problems, although they still don't know their basic facts. Now I could have spent all year making sure they know their basic facts, but it doesn't matter, they go on to problem solving anyway. And then they come to me and say, 'Yeah, but I don't know what 7 x 6 is.' So I ask, 'O.K., what are we going to do about it?' And then they decide to develop their multiplication charts and work on them until they are learned.

The same sort of thing happens with language arts. One year I had a group of grade 7 boys whose skills were non-existent. So I got them started writing anything they chose, and I did not look at skills like sentences, paragraphs, grammar, punctuation, spelling, or anything like that. I wondered if I should limit them to some definite tasks or plunge right in, and I decided to plunge. I gave them the same list of items for writing that everyone else in the class got, and I said to them, 'I want some limericks and Haiku poetry and reports, but novels and sonnets are optional.' So they decided to write novels and I got paragraphs that were seventeen pages long. But they wrote.

```
                        What You Will Write

        fantasy              reality              essays
        friendly letters     business letters     journals
        theme stories        tall tales           myths
        legends              Haiku poetry         limericks
        rhymed verse         blank verse          sonnets*
        novel*               short stories        speeches
        plays                advertisements       reports
        announcements        other projects of your choice

        *these assignments are a special challenge and not all of you
        may wish to tackle them

        Have fun!!!!!!!!!!!!!!!!!!!!!!!!!!!!!!!!!!!!!!!!!!!!!!!!!!!



                        Writing Skills

        These are the writing skills that I expect all the grade seven
        students to master by the end of this school year. The grade sixes
        should master at least 80% of them. You might find it useful to check
        off these skills as you and I agree that you have mastered them.

            good sentence structure

            good paragraph construction

            proper use of capitals

            proper use of punctuation

            creative use of words

            use of quotations

            awareness of story style

            good use of grammar

            good lead paragraphs and/or sentences

            good use of syntax

            correct spelling

            knowledge of the importance of a good title

            correct use of an extensive vocabulary

            ability to capture the reader's attention

            sensible sequencing

            proper use of tense

            proper use of agreement

            ability to edit

            ability to evaluate your own work
```

Making requirements explicit helps Bev Schreiber's students settle down to work.

To help students get started on their writing I have them take turns reading to the entire class from works of their choice. One student brought in her older brother's high school poetry anthology and read from that. Based on that model, they started writing poetry. They looked at other books to give them more ideas. Some were actually writing poetry without any idea of formatting and yet they were writing. And that was the start. By the end of the year even my group of boys were talking about syllable counting and scanning and were starting to develop skills.

Their writing was coming along, and now they *wanted* the skills. If they handed me a piece of writing that had no format, I'd just write 'format?'

on the page and they'd be right at my desk. 'What do you want me to do?' So I'd ask them, 'Shall we get started together, or what do you want?' They usually asked for a start and then they'd go right on from there. When they began their writing, all I got was tales of violence. I let that go without comment, and they would compare notes on their horror stories. Then before Christmas I told them, 'I'm tired of violence. I'll give you two weeks to finish up with it, and then I want something different.' So they accepted that, and then in their poetry they'd write about nature and some were motorcyclists, so they'd write about that. They'd talk about soaring and flying on their motorcycles, and then they'd use that sort of imagery in their poetry. Through letting them simply write, without insisting on any of the conventions that normally apply, they evolved their content first, then they began to develop the basic skills they presumably needed before they could put pen to paper.

The interesting thing with this group is that they would read! If I let them go on, they would have read all day. I just told them. 'You always have to have a novel at your desk or you're in big trouble.' But I didn't give them worksheets and I didn't give them basal readers. I just had a good-sized collection of books in my room that I had accumulated over the years, and I had four student 'librarians' who checked the books in and out. Here again the students did the choosing and followed their own interests, which at times were far beyond what their skill levels would suggest.

KNOWLEDGE OF THE CURRICULUM
REMAINS THE SOLID GUIDE

But there are things that all kids need to learn, and they don't all learn them automatically. As teachers we need to be aware of that. If we don't learn to observe and interact with sensitivity and solid background knowledge, we may find ourselves in the same situation that has arisen before, where a significant number of kids don't learn because they needed to be taught rather than left to their own devices.

If, in our move toward holistic ways, we throw out curriculum guides, then teachers may not have anything to go on and be unaware of the specific areas that need to be covered. For instance with the group of boys, if I hadn't specifically and consistently referred back to what I knew they needed to learn, they wouldn't have got it. I could give them that input because I could still refer to the curriculum guide where there was something definite on paper. With that aide, I could look at a kid and say, 'Now you should be doing this level of writing. So how are we going to get you to that level? What's missing, and what do we need to work on?' I still need to keep that knowledge in the back of my mind all the time.

Another thing we need to be aware of is that kids get stuck, and we need to be intelligent enough to get them over the hump. It's like the kids I used to get in counseling from Sundance School. They'd be in grade 4 or 5 and they wouldn't be able to read. There was no reason for that except nobody had nudged them over the hump to get them out of that stuck place. If we don't talk about these kinds of necessary interventions, we are not making it clear for teachers what this whole-language approach to teaching is all about, and teachers may actually begin to feel guilty about actively teaching.

So while teaching and learning are open and flexible, there is no question about abandoning reference to the curriculum. All the teachers we observed and/or talked to are very clear about the knowledge and skills their students need to acquire, but they are also clear about the ways in which their students learn best and most naturally. That combined knowledge and a deep commitment to fostering maximum learning are the factors that create the climate of learning that is also a climate of delight.

MOVING TOWARD COMBINATION CLASSES AND THE NON-GRADED ELEMENTARY

7

The non-graded elementary school acknowledges that children mature at different rates

CHILDREN MATURE AT DIFFERENT RATES. They bring diverse backgrounds of learning and experience with them when they enter school, and their individual personalities and talents are unique. As teachers we know that the range of students' experience and developmental stages is broad; yet in the past, traditional curricula for the different grades have prescribed the same work for all students and have laid down guidelines regarding the sequence in which skills and topics were to be introduced. Age and/or placement in a grade have governed the work that students were expected to do at any given time.

Educators have always been aware of the need to make adjustments in the curriculum. They have encouraged more mature students to move ahead and have offered extra help to those less experienced or less mature. But they have always felt the pressure of meeting specific deadlines in order to promote students to the next grade. Having students repeat an entire grade when they needed extra work in only one or two subjects has not been entirely satisfactory, nor has it been beneficial to remove children from their own age group. "Social promotions," intended to keep students with their peers, have been one answer to the dilemma. But if the work then proved to be too advanced, late bloomers fell further and further behind. Their self-concepts suffered and they did not gain from the promotion. Neither holding students back nor promoting them on social grounds fully served their needs.

Placing students in combination grades has been one solution. There is a move here in British Columbia – and in other places throughout North America – toward integrating the primary grades, and now the intermediate grades, to create a non-graded elementary system. The intent is to acknowledge – in fact as well as in theory – the divergent levels of maturity in students of the same age. Instead of having to work as a single group on the same task, under the new system, each student is encouraged to work at his or her own pace and sequence of learning. Students' individual strengths and areas of need are

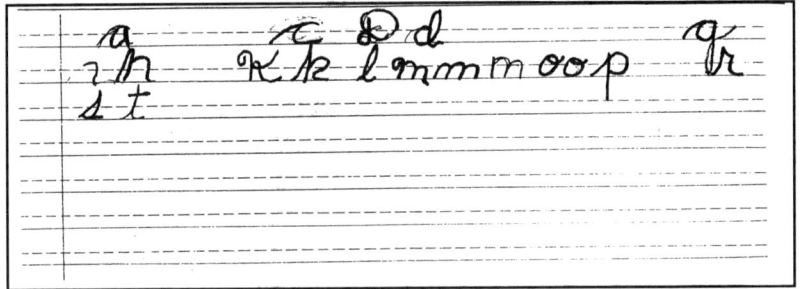

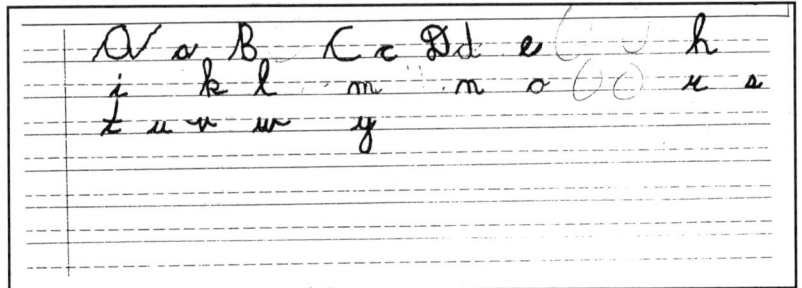

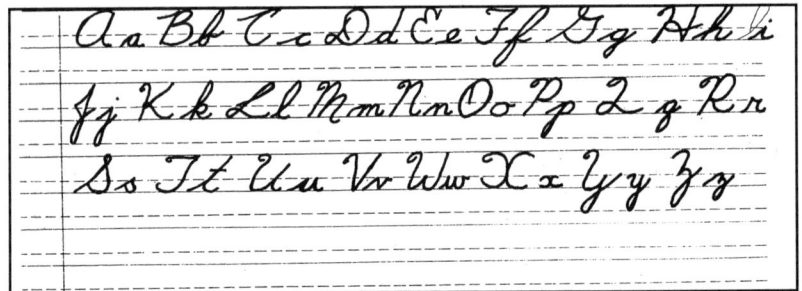

Samples of handwriting taken early in September in Liz's class reflect the diversity among students' maturity and skill development.

241

*Moving toward
combination classes and
the non-graded
elementary*

acknowledged, and learning is fostered in positive, non-threatening ways. The concept of continuous progress is part of the move toward integrating the elementary grades. By moving toward "family groupings," students are given the opportunity to move ahead in areas of strength while taking extra time with difficult topics.

Eliminating the need for annual promotions according to the guidelines of a set curriculum allows for greater flexibility of teaching/learning and removes the stress of deadlines. Both the teacher and the students are free to let learning evolve naturally. As we have emphasized before, this does not mean the abandonment of discipline or the adoption of an attitude "that anything at all will do," but it does mean that attention shifts from the curriculum to the learners. Though the curriculum is used as a general guideline and as a resource for goal-setting, the students, rather than the curriculum, determine the sequence and pace of learning.

Whether you are working in a combination grade (4–5, 5–6, 6–7) or a non-graded elementary system with the kinds of family groupings based on age or level of maturity described later in this chapter, you will find that the mix of students – working at different levels – becomes the stimulus for greater independence of learning, a lot of peer modeling, and good social integration among children of differing ages. In such a setting, the spirit of cooperation that is always an important element of teaching the learners' way comes to the fore.

Most of our in-class observations in intermediate classrooms have been made in combination classrooms. As you will have noticed, our three collaborators all teach two- and three-level combination classes, as do several of the other teachers we visited and interviewed. So our suggestions in this chapter are based on actual classroom experience. Though we have referred to mixed groupings and buddy work in other chapters, here we will address teachers' specific concerns about being shifted into new ways of grouping their students. We will offer many practical examples and suggestions.

How to make the transition to teaching combination classes

If you keep in mind that in a family everyone – regardless of age – participates in the usual day-to-day activities, you will find it easier to accept that every student in your class can participate in learning activities at his or her own level. Once you shift your teaching from prepared lessons with definite levels and narrowly defined learning outcomes to more broadly based activities – reading, writing, math, social studies, and so on – then the learners in your class can select materials and levels of participation that fit their own levels of maturity and experience. The hard part for you – as it was for us at the outset – may be to let go of the need to look for the same "teaching outcomes" for all your students and to observe instead how individual learners interact with the learning materials, with you, and with each other. As you do, you will start to note steps forward related to each student's level and background – active participation, new skills, greater productivity, willingness to try something new, the gradual accumulation of subject-area knowledge. Instead of gauging success by measuring students' performance against predetermined performance objectives, you will look for progress in terms of the individual steps forward made by each student. As you show students that you trust them to work independently, they will rise to your expectations and read, write, do their own filing, clean up, participate in peer editing, or do research, leaving you free to work with those individuals or small groups who need special attention or help.

If you adopt the same attitude for your own growth as the one you apply to the students – allowing for gradual development, accepting less-than-perfect performance at the outset, and building on strengths – you will soon notice that you and your students are collaborating in the day-to-day work of the classroom. You will find that you are learning with the students and that you appreciate them as learners and peer teachers. When you let go of "having to teach specific lessons" and instead focus on the learning environment – making diverse materials available, giving plenty of choice, integrating skill building with the acquisition of new knowledge – your students will respond eagerly. And, as long as you convert to these new ways gradually, you will enjoy your work.

Adapting the learning climate to the needs of multi-age grouping

**MULTI-AGE GROUPING FITS
THE STUDENTS' NATURAL WAYS OF LEARNING**

Multi-age grouping is simply a logical extension of the philosophy and practice of adapting teaching to the students' ways of learning. By extending the ages and developmental levels of

243

*Moving toward
combination classes and
the non-graded
elementary*

children in a class, the learning environment comes closer to approximating the home learning environment where children learn from peers and are constantly surrounded by new challenges that extend their language, social skills, general knowledge, and ability to solve problems and think creatively.

Just as parents don't talk separately to each of their children at home, so teachers need not deliver separate lessons to each student in their classes. In class, as at home, teaching by modeling, practice, and feedback gives children of diverse ages the chance to respond at their own levels.

Using mixed-ability grouping for most of the classroom activities enhances peer modeling and fosters continuous learning for students – each at his or her own pace. The spirit of cooperation allows each child to participate in group projects to his or her own ability and level of development. If Julia is a particularly good artist, then she may contribute the illustrations to a writing project that is carried out by a group of students. If Jeremy is the most knowledgeable sports enthusiast, he may contribute the sports section to a newspaper project. Sharing responsibilities and jobs gives each student the sense that he or she is part of the team and is making a valuable contribution. Self-confidence is enhanced, and students see themselves as effective learners – a viewpoint that can be sadly lacking when all students are supposed to work at the same job and to advance at the same pace and in the same way.

The ongoing assessment and close observation of students' progress that are integral to teaching the learners' way are ideally suited to working with students of differing ages. Work accumulated in student folders will demonstrate solid progress throughout the year. There is no need to compare students to other students or to a fixed standard when each is moving forward in the non-graded elementary system. If each student's performance improves over time, all is well. That reassurance, along with the pleasure of teaching students who are eager to participate in the daily activities, will help to convince you that multi-age or "family grouping" really works – both for you and the students.

ACCEPTING FAMILY GROUPINGS AS NATURAL AND BENEFICIAL

Since we have a strong tradition of grouping children by age for purposes of schooling, a first step in setting a favorable learning climate is to accept that family grouping is both natural and beneficial. A look at how children learn outside school makes it clear that only in school are children confined to learn in the exclusive company of children of their own age. Everywhere else, siblings, neighbors, friends, parents differ in age. Families certainly have a mix of ages, and this mix helps young children to learn rapidly. They have models of varying ages and levels of development to follow, and their own attempts at doing what "the big guys" do are accepted and encouraged. Looking at it that way, moving toward the non-graded elementary looks completely natural.

Think of your own learning and try to recall a time when you learned from a more experienced peer, someone you looked up to but who was not so far above you to take on the aura of a teacher. Perhaps participating in a sport or a hobby, or simply playing a game, provided the opportunity to watch and then emulate your hero. Did you find it easier and more fun to learn that way than by following a structured lesson? Do you still remember what you learned? Did it have lasting benefits? For young children, being allowed to stay up late like the big kids or go camping for the first time is far more apt to bring out "grown-up" behavior than being admonished not to act like a baby. Watching a small child trail after a group of older children at play reveals the most amazing concentration, attention span, and persistence at trying something new and difficult.

Inherent in these examples is the knowledge that children learn well in learning communities that include peer modeling and work or play that moves beyond their own experience. Curiosity, interest, and the desire to do "what Jim and Bonnie are doing" activate learning and persistence. At the same time, the effort and stress for "the teachers" are minimal. Both teaching and learning function naturally and effectively. Collaboration is fun, exciting, and generates new knowledge.

Sharing in family groupings also builds social skills. If you model courteous, considerate behavior and ways of getting along, you will establish a climate for learning and build the students' confidence in school and out. Keeping students together and with the same teacher for two or more years removes the anxiety of year-end deadlines, the fear of academic failure or losing friends. The non-competitive atmosphere leaves late bloomers ample time to catch up to their more mature peers, and the continual focus on strengths and on steps forward keeps learning positive.

Treating all students as responsible members of their learning community encourages them to take charge of their own work. Since you are not talking down to any students and are offering everyone the same interesting materials and lessons, they are most responsive and show themselves to be independent workers.

CREATING THE RIGHT PHYSICAL ENVIRONMENT

To foster collaborative work among students of varying ages, you will need to rearrange your classroom to make space for physical movement and ease of sharing. Desks set in neat rows take up extra space and inhibit student interaction. Pushing

Working as buddies to younger students builds skills, self-confidence, and leadership qualities.

tables or desks together into sets of four or six will give students the opportunity to work together and will also create space for carpeted areas, learning centers, and storage of the wide range of books and materials required to satisfy the needs and interests of all your learners.

A good supply of cushions, a sofa and/or bean bag chairs in one corner, space under tables or near the wall invite students to congregate in small groups to share reading and talk, or to withdraw to a quiet spot that admits just two. If the hallways in your school can be used for quiet meetings, then your classroom can expand to incorporate that space as well. When engrossed in a special project, students love the privacy and quiet that that kind of space provides, and you will find that they stay right on task – often more successfully than they do in the classroom where there are distractions.

Shifting seating arrangements at intervals, with students selecting where they want to sit, adds fun and variety for children in the primary grades, but by grade 4, students generally prefer the stability of fairly fixed seating arrangements. Working in different groups for projects, gathering as a group on the carpet, and occasionally rearranging the classroom seating plan, satisfy students' need to socialize with special partners and friends. To enhance group sharing, Hanne MacKay asks her students to sit in a circle for class meetings. Because she is part of it, the circle creates a sense of equality and students feel free to speak up.

The open-area of a grade 5–6 class at University Hill Elementary School in Vancouver allows for lively interactions among students.

247
*Moving toward
combination classes and
the non-graded
elementary*

*The classroom stays
organized with the aid of
movable carts and storage
units.*

   Though learning centers may not be as prominent in the
intermediate classroom as they are in primary grades, you will
want to set aside special areas in your classroom for books,
writing materials, art supplies, and science/math equipment.
The reading corner with its books and magazines will be ever-
changing as you and the students restock it at frequent intervals.
You may want to arrange books by genre – novels, drama, poetry,
non-fiction – to make it easier for students to choose reading
materials and to increase their awareness of the variety of books
available. Designated conference corners, a "quiet" area, and a

bookshelf

bookshelf

in class library

bookshelf

computer

computer

Science and exploration centre

sink

sewing box

table (mechanics box)

desks and tables

drama box

cupboard

couch

counter math-games and storage

desks and tables

writing and art table

desks and tables

plants on all windowsills

listening centre

bookcase

teacher's desk

couch

carpet

social studies centre

T.V.

bulletin board against wall

door

blackboard

door

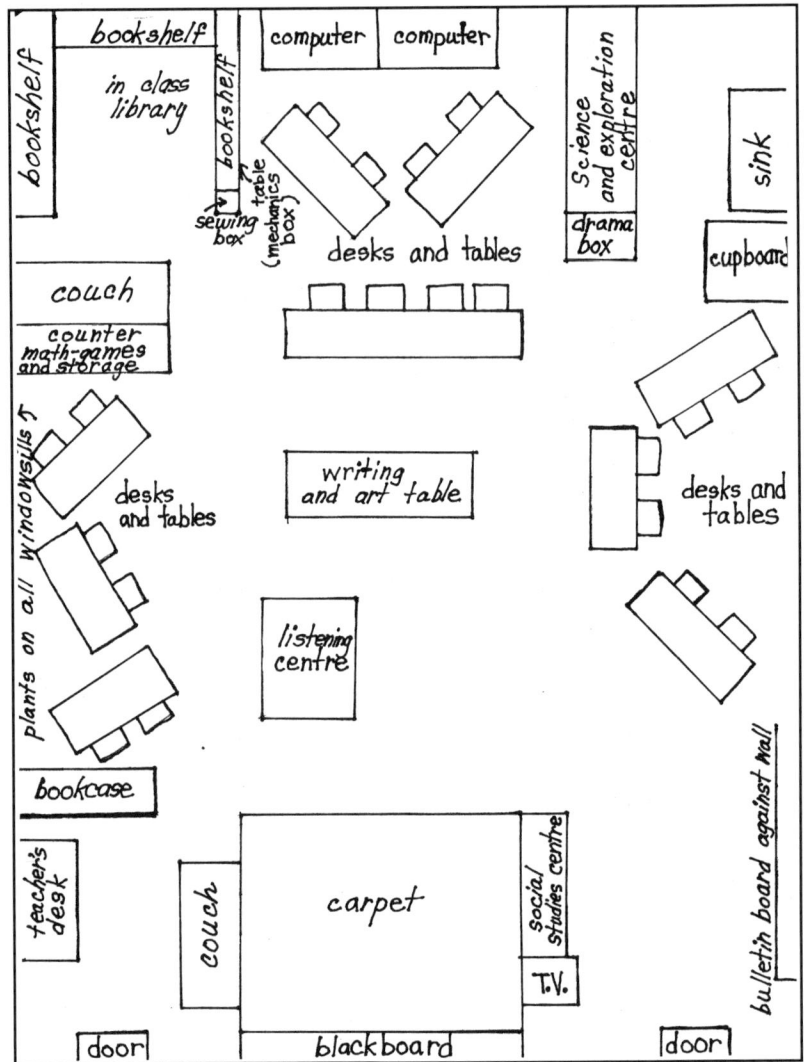

Classroom layouts change. Here is Liz's current classroom layout for her grade 3–4 students.

publishing area promote writing activities and the work of student authors who are busy getting their compositions ready for publication.

USING TEACHABLE MOMENTS TO CREATE A COMMUNITY OF LEARNERS

At home, children, through their daily interactions with their parents and siblings, learn to talk, think, and solve problems. There are no special lessons about taking things apart, about cause and effect when a glass of water is tipped over, or about how to succeed when trying to join a group of older children at play. Talking and learning skills evolve in the context of everyday life, and children of all ages not only acquire specific knowledge but also develop highly effective problem-solving and learning strategies. They don't wait for a "lesson" but act on the impetus of interest and curiosity to learn what the moment has to offer.

The activity-centered learning of a whole-language classroom offers the same spontaneous, integrated learning. When Marne told her class about her family's tradition of reading Dylan Thomas's "A Child's Christmas in Wales" as an after-Christmas-dinner digestive, a student brought in a copy of the poem to share with the class. Marne read it aloud, then brought in the BBC video production for the class. Based on the pleasant interlude of a read-aloud and a video, the class decided to illustrate the story and then act it out. This became their contribution to the school Christmas concert.

The students decided upon and took charge of the production. First they selected their favorite part and illustrated the episode on a piece of acetate for later use on an overhead projector. That helped them to get to know the different characters. Planning the play evolved from there.

The students used the poem as a basis for creating a script and they, not Marne, assigned roles and decided on scene changes. The process of creating the production evolved spontaneously and naturally right down to the last-minute planning. As the one and only full-scale rehearsal took place the day before the concert, the production kept its freshness and zest.

The production was a fine example of students fitting in at their own levels as they all chose their own roles and did their own drawings. By the time they staged their production, all students knew and loved the poem. A personal anecdote full of good feeling had started the process, and the students took over from there. Aside from becoming thoroughly familiar with a gem of literature, students learned about cooperative planning, stage management, script-writing, and character development. Their production was a marvelous success, and they also learned about the joy derived from throwing yourself into your work. Their excitement and involvement had already been the best reward for dedication.

The same spark of interest that led to a full-fledged drama production in the example above can be picked up any time during the year if the teacher listens carefully to the students'

discussions for an undertone of excitement and total involvement. Enthusiasm for mystery stories started a project on
detective work in one classroom; in another, interest in court-
room procedures led to a simulated trial with research and role-
playing that involved visits from professionals and careful
library research; in a third, dreams about the "perfect home"
produced research into house design and construction, which
included color coordination, estimating costs, and drawing up
contracts. A visitor to the classroom, a chance remark by the
teacher, or a question raised by students may provide the spark.
After that, all it takes is the decision to alter present plans to
launch on an absorbing new venture.

MAKING ROOM FOR PEER MODELING
ENHANCES THE LEARNING CLIMATE

When you have a classroom filled with students of approximately the same age, peer modeling is not nearly as extensive as
it is in family groupings. Younger members of the group are
eager to learn what their older classmates are doing: More
mature students band together to form special interest groups
to work on projects and learn from each other, but they also
become reading buddies, mathematics mentors, and art partners for the younger students in the class and greatly enhance
their own learning while teaching their younger peers.

When reading about ancient Rome proved too much for
George, both he and Sylvia were ready to give up and declare that
unit a lost cause for George. But Dan (an older student) decided
otherwise. "I'll tell you what's in each of the chapters, and you
can take notes." A fine note-taker, George proceeded to gather
the necessary information, and both he and Dan gained some
solid knowledge – much to Sylvia's relief and pleasure. In the
process, Dan modeled summarizing skills for George, and both
modeled peer cooperation for Sylvia.

Since projects form such an important part of day-to-day
learning, students who can offer special information or knowledge on topics like fashions, sports, piano playing, or current
events at times become information-givers for a group of
students or the entire class. And these "experts" are not necessarily the more mature students. When working on lyrics for a
particular piece of music, Naomi, though the youngest of her
team, added her skills at the piano and helped team members fit
words to the music.

Gabrelle & Katherine

What happened this morning

This morning I woke up and I had a special breakfast. My special breakfast was yogert and muffins. After breakfast I watched the movie Bednobes and broomsticks. But after I watched T.V., I had to take a bath so I could be clean for school. After that I went outside and I played in the snow and made a snowman. I put coal on for his eyes and a carrot for the nose and a bananna for a mouth Then I gave him stick arms and a broomstick, and I called him frostey! Then I gave him a glass of water.
Then I came to school.

Dictated by Gabrelle- Scribed by Katherine

Gabrelle, the younger child, is practicing her composition skills with the aid of her older buddy "scribe," Katherine.

BUILDING COOPERATION AMONG STUDENTS MAKES LEARNING SAFE AND PRODUCTIVE

Cooperation and sharing are as natural in school family groups as they are at home. The production of books, the presentation of plays or reader's theater, the creation of new centers, and the stocking of the library corner invite cooperative learning that often brings mature and emergent learners together. The students themselves choose their partners, and they do not limit themselves to partners of their own age or level of performance. Working with children they like and with whom they share interests often forges highly productive partnerships between children of divergent ages.

As they work together, students will follow your lead as you model attentive listening, genuine caring, and quiet ways of talking. But the introduction of mixed-age grouping may require some extra effort to make students aware of effective ways of working together. From time to time you may need to remind more advanced learners to give other students a chance to speak up or to do a job without interruption or a chorus of voices in the background. Similarly, you may need to provide a gentle nudge to urge your independent readers and writers to work on more challenging tasks than those pursued by their less mature classmates. Knowing that Jessica was able to read more demanding novels than The *Babysitter's Club,* Marne asked Jessica in her reading response journal if she had ever read *The Secret Garden.* Jessica responded that she had started it but found the book too

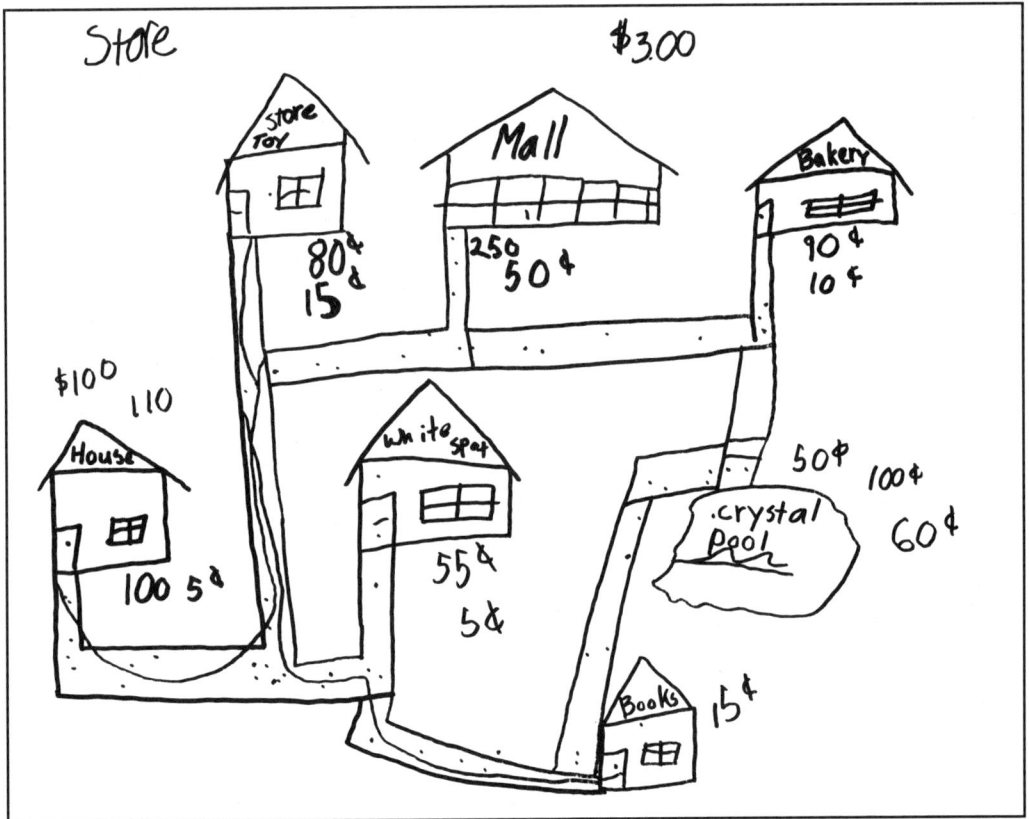

Jessie   May 9

<u>My account</u>

My buddy just adored my math games. She had lots of fun. After we had played it, once, she wanted to play it again!!

My buddy is pretty good with money. She had to make a few guesses for a few of the questions, but other than that she was really good.

The expresion on her face was obviosly happy.

When the questions got a bit harder she thought about them a bit and then guessed. I think that that means that it's a fuerely good game because it isn't to hard and it isn't to easy.

I think that I will make up another math game just for fun.

The design of a math game (see opposite page) for the younger buddy was a learning experience not only for Jessie but for her younger buddy.

difficult, and Marne didn't mention it again for some time, but after another casual comment about giving *The Secret Garden* another try, she received an enthusiastic response, "I'm reading it now, and I love it!"

FLEXIBLE GROUPING AIDS BOTH CONTINUOUS LEARNING AND CONTINUOUS PROGRESS

To make certain that all students receive the personal attention, challenge, or reassurance they need, the non-graded elementary school will include a number of different class groupings.

Depending on the size of the school and the number of students at the various levels, there may be both two-year and three-year groupings. Unless class sizes are small, extending the integration over four years could overtax each teacher's ability to meet the needs of all students, but we have found age groupings that span three years quite workable. The majority of students usually represent what would have been two grades with only a few older students added in. These students may need additional work in one or more areas and often are socially less mature than their peers. In the non-graded classroom there is no stigma attached to being with a group that is slightly younger in age, and since cooperative work pervades the day, all students feel a part of the class.

If there are enough students in the school to permit two-year groupings, the option to move students to the levels that fit their particular needs is that much greater. Students who advance rapidly may move up early and complete the elementary levels in less than the usual number of years; however, students who are ready to advance but still need some extra support may work best if they are moved to a class spanning the last three years. That way they can continue with some of the lower-level work while building social as well as academic skills. Late bloomers or more immature students may spend a full three years in their initial class and then move on for one or two years in the upper level group. The combinations can be varied to match the specific needs and talents of the students to the special talents and strengths of the teachers working at the different levels.

The relaxed atmosphere and freedom of movement in the non-graded elementary may seem like poor preparation for the rigors of junior high or high school. But students who are trusted to work at their own pace and in their own ways develop very responsible work habits. And the reliance on projects and writer's workshop fosters the research and writing skills so essential to effective study. As they approached graduation, most students in Sylvia's class were confident about their move to the more formal atmosphere of high school.

The climate of cooperation includes teachers as well as students

Keeping the same students and teacher together for more than a year builds a special bond between teacher and students. It also helps to settle new students into the classroom as they enter during or at the beginning of the school year (when many have been promoted to the next level). Whenever new students join your class, students who are already there and who have

Dear, Sylvia

Hello. How are you doing? I'm fine an so are most of the other kids in Grade eight. Well, what's It's like teaching a whole new bunch of cheery kids? For me being in grade eight is so fun and exasperating. But I really miss being in your funclass. Grade seven seems like it was years and years ago because so much has happened for me.

I feel so much more confident about myself now. Being in grade seven we felt so big, but then the minute we hit hight school it felt like we stested all over again in Kindergarten.

When I left South Park I felt like I was taking a memory that I knew I'd never forget I loved being in your class. You taught me so much about the real world and you really prepard me for grade 8 9 and 10. Sometimes you were tough!!, but we all got through it. Thanks so much Sylvia!!

Students may not always show their understanding or delight when they are with you, but as this letter to Sylvia demonstrates, in retrospect they perceive the benefits they derived. (Letter continues next page.)

experienced "the climate of delight" will make the newcomers welcome and help them settle into classroom routines. That settling-in period will be eased even more if you have been in close contact with teachers working at levels above and below yours. A knowledge of students' strengths and their special needs and interests will help determine who goes into which classroom and will give teachers the opportunity to welcome newcomers with a good sense of knowing and valuing them.

In schools where buddy systems or joint activities bring students of all ages together at frequent intervals, there is

Page #2

The first day I got to Central I was terrified but now I feel like I fit in a bit better the work is hard but I Love it. well maybe not all of it but most.

Did you have a good summer? I did. I went to the Sunshine Coast Toronto and I went to Banff with Alyssa Bishop. We had a blast.

You were and still are my favorite teacher I had so much fun with all the things we did like the trips, Projects and most os all just having you as a teacher

Now J finally realize how lucky I was to have gone to South Park. I love yoo Sylvia for all the differente things you gave me, caring sopport preperation and most of all all the memories

Love,

Erin

already a bond between teacher and new students, as they have worked with them before. To help newcomers settle in and old-timers feel happy about welcoming new classmates, you may find it a good policy to help your continuing students discuss how they can best welcome the newcomers, make them feel comfortable in their new class, and help them learn. Suggesting that, as experienced learners, they have much to offer brings out the best in students, and discussions about the special needs, hopes, and fears that the newcomers may bring with them

257
*Moving toward
combination classes and
the non-graded
elementary*

establish a learning community more solidly than simply laying down rules of conduct. In turn, the newcomers may spark renewed enthusiasm for learning activities that are fresh and new to them but familiar to the rest of the class.

By asking students to share the responsibility of welcoming newcomers you reinforce peer teaching and peer modeling. More often than not, the students, rather than the teacher, show inexperienced students where things are, how to do things, how to behave, and what *not* to do. Encouraging a buddy system in which two or three students work cooperatively smooths out the entry process that much more. Joining other classes in special events, group projects, or team teaching enhances academic learning and prepares students to move to the next level.

COOPERATION MAKES FOR
A SMOOTH MOVE INTO THE YEAR 2000

Education week is a time for drawing parents, students, and teachers closer together. At Berkshire Park School in Surrey, B.C., teachers chose to make their open house a tangible demonstration of the cooperative, holistic learning that is expected to characterize education in British Columbia by the year 2000. One group of teachers decided to concentrate on getting students to research the various eras of the twentieth century and then to create a series of displays. Anne Peterson, Marg's daughter, describes how close cooperation among teachers, students, and parents created solid learning for everyone involved. Her description provides evidence of the potential for learning and social development that is inherent in multi-age or family grouping.

The month before education week the six teachers in our group chose different periods of roughly two decades from 1900–2010 for their groups of students to study. To help the students of all six classes to decide which era each of them would like to research, we talked briefly about the different time segments – the twenties, the depression, the years of World War II – extending into the future to the year 2010. We then asked the students to choose the time period that appealed to them most, and, depending on their choice, they joined one of the six teachers. So each teacher had a complete mix of students ranging from grade 2 to grade 5. And that worked so well!

Because the research extended beyond the school, the teachers learned almost as much as the students. The teachers started by talking about what they knew, but from then on most of the information came from students' homes. We got personal photos and clothing, and one of my kids brought in a whole set of war newspapers from England. So we got a feel for those years. I hadn't really known what the forties were like.

The students also interviewed parents, grandparents, anyone they felt would know something about the era they were focusing on. Then they brought back their interview sheets and we compiled the information and made lists on the chalkboard. To get started, I would say, 'O.K. who has information about what the clothes looked like? Who has information on . . . ?' We would look at what we had gathered, sort out what was important, fill the gaps, and then ask a parent to give us a hand with typing or recording what we had collated on the board.

The students loved the whole project and they learned a tremendous amount. But in addition to the factual learning, they found out what it was like to work with each other. At first the younger children were leery about working with the older ones. I think they were scared that the fifth-graders would laugh at their artwork and things like that. And to begin with, the older students asked too much of the younger ones, but then they learned what the second-graders could contribute, and they accepted and appreciated that. It was a wonderful demonstration of just how well the non-graded concept can work – for the students, the staff, and the parents.

Interest and involvement were high, and students stayed fully on task. In the process they learned first-hand what research is all about. They did a great deal of reading. They built their listening skills during the interviews, and these also involved note taking. To come up with the radio news reports for their presentations they had to listen to newscasts to pick up how to do that kind of reporting, and to develop newspaper headlines they scanned the newspapers to see what would look authentic. Telephone skills were required too because a lot of the kids called grandparents to gather information. There was even physical involvement and peer teaching, because the dancers had to learn the dances of their era at home and then come to school to teach their group.

The staff, too, gained. We found that this kind of cooperative project was a great way to get everybody together. We had never done this sort of age-mixing, and we needed to meet again and again to discuss how things were going and what the kids were getting out of the work. It was stressful to begin with, but then we began to feel really positive about it, and in the end we had a wonderful show for the parents. All along we felt as though we always had somebody to turn to, that we didn't have to do the work all alone. Naturally we also included the librarian and she really enjoyed her active involvement. By bringing everybody together into one big project we could see how others worked and could pick up new ideas. Having choices really helped, because nobody felt on the spot to do something that went against the grain.

259
*Moving toward
combination classes and
the non-graded
elementary*

DO YOU REMEMBER...

THE 1940's ?

What did the clothes look like? Women-slim skirts, black gloves,hats
skirts medium length   Men- baggy pants, suspenders, wide
ties, hats   Zoot-suits

What did the kids play with? baseball,home-made toys, marbles,
jacks,hopscotch, bola bats, street hockey, dolls, playhouses,
coasters, matchbox cars,stick ball skipping ropes, rubber balls

What things did families do together? picnics, Church, movies,
visit other families,trip to the beach, family dinners, camping,
listening to the radio, bingo

What songs were popular? Big band music,Nat King Cole,Boogie Woogie
Bugle Boy, Vera Lyn,Benny Goodman,Red Sails in the Sunset, In
the Mood, White Cliffs of Dover, War songs

What kind of dances did people do? Waltz, Jitterbug,
Bunny Hop, Fox Trot, Samba , Tap dancing - Shirley Temple

What were the furniture and appliances like? ice boxes, ringer
washer, gas stove, coal furnace,iron beds, water pump,heavy
velveteen couches, small coffee tables with glass inserts,phonograph
Brownie cameras
What were the important news flashes of the decade?End of world war-
1945, jet planes,bombings of Pearl Harbour and Hiroshima,, Glen
Miller killed overseas,German planesshot down,

What kind of meals did the families eat? Fresh fruit and vegetables,
homemade bread,porridge,fresh meat and fish,preserves in Winter
Some food was rationed - coffee, tea,chocolate

What did the houses built in the 40's look like? Two or three bedrooms,
One bathroom, wood and brick strutures, small houses, narrow
windows,storm cellars,stairs with large bannisters

Thank you for your help.

If this kind of cooperative work began early in September, the whole school would become a family group. It helps to get started early in the year by having older students act as reading buddies for children in the lower grades, but drawing the whole school population together as we did is that much better. When a grade 5 student sees a kindergarten kid in the hall, knows his name, and can say, 'Hi, Jamie,' you know you're off to a great start.

Anne Peterson's description of her school's short-term project and its benefits leaves no doubt about the possibilities inherent in drawing together an entire school to work cooperatively. The social and academic benefits that Anne enumerates are open to all of us who work in family groupings, and they could be enhanced that much more if time was open-ended to give students the opportunity to do more of their own compiling and sifting of information. Knowing about successful experiences such as this one helps to minimize the concerns about having to adapt teaching to fit diverse groups in the classroom.

Adapting activities to fit the varying needs of students

How to adapt teaching activities to the varying needs of students of divergent ages and levels of maturity is the chief concern voiced by teachers when they are moving toward non-graded classes. They worry about having to offer separate lessons to each group in order to meet all of the students' needs. As long as teachers think in terms of carefully prepared and sequenced lessons, that worry will persist. Textbooks and lesson plans address specific skills and information, and they generally follow a linear development in which one step is supposed to build on the next one. But natural learning works in more global ways, and students increase their store of factual knowledge by

The New Century. 1900's	Chris 1920's	1930's	Anne 1940's	'50's	Suzie '60-75's	Brenda high tech 90's
lantern stove table library marbles	radio Stacy's records Shirley Temple flapper costumes radio broadcast.	monopoly jacks	electric train Frank Sinatra	poodle skirts saddle shoes hula hoops yo-yo's radio (Anne)	Mrs. Beavely	microwave robots

261
*Moving toward
combination classes and
the non-graded
elementary*

building upon their own unique backgrounds and abilities. If they are encouraged to follow their own specific interests in pursuing a theme or topic, they find their own level of participation. Because they are personally involved in seeking new knowledge, they will acquire more factual information and more in-depth understanding than a teacher-designed lesson is likely to convey. To provide some suggestions for catering to the special needs of non-graded classes, we outline some adaptations of the holistic ways of teaching/learning that we have described in preceding chapters.

READER'S WORKSHOP

Since reader's workshop offers students the opportunity to choose what they want to read, it lends itself well to multi-age grouping. But you will need to make some extra options available to give all students the opportunity to enjoy the sessions. The more mature readers in your class may want to withdraw to the designated quiet corner or the hall to become totally absorbed in their reading; less proficient readers may need to do some writing, drawing, or quiet talking in connection with their reading; and all students should have the option of selecting several books (or other reading material) before settling down to read. Keeping the time devoted to reading flexible becomes particularly important when you are working with students whose ages range over several years. The process of gradually lengthening the time devoted to reading is one way to make sure that your mature readers have ample time for sustained silent reading, and the option to do some reading-related work assures that the session remains enjoyable and profitable for everyone.

Encouraging students to read to and with each other can become the beginning of small-group and then whole-class discussions of novels or non-fiction works. Many mature readers enjoy reading to their younger classmates, and this becomes a way of introducing novels that some of your students would find too difficult – or too tedious – to read. Sharing a chapter of a novel often leads to quiet personal exchanges that enhance the pleasure of reading and open the door to further discussions in a larger group.

If you select a wide range of books of all types and levels from the library at the beginning of the year, students will quickly reveal both their special interests and their favorite authors. As soon as you have established a library routine, the students themselves will restock the materials in your classroom and

---

NOVELS WE WILL READ AS A CLASS

LITTLE HOUSE IN THE BIG WOODS
WARTON AND MORTON AND THE KING OF THE SKIES
CALL IT COURAGE
MY SIDE OF THE MOUNTAIN
ISLAND OF THE BLUE DOLPHINS
THE CAY
ALICE IN WONDERLAND

NOVELS THEY WILL HEAR

CHITTY CHITTY BANG BANG
WARTON AND THE CONTEST
THE TRUMPET OF THE SWAN
HARRY'S MAD
FROZEN FIRE
HOUSE OF SIXTY FATHERS

Student suggestions and the teacher's knowledge of required books resulted in this list early in the year.

augment them by bringing in their own books. At this point the benefits of family grouping make themselves felt. Watching other readers enjoy more advanced reading material and hearing comments and discussions about them will challenge the younger members of the class to expand their reading. At the same time, more mature students will be reminded of old-time favorites and the fun of interspersing some easy reading every now and again.

Love of literature draws young and mature students together as they exchange comments while they browse through your display of books: "Yeah, I really liked that one!" "Oh boy, there is one by _____ that I haven't read." "You would really like this!" Reading is not a passive activity but imbued with energy and eager anticipation. Young students reach far beyond what you might expect, and their older peers develop leadership qualities and communication skills as they interact with their classmates. At the same time, mature readers deepen and broaden their appreciation of favorite classics as they re-read and discuss them.

As you listen to their comments, you will notice how readers draw what they are ready for from a book or story. Depending on their age and maturity, students identify with characters and events that fit their experience. Then, on rereading the book they will shift their perceptions and pick different characters with whom to identify. These shifts are reflections of the students' own growth as well as their growth in reading ability. Just as parents don't berate their young children for acting their age, so the older students do not belittle their classmates for their unsophisticated perceptions of what they have read. Instead, the more mature students take pride and pleasure in the growing ability of their reading partners and revel in savoring favorite stories again and again. In the process both they and their young peers move toward fluent reading that moves beyond taking in facts and extends to reflection and thoughtful interpretation. For you as well as your students, seeing the same stories through different eyes makes for extra interest, and the multi-age grouping in the class adds a richness and variety that is rarely found in a traditional classroom.

READ-ALOUD SESSIONS

Read-aloud sessions lend themselves particularly well to family grouping. Here is your opportunity to introduce interesting reading without straining the capacity of your slower readers to keep up. You will find that they model their attention spans on their more mature peers, and that their contributions to discussions add unique and sometimes unexpected viewpoints. If you occasionally draw a smaller group together for a read-aloud session while their peers are working on a special task or project, you will find that students not originally included in your group are drawn to your reading regardless of their own work.

So, read-aloud sessions are often a good way to draw all of your students together. If your reading is full of feeling, drama, and expression, students will listen intently whether the story or chapter is a challenge or a pleasurable rerun. Being open to questions, using pictures to illustrate difficult text, and keeping track of incipient restlessness will keep your readers with you throughout. Here, as in so much of classroom work, it becomes important that you pick books, stories, poems, and other materials that *you* find interesting and enjoyable. Even if they cannot quite follow you, students will be intrigued and delighted with the obvious enthusiasm you bring to read-aloud sessions, and age or level of maturity is no impediment to that enjoyment.

WRITER'S WORKSHOP

Like reading, writing gives students the option to work at their own levels and pace. If you start the year by modeling idea-generating and then making drafts to get your thoughts onto paper, students will respond at their own levels, bringing their experience and levels of expertise to bear. The amount and polish of the writing will vary according to students' interests and maturity, but all of them will be ready to write if you make it clear that you are interested in reading what they think and feel. To some, illustrations will remain the starting point for writing, for others illustrations may be a thing of the past as they work at producing their own mystery novels or polishing their poetry. Including some of the finishing work of book binding and special layout work gives more active students a chance to move about, to do something other than lean over an empty page.

At the lower levels you may want to couple writer's workshop with center time. To make certain that everyone gets some written work done during the session, you can set minimum standards of writing that must be met and then give students the option to choose activities in centers you have available around the room. You will find that while some students will gravitate toward the library center, the art center, or the science center, others will eagerly fill every minute of writing time and may even take the unfinished page out to recess to continue their work in some quiet corner. And the eager writers are not necessarily your most advanced students. As emergent writers find that you value the content of their writing even when its form is less than polished, they become much more expressive and willing to venture into the new genres of writing that they have observed in their reading or in the writing of their peers.

Conference sessions also do much to involve everyone in positive ways. You will notice that students of quite divergent

265
*Moving toward
combination classes and
the non-graded
elementary*

backgrounds will choose to work together. Group sharing and advice seeking involve everyone and bring new ways of dealing with writing to the attention of emergent and mature authors alike. The diversity of levels inherent in family grouping adds extra interest to these discussions, and students sharpen their communication skills as they work on each other's writing in productive ways. They acknowledge steps forward just as you would and keep their comments positive. In your own conferences with students, you do not assess writing against some pre-set criteria but simply watch for individual steps forward. Because of this, you will find that the sense of moving forward keeps students writing – and enjoying it – no matter what their level of maturity or experience may be.

MATHEMATICS

When working with mathematics it may seem impossible to avoid separate lessons for students of widely diverse levels of skills and knowledge, but here, too, the principles of moving from whole to parts and concrete to abstract negate the conventional wisdom. Just as reading does not have to start with learning phonics but can build upon students' interest in stories and information gathering, so mathematics does not have to be learned in a linear progression of discrete skills. Turning math upside down and beginning with real problems instead of the careful introduction of specific concepts or skills results in eager student participation at all levels of the intermediate grades. Calculators, estimating, and concrete manipulations or model building draw students into thinking of mathematics as practical problem solving. They are intrigued and empowered by working on real-life problems, and once again neither age nor ability level is a barrier to participation.

Collaboration and discussion serve all students and prepare them for more formal presentations and then practice of math skills. Because the problems are reality-based, students will work hard to find answers, and the perennial question, "Why do we have to do this?" does not arise. Instead, students formulate questions about ways of solving the problem at hand. They hypothesize, debate, and ask the teacher for input so that the question becomes "How do we do this?" Genuine desire to find solutions turns math work into a succession of teachable moments and students into eager learners. Since the work deals with actual problem solving, here, as in other project work, students of varying abilities will collaborate to make their contribution. All learn, and there is no question of "the low group" being stuck with endless drill for a skill that has little meaning and low transfer value to problem solving.

Problems tackled may range all the way from working on collecting and accounting for monies connected with various school activities, to converting measurements in recipes or working with the large numbers connected with space travel in conjunction with an astronomy unit. Problems of geometry and trigonometry present themselves in building models or designing better use of space around school, and making maps for field trips introduces the concept of scale drawing. Science projects offer the challenge of working with formulas and ratios as students convert Celsius to Fahrenheit and compare the results of experiments.

Though you may be working with students ready to enter junior high school, you will find that concrete examples and physical manipulation of materials remain important parts of solid learning in mathematics. The need to move from the concrete to the abstract is not limited to young children. If you think of your university days and the struggles you had with understanding abstract theory or the meanings of new vocabulary, you may recall the relief you felt when finally some very concrete examples brought home to you just what is meant by "standard deviation," "т scores," or any of the other mysteries of statistics. For us it was a matter of struggling through and then looking back to try and figure out just what all those calculations and high-sounding terminologies really meant. Thinking in these terms makes it easier to accept that students at all levels need to work at a concrete level before abstract ideas will become truly theirs.

If you build on that concept, teaching math to a group of students at divergent levels becomes far less daunting. Physical demonstrations of fractions using blocks, drawings, cut-up apples – anything that lends itself to being divided – will be accepted by all students. Practice, preferably in the company of buddies, and lots of talk and comparisons will solidify understanding. Here, as in other areas, students will work at their own levels and depth of understanding. Some will need lots of extra practice, others will see the work as an easy review of familiar material and will move on to more sophisticated practice and exercises offered by you, the textbook, or their own imagination. As more mature students become mentors to their less advanced buddies, everyone gains. Often a peer who is just a step or two ahead of the learner will have better success in conveying what needs to be learned than an expert who is too far ahead. So to teach math in the non-graded class, rely on real-life problems, concrete manipulations, buddy work, and lots and lots of practice and discussion.

CONTENT AREA LEARNING

At times intermediate teachers will say to us, "That's all very well for building the basic skills in reading and writing, but I have to see that my students learn some solid content in science, social studies, and . . . ." No one would question that students need to acquire specific bodies of knowledge. Curriculum guides for the various grades offer guidelines for the knowledge to be gained in each subject and for each grade level, and textbooks authorized by the education authorities contain neatly defined lessons for conveying that knowledge. The trouble is that the carefully designed sequence of presenting information does not necessarily appeal to the students or, indeed, make sense to them. The fact that textbook writers strive to present information objectively tends to make the lessons abstract and less than thrilling, especially to young students.

Over years of observing students in many classrooms we have been struck by the temporary nature of much of their "solid fact" learning and, by contrast, the depth and integration of knowledge that they have acquired through work in which they actively participated because their interest and feelings were involved. They enjoyed the work, and the activities themselves were more important to the students than the information they gathered. In fact, learning factual information almost became a by-product or bonus. Yet the information gathered in these personal ways made a far more lasting impact on students than the most careful lecture or textbook study.

Engaging students in acquiring facts can be a challenge at any grade level. This is an even greater challenge when working with a multi-age group, but projects, personal engagement, and activity-filled work are sure ways of meeting that challenge. They draw all students into the excitement of discovery and generate much more learning than you can envisage as the work begins. Anne Peterson's way of teaching Canadian geography through involvement with Canadian literature is a fine example of engaging students – solid content learning became the "bonus" for reading enjoyable books. And along with knowledge about Canada, the students acquired a strong sense of the scope and utility of geography. They learned how and why to use maps, how much information can be gleaned from maps, and how to integrate the use of geography with the study of other topics. Instead of abstracting specific facts, students integrated information into a larger system of knowledge. They learned to transcend the facts and move to a higher level of understanding.

DRAWING ON LOCAL HERITAGE TO UNITE GRADES 4 AND 5

Social studies offers the same wonderful opportunity to involve students in ways that help them to connect what they learn with their own knowledge, interests, or feelings, and to draw them together as a group.

Vicki Green speaks of her work with students in the small rural community of Armstrong in the interior of British Columbia:

I had a grade 4–5 classroom, and I really wanted to establish that we weren't grade 4s and we weren't grade 5s, but were just a group of people working together. And I wasn't about to do a unit on the Haida Indians in grade 4 like other classes and then switch into something else, say communication, with the grade 5s. I wondered, 'How do you get this age group together? How do you get people – yourself too – to break the usual mind-set about how to teach these kids?' So I contacted Ken Mather at O'Keefe Ranch (a reconstructed pioneer town) and got his permission to have the kids come there and recreate some of its history through research and acting. Then I talked to a friend, Hugh Caley, who produced a program called "Places and Things" for television, and he agreed to have the students' performance at the O'Keefe Ranch on his program. So we had a definite goal to work toward.

Since the ranch was closed to the public at that time but available to us as a resource, the kids were able to explore the whole site. They defined the areas that were of particular interest to them. Some of them liked the general store, some were interested in the church and its graveyard, and others were drawn to the blacksmith's shop.

As we worked and practiced for our big day, the parents became a wonderful help. The kids who had picked the church as their area of interest had decided to have a big wedding, and one parent worked with them. Another parent worked with those who wanted to do the general store, and she took them through the role-playing that they were going to do for the cameras that day. They could dress up in old clothes and touch the artifacts and share with the parent, and because of that a lot of things came out that might not have come out if they only thought in terms of doing things for school.

269
*Moving toward
combination classes and
the non-graded
elementary*

Four kids became fascinated with the archives, just absolutely over-whelmed with the amount of information that was there. Now these were kids who were just becoming aware of factual information, and so they loved to find out stuff that no one else knew. Their work really helped to fill in the gaps.

The day we were filmed, Hugh found that his crew wouldn't have time to film all of the sites with all of the kids. But the kids who were cut out had created questions for Ken Mather, so at the end of the film they can be seen asking him a lot of questions that really divulged a great deal of information about the ranch.

In the show itself they acted out a number of scenes: one in the store where some were filmed purchasing things and others mailed letters; another in the kitchen of the old house where three of the girls were preparing food; a third scene of a pillow fight in the bedroom. It was a wonderful show. But we could have done it quite differently. If I did it again I would not give as many directives. This would have made the work that much more effective for them and even more fun for all of us. But I had to go through the process once to be comfortable enough to let the students take over.

Working with the children in that way is of real appeal to me because I want to find out how to break the mind-set: 'I'm doing Peru'; 'I'm doing the gold rush'; 'I'm covering that content.' To break that mind-set, I think you have to go out of the school to informal sites: You have to go to the pond, to the park, to the store, whatever. So much of that is done at the primary school level, and I wonder why it stops when the kids get older. The kids themselves could plan great field trips. I love projects and field trips that have an historical perspective because they allow you to pretend that you can go back into the past. The kids really get into their roles. And some of our most powerful writing emerges from that kind of work.

No one could question the personal involvement on the part of Vicki's students. They were reliving the history of their community and all of them participated. The more advanced readers delved into the archives, while younger members of the group engaged in role-playing and more physical explorations. Vicki's points about the importance of moving learning out of the school environment and involving parents reaffirm the need to see learning as a much more global, inclusive process than traditional textbook study. Students participating in living his-tory gain so much more than factual information. Knowing that dates and names concern real people and being able to get a sense of time and place give a whole new dimension to the study of history. If it came to meeting specific curriculum require-ments for a social studies unit, students could build on their personal work on local history to imbue the study of more remote times with interest and life.

SCIENCE

For science, too, multi-age grouping works well if teaching is primarily done through projects, hands-on work, and active exploration both in class or in out-of-school settings. Concrete ways of involving learners allow everyone to participate, and the emphasis is not so much on conveying textbook information as it is on becoming familiar and comfortable with scientific enquiry: information gathering, learning from observations and experiments, keeping track of observations, measuring and recording data, becoming familiar with scientific terminology. When textbooks are used only as back-up material to the concrete work, developing enquiry methods, hypothesis testing, and preparing reports take precedence over memorizing formulas or the parts of insects or flowers. Here, too, acquiring specific information becomes the by-product of learning that is process-oriented and actively engages the learners. With that approach, students of all levels can participate in studies of biology, chemistry, or environmental science.

Evaluating progress

When working with students whose ages and ability levels range over two, three, or even four years, fixed criteria for measuring progress and comparing students' performances become unrealistic. To keep track of individual students and their progress, descriptive notes rather than marks on worksheets form the basis for recording and reporting how students' learning evolves. Along with information on academic work you will want to keep records throughout the year that include notes on problem solving, discussions, artwork, social behavior, and willingness to participate in or try new work.

Since your students will function at quite diverse levels, using assessment as a tool for guiding day-to-day learning becomes crucial. As you record how individual students progress in their writing, reading, and content learning, you will become aware of areas that need special attention or reinforcement. If your independent readers and writers are shifting to more sophisticated reading material and lengthy written work, you may need to work with them on critical evaluation of their reading, on the organization of lengthy writing, or on advanced spelling. If less advanced readers and writers seem stuck in a repetitive pattern, you will want to help them find more exciting reading material and work with them on brainstorming for new topics to cover in their writing.

If you are concerned with being accountable, refer to the curriculum guides for the grades that are combined in your class. Use the guides or your scope and sequence charts as checklists to mark which requirements have been met and note which opportunities of learning you need to create to meet additional requirements for some of your students. Such reference work will reassure you, your supervisors, and the students' parents that the learners are moving forward in meeting curriculum requirements. When you take the time to do such careful cross-checking, you may be surprised to find that younger students are beginning to meet requirements set for their older classmates, and that your more mature students occasionally have unexpected gaps in skills or knowledge – as defined by your charts – even though they are making progress.

In some districts continuous assessment goes hand in hand with continuous promotion, and students may move to a higher level in midyear. The classroom teacher, more than standardized tests, will determine at what point students are ready to move on to the next level.

KEEPING PARENTS INFORMED

If the non-graded elementary school is a new development in your area, it is important to keep parents informed of the new ways of teaching/learning. They may want to be reassured that family groupings do not mean the abandonment of standards or less learning for their children. Beginning the year with a parent information session – perhaps an evening discussion or a tea at which the students serve their parents refreshments – then following it up with regular newsletters about new developments, projects the students are working on, and their strides forward will demonstrate that the non-graded elementary is fostering learning in a positive way.

Just as you build on strengths when working with your students, so it helps to be very positive when communicating with parents. They will no doubt have questions and concerns, but if you can point to all the solid benefits their children will derive from the non-graded elementary, parents will often become your strongest allies, supporters, and helpers.

If you remind parents of their own ways of learning and the ways their children learn at home, they will see that the integration of classes will help rather than hinder their child's learning. Drawing the parallel between learning within the family and in family groupings at school will draw attention to the benefits of peer modeling. Parents will see the advantage of having children participate in interesting, meaningful work and of working with peers who are more experienced. Once their children are launched into the program, they will note the independence and responsibility engendered by the integrated ways of learning. The absence of anxiety and stress will certainly have the parents' approval. They know their children will learn more easily if they are not worrying about what lies ahead – meeting deadlines, getting a poor report card, facing a new teacher, more and difficult work, losing their friends, and/or having to cope with a lot of strangers.

The fact that students are free to move ahead in areas in which they work well without having to wait for other students to catch up will show parents that you are not interested in holding their children back. At the same time, allowing extra time to have students evolve their writing or spelling skills will seem less worrisome. If you keep track of progress by means of reading and writing folders, you will be able to point to solid steps forward when you meet with parents each quarter.

As soon as they perceive their children's enthusiasm for projects and other learning activities in class, parents will be receptive to your comments about ways of encouraging their children to expand their school learning at home. Seeing their children read, write, and solve problems creatively will make it easier for you to reassure parents that students are indeed learning basic skills and solid facts even though these are not taught in traditional ways. If you discuss the importance of learning and thinking skills, parents are sure to agree with the activity-based work of your integrated classroom. But your own obvious joy in teaching in an interesting, challenging classroom is the most telling message to students and parents alike.

Because teaching in family groupings makes greater demands on teachers, you may receive extra support by way of reduced numbers of students, extra materials, and the help of aides. If integration is just being introduced in your area, your school district, supervisor, principal, and other teachers will offer you extra training, advice, and reassurance. As a result you will quickly adjust to the needs of students of different ages and levels of ability. Our best advice to you is to trust the students to learn, give them lots of room to develop their own interests and projects, and hang in there! Children are wonderfully creative learners as long as you stand back and give them room to learn their way.

What teachers say about working in multi-age classrooms

At University Hill Elementary School in Vancouver teachers have worked with multi-age grouping for some time, and they have prepared a special booklet for their visitors that concludes with the following "Comments from the Staff."

- "I have taught a variety of grade combinations including straight grades, split classes, and multi-age classes. I find multi-age group teaching the most rewarding, as the focus is truly on the individual child."
- "This way of teaching was not imposed upon me in any way. It represents my own slowly developed and positive solutions to problems I encountered during my first years of teaching young children. For that reason it is not harder – it is easier and certainly more satisfying. What a joy it is to have found a whole staff who shares my feelings about what education should be!"
- "I enjoy teaching within the family-grouped structure. It enables me to create an environment where children flourish and develop a myriad of social and academic skills."
- "I have experienced a wide variety of teaching environments but none have been as satisfying nor have met the needs of developing the total child and his or her learning environment as does a multi-age class."
- "The most notable difference is in the children, particularly in their attitude towards each other. Despite diverse backgrounds, there is a remarkable level of tolerance and harmony. Children seem more willing to take chances creatively and are more comfortable with people of all ages (including teachers!)."
- "For me, one of the many advantages of a family-grouped class is the opportunity to know individual children over a two to three year period and to observe them develop and change their roles within the group. I also notice much greater acceptance of differences and less peer competition among children in this environment."
- "Learning to teach a multi-age group is an on-going process, which makes it an experience that is challenging, stimulating, and rewarding. Children and teachers are engaged together in a continuous process of growing and learning."

> • "It has been my experience that children learn more in a cooperative, non-competitive environment where it's O.K. to make mistakes and where each child is encouraged to measure progress by how much more he or she knows in June than in September. I have taught in both types of classrooms – traditional and centers-oriented multi-age groupings – and would leave the teaching profession rather than return to a traditional classroom. Initially, there's more work/input needed from the teacher, particularly in the whole language area, but I've found it well worth the effort."

Worries and fears about the non-graded elementary

Both teachers and parents who are unfamiliar with the benefits of family grouping have expressed their concerns. The kinds of concerns shown below are readily answered by a point-by-point reference to the list of strengths.

TEACHERS' CONCERNS

- A curriculum that stretches over several grades is too vast to be handled by one teacher.
- Teaching a non-graded class will be like preparing and teaching two or three separate lessons for everything – math, social studies, science . . .
- Organizing the classroom will be too difficult when students work at such diverse levels.
- The work for advanced students will be watered down and too concentrated for the younger ones.
- If they all have to work together, older students will be exploited, younger ones will be lost in the crush.
- It seems impossible to individualize work for students when they are at such different levels of maturity.
- Grouping students effectively becomes unworkable with widely divergent ages.
- Promotions cannot be fair and equitable when students are working at such diverse levels.
- Discipline will be a problem, and the older students will bully and override the younger ones.
- Distractions will disrupt learning as students of different levels work together in one classroom.

PARENTS' CONCERNS

- My child will not receive proper instruction in such a mixed group.
- My child should not be grouped together with a bunch of younger [older] children.
- How can the teacher keep discipline when he or she has so many different jobs to do?
- There will be too many distractions for serious work when all those young kids are in the same class as older ones.
- How can you challenge the older children when you have to keep your eyes on the younger ones?

- Years of working in combination classes that had family groupings and gave teachers and students the opportunity to work together for two or more years has shown us the strengths and benefits of the non-graded elementary.
- Students of all ages are able to participate in classroom activities much as they are able to participate in activities at home. The teacher is relieved of teaching several versions of the same lesson because peer modeling is an essential ingredient in a learning environment that encourages each student to work at his or her own level in reading, writing, math, other content areas, and special projects.
- Family grouping helps the teacher keep the focus on the students. He or she teaches learners, not a curriculum.
- Work on projects opens the door for a wide range of activities, and the teacher can easily assure that students become aware of many ways of approaching the work. In that climate, students will draw what they need and want from the work at that time – without boredom or stress.
- Since the students initiate and suggest many of the topics for discussion and study, there is no question of coaxing a class of bored learners into completing assignments. Lessons arise from the students' own interests.
- If the teacher establishes a climate of cooperation and consideration, older students not only model learning and social behaviors, but also become reading buddies, research partners, and mentors for their younger classmates. They develop leadership qualities and social responsibility. Both they and the younger students thrive in that climate of cooperation.

Strengths and benefits of the non-graded elementary

- Integrating the day – weaving reading, writing, mathematics, and any subject on the curriculum into the varying activities of the day – builds the foundation for full, functional literacy and "learning for living." It also frees the teacher to work with individuals and small groups who need or want extra attention.
- The independence of working on projects and group activities inculcates thinking, learning, and problem-solving skills, freeing the teacher from the need to plan the students' every move. In most instances, the students, not the teacher, decide on their work partners or groups.
- Skills emerge naturally and in the students' own time-frames. A student may be in grade 6 in math, grade 4 in writing, and somewhere in between in other work. With family grouping, that student is free to surge ahead or linger based on his or her needs, and will move smoothly to the next level.
- The students themselves become the co-creators and keepers of classroom rules.
- The excitement of working with interesting, innovative ideas and projects keeps the classroom bubbling with language that expands students' vocabulary and thought. Purposeful work keeps the entire class busily on task.
- The freedom to participate in work suggested by more advanced students shows younger children where they are headed and what new challenges and excitement lie ahead. Since all students in the class are free to perform at their own levels, they gain, rather than lose, from working in family groupings.
- The entry/presence of students of different ages adds new spark and enthusiasm to the entire group. The spontaneity and creativity of the younger students complement the work done by more experienced learners.
- Social skills and empathy develop in family groupings in which the teacher becomes a model of positive ways of interacting and dealing with interpersonal relations. A teacher dedicated to family grouping will have fewer – not more – discipline problems to contend with.
- When work is activity-based and closely connected to the students' interests, attention spans are long and concentration is intense. Skills are internalized in ways that move far beyond the ability to give right answers on a worksheet. The students themselves will minimize distractions that keep them from focusing on work of interest to them.

Family grouping enhances the functioning of the learners. As they interact with each other, the teacher, and the learning environment, students generate rules of reading, spelling, grammar, writing, and problem solving. They become active, self-initiating learners who are confident in their ability to tackle new and unfamiliar tasks. They enjoy learning, and they move ahead at their own pace and in their own way. They are challenged more, not less, in that kind of learning climate.

ASSESSING PROGRESS –
BEING ACCOUNTABLE

8

The *why* of fitting assessment to learning

NEW WAYS OF FOSTERING LEARNING call for new ways of evaluating progress. In the interactive atmosphere of a whole-language classroom, assessment must become an integral part of the philosophy and practice of holistic teaching/learning and involve students and parents as well as the teacher. The focus on process as well as product has to be reflected in ways of measuring progress, and the reality-based learning is best mirrored in assessments that draw upon the ongoing in-class work of the students.

Traditional tests are unidirectional. The teacher sets, administers, and scores them; students have no input and little recourse. Yet the essence of teaching the learners' way is to foster growth through interactions in which teacher and students become co-learners. That interactive quality needs to be part of assessment as well. In writing conferences the student presents a draft, discusses it with the teacher, considers questions and suggestions, and then revises and improves the work as the next step in the upward spiral of learning. Students do not hesitate to share and discuss their first drafts as there is no threat – they are neither being tested nor is their performance being measured against a fixed standard. Instead, in these interactive sessions both teacher and students learn about gains made and steps yet to be taken.

Teachers have always known more about their students than test scores have revealed. By fitting the assessment of progress to the ways in which students learn, teachers deepen their understanding of students and their work. Instead of interrupting the flow of learning by tests, which take valuable time and often produce anxiety, whole-language teachers use assessment as part of the day-to-day work and enhance, rather than interrupt, learning. Just as the conferences help students to upgrade their writing, so they inform the teacher about areas of need that can become the focus of work with individuals or of group mini-lessons.

Since work in class is broadly based, so is measuring progress. Teachers use a variety of ways to observe and record how students are advancing, and the methods used in making evaluations extend well beyond pencil-and-paper tests. Students make their input through self-evaluation and through accumulating records and examples of their work. There is genuine collaboration in assessment as well as in learning, and that collaboration extends to parents as well. Because the assessment methods are firmly based on the concrete evidence of in-class work, they yield both valid and reliable information about students and their work. The bonus for everyone involved is that assessment becomes as positive and productive as the day-to-day work. And for you, the teacher, there will be renewed interest in observing your students closely and noting their every step forward.

How to shift to new ways of measuring progress

OBSERVING LEARNERS IS A NATURAL PART OF TEACHING/LEARNING

Whole-language teaching developed as a result of intensive in-class observations. The same kind of observation – simply noting and describing what students are doing – is very effective for keeping track of students' progress. Learning to describe, without making value judgments or comparing students' learning to fixed teaching objectives, takes practice and patience. But there are wonderful benefits. As you watch you become aware of your students' every step forward. You focus on what they *do* rather than worry about what they have not yet learned. At the same time, you become a researcher in your own classroom and renew your interest in discovering how students process information. Observing and recording how creative their thought processes can be is well worth the effort and can cultivate and sharpen observation skills.

Your observations begin as you greet students at the door, and then continue throughout the day. You can track students' progress by making brief anecdotal notes, or you may want to move toward preparing observation checklists for fairly predictable developmental sequences such as spelling:

- Uses vowels as place holders
- Shows awareness of suffixes/prefixes
- Generalizes known spelling patterns to new words
- Looks at meaning to help spell words
- Develops mnemonics for remembering the spelling of difficult words
- Checks the appearance as well as the sound of words
- Uses vowels more accurately

But when you first use observation to measure progress, it is good practice to make your own notes on students' learning behaviors. We have found that when we used observation lists – even those we developed ourselves – we developed tunnel vision and noticed only those behaviors we had listed. Observation lists, of course, can be useful at times, but their use does not help you get into the habit of describing to yourself exactly what it is that students do.

Since writer's workshop has a fairly set routine that gives you time at the beginning of the year to make notes while the students are getting their first drafts under way, it may be a good place to start observational notes. If you do, you will quickly get to know your students because you will be paying close attention to what each one of them is doing. Whether you write your notes or simply compose them mentally, resist the temptation to make a value judgment about what a student *ought* to be doing. Get in the habit of describing first.

- "Jonathan needs at least five minutes of thinking time before writing."
- "Melanie begins her work by drawing first."
- "Christian gets tense and clutches his pencil when he tries to write."
- "Alexis and Jessica are beginning to collaborate through conferences."
- "Rhiannon is doing some reading research for her writing."
- "Lee is consulting his list of ideas to get started."
- "James needs to talk about his ideas before he can develop them."
- "Sean has produced three pages already."
- "Breakthrough! Meghan is using webbing to generate ideas."

From these simple descriptions you will move to more details about the specific features of their composing and spelling and will share with the students your observations about good lead-ins, appealing descriptions, ways of making writing suspenseful or more lively.

You will find that, aside from helping you keep track of progress in writing, the simple behavioral descriptions will tell you a lot about your students' learning styles and how they function best.

- "If you leave Jonathan alone, sure enough, he suddenly starts to write after staring – seemingly vacantly – into space for a considerable time. Once he gets started, he ends up covering three pages."
- "Melanie's need to illustrate before she writes leads to beautifully imaginative writing; drawing is her way of organizing her thoughts."
- "When you show Christian a relaxed way of holding a mechanical pencil, his trips to the pencil sharpener stop, and he relaxes enough to let thoughts flow."
- "Suggesting to James that he talk his ideas into a tape recorder leads to a veritable outpouring of composition."

By noting and honoring how students are proceeding, both you and they are freed of the tensions and frustrations that so frequently accompany writing sessions.

Reader's workshop provides you with the opportunity to become familiar with your students' personal interests and reading preferences. As you note who is selecting which books and how long it takes them to complete their reading, you will have a fair estimate of reading levels and who needs extra encouragement, a reading buddy, or some extra practice. Once students begin to exchange thoughts on their reading in their reading response journals, your casual observations will be enhanced by the students' own comments. The responses you make in their journals can become the impetus for students to delve more deeply into their reading, to select more challenging books, or to try new genres.

AUDIO-VISUAL EQUIPMENT
CAN AID RECORD KEEPING

Using a tape-recorder adds further detail to your observations. If you ask individual students to read aloud for you early in the year, then again around Christmas, in spring, and toward the end of the school year, the recordings will form a valuable part of your overall records. Similarly, tape recordings of discussions, poetry readings, oral reports prepared and presented by students are excellent ways of reviewing at leisure how students have progressed during the year. Having such records available during parent conferences can add weight to your remarks about students' learning and a warm personal note to your discussions with parents.

In addition to keeping track of progress, tape recordings are an effective way to coach students in the preparation of reports and oral presentations. Having the opportunity to listen to themselves helps them to find what went well and which areas they need to improve. Turning the tape-recorder over to students encourages individual practice and buddy work.

Talking your observations onto a tape rather than entering them in a notebook can reduce your in-class writing load. Transcribing selected parts later on will act as a memory jogger either then or at report-card time. Tape recording writing conferences can at times be useful to give you and the students a chance to play back the tape to find out to what extent your comments have helped their writing evolve.

At the same time, listening to such tapes gives you a chance to reflect on your ways of commenting. If you are as positive with yourself as you strive to be with your students, reviewing tapes will be an excellent way to improve your skills.

- "Next time I'll focus more on the *feel* of the writing."
- "When Brooke was hesitating, I could have asked her what *she* felt was needed to bring her reader more into the picture."
- "Accepting Kamil's judgment about that piece of writing would have been better than insisting that I think it's marvelous. Having him explain what he would change would have acknowledged him more."

Those kinds of musings will not only deepen your understanding of the students' work but will help you relax and enjoy your conferences that much more. Just be sure the feedback to yourself is as positive and descriptive as the feedback you give your students – matter of fact and free of "shoulds" or confusing undertones.

The use of video equipment adds a further dimension to observations as videotape will capture body language, gestures, and visual images of the students' work in progress. Whether you use the video recorder for everyday classroom interactions or for field trips, drama, or special presentations, students will be intrigued to view their performances, and the videotapes can become a tool for both teaching and evaluation. Since you can record work in progress, students can compare their own ways of working with those of other students and can look for models of effective ways to approach different jobs.

Vicki Green found that students kept referring back to the videotapes she filmed during a field trip to Victoria. Having separate fifteen-minute tapes of each of the various sites visited allowed students to review parts of the trip they particularly enjoyed. As they kept returning to tapes of their choice, their reports and descriptive writings gained in richness of detail, and their powers of observation and description were sharpened. Needless to say, the tapes also helped to recapture the fun and excitement of the trip.

For physical education, drama rehearsals, and work on science experiments the video camera becomes an impartial observer/describer. Taking a close look at students' work and being able to review a specific segment several times can be very helpful in noting problem areas and helping students to polish their performances – with your help, through peer interaction, or through self-observation and correction. Here again, successive tapes can really highlight students' improvements. With drama, if you have filmed rehearsals at the beginning, midway through, and just before a performance, the differences will be marked. Having a record of such progressive improvement can reassure those students who feel unsure of themselves or who are unwilling to acknowledge that they are making progress. Seeing a progression of steps in one area often opens the way for progress in other areas. Success does build upon success, and the focus on strengths in evaluating progress is productive for teacher and students alike.

Keeping records of progress takes many different forms

ANECDOTAL NOTES ON OBSERVATIONS

Whether you simply observe or use a tape recorder or video equipment, at some point you will want to write down some of your observations. Margaret suggests keeping a notebook handy to record highlights of the day. By cutting a narrow strip off the side edge of most of the pages you can write a list of students' names in the margin of the page that extends out and can then make notes on individual students in an organized way. Such notes might record firsts: speaking up in class, selecting a novel, starting to use watercolors, trying poetry as a means of expression, or choosing a partner for math. The records can also function as reminders of personal or academic needs: "seems worried today," "still struggling with paragraphing," "is going over negative numbers again."

While such cryptic notes may not seem like much of a record, they not only keep you focused on the learners and their ways of working, but they also become a record of progress in areas that are often neglected in regular assessment: personal feelings, expressive ways of working in the arts, the persistence and practice some students will bring to certain areas of their work, at what point a change or step forward occurred. Looking back over these notes can be useful for completing notes on report cards, but more important they will reveal trends or underlying currents that help or impede students' work at various points of the year. Without having to pry into their personal lives, you will be able to give extra moral support, allow extra time to complete work, be understanding of seeming sullenness or anger. When working with adolescents whose hormones are beginning to percolate, such personal sensitivity and support will go a long way toward establishing a climate of delight in your class.

If focus on all individuals within the class seems overwhelming, singling out several students for close observation each day can be a good way to track progress. Liz makes a chart of her students with blank squares the size of small Post-it Notes and then singles out two or three students for a close look. As she interacts with students she makes brief notations on her "stickies" and then transfers these notes to her chart. By observing students who work together or are seated together, her note taking becomes quite manageable and does not interfere with students' work. Making notes assures that everyone comes under close scrutiny at regular intervals, and that observations are not limited to special groups.

EVALUATION FOLDERS

Keeping an evaluation folder for each student is perhaps the most widely used means of tracking ongoing work. Your own notes on the student's progress may form part of the content of the file you keep on each student, but the folder generally bulges with the student's own work: examples of writing taken at weekly or biweekly intervals; math exercises or quizzes; reports completed at the end of a project; photocopies of particularly noteworthy pages from the reading response journal; learning center logs; diorama evaluation forms; spelling exercises; artwork; audio tapes of the student's readings; miscue analysis sheets to go with the tape recordings – anything that gives evidence of the student's work during the term.

Reviewing the folder at intervals reveals how each student is progressing and serves as a reinforcement of your daily observations about learning styles, strengths, and areas of need. If you are doing goal-setting interviews with your students, each folder will have the record of contracts (see page 291) or goal interview sheets. The content of the folder then becomes the basis for your meetings with individual students to discuss if they have achieved their goals, exceeded them, or are in need of revising or updating them.

Depending on your year-end reporting needs, you will want to keep certain pieces of information in the folder throughout the year. Most of the work can be sent home with students and/or parents at the time of the term interviews. But, whether you keep the material for the duration or relinquish parts of it at intervals, the information in their files is always accessible to the students. In other words, there are no anxieties about report-card time and no unpleasant surprises in store for anyone. In fact, to a certain extent, students are the ones who determine what goes into their files. They are the ones who decide what pieces of writing they would like you to use as a basis for evaluating their achievement during the term or the year. Here, as in all the students' work, the focus rests on strengths and steps forward. Messy drafts, false starts, new ventures that did not quite succeed are considered as the soil in which successful work took seed and then flourished. The only reason for analysing the soil is to find out how it produced growth and how it can be nourished to become even more productive.

STUDENTS' OWN RECORDS

In addition to the student folders *you* maintain, each student will have a writing folder, an art portfolio, a music folder, a reading log, and any other collection of work that may be part of his or her regular work. Drawing upon student records – both for your ongoing observations and for term or year-end reporting – assures that you and the students collaborate closely as you monitor progress. If you keep your eyes on the content or message more than on the form, you will not get overly concerned about: the jumble of notes in Shane's folder; the absence of an idea list in Morgan's folder; the messiness of Alexis' draft; the non-existence of can-do lists in many of the folders. (See page 292 for examples of can-do lists.)

```
                    Student Portfolio

                    Name  _____


(WARNING—DO NOT LOSE THIS PIECE OF PAPER!!!!!!!!!!!)

Each month you will make sure that you have collected examples of the
work that you have done for the preceding month. This work will be
marked with the date, stapled together, and given to me to file. This
material will be used to show your parents and Mr. Casey the progress
that you have made. It will also be used by you and I when we do your
report card. IT IS THEREFORE VERY IMPORTANT MATERIAL. PLEASE TAKE THIS RE-
SPONSIBILITY SERIOUSLY.

Each month you should staple together the following pieces of work.

  1. A book review or related activity from a book that you have read
     that month.

  2. One piece of writing. This could be work that you have just edited
     or it could be a finished piece of work.

  3. One piece of art.

  4. Any tests that you have taken.

  5. Any reports that you have completed.

  6. Something of particular interest to you.

  7. Something of which you are particularly proud.

  8. A summary statement on how you feel about yourself as a student at
     that particular time. (This must be done each month.  You may
     refer to your work journal.)

  9. You may wish to tape-record (audio or video) presentations you have
     given to the class. In that case I will give you a tape which
     will be yours and which will be included in your file.

I can photocopy any material which you wish to put in your file but
which you also wish to remain a part of your notebooks.
```

*The student portfolio
contract serves as a basis
for renegotiating and
evaluating.*

Writing folders are perhaps the most productive evaluation tools. They include drafts, finished products, idea lists, and can-do lists. The students are supposed to keep their folders in the classroom at all times so that nothing is lost, and students are expected to save every scrap of their writing. In practice they do not follow both of these rules all of the time, but enough solid information is gathered in the folders to serve as a basis for analysing progress in idea-generating, composing, spelling and grammar, and their use of different genres of writing.

```
CENTRE   LEARNING   LOG
```

DATE: *Nov. 14*

Today I went to the *Imagtion* centre.
A question I had was *how to make a car out of wire. (and suckseed)*

What would help to answer it? *someone who knows how to work with wire*
One thing I learned was *it is hard to make wire bracelets and wire cars*

Something I would do another time is *go to the Discoverery center*

Tomorrow I will *go to the writing center or maby the sewing center*

How was my performance at this centre? *vary vary vary vary VARY GOOD*

Analysis of the content of the writing folder can range from a count of the number of pages produced to the examination of idea content. Instead of comparing the writing to a fixed standard or to that of other students, looking at each student's evolution becomes more productive. As you discuss students' writing with them or make notes about specific aspects for your term reports use descriptive comments:

- "Your ideas are really beginning to flow. You have three whole pages here!"
- "I like the way you describe that scene. Your words wake all my senses."

- "Your spelling is coming along. Now you have most of the endings right."
- "Your use of bigger words is very effective, and the spelling is right."
- "That is a very complex story. You introduce me to your characters, show me what is going to happen, and then bring in suspense and excitement."
- "I see you branched out into poetry. Following the pattern of the poem we read seems to have worked well for you."

CENTRE   LEARNING   LOG

DATE: _____

Today I went to the _maze_ centre.

A question I had was _why dose danny have to work on the maze_

What would help to answer it? _ask teacher_

One thing I learned was _how to solve a big problam_

Something I would do another time is _solve the problam with out arguing_

Tomorrow I will _try not to get in arguments_

_____

How was my performance at this centre? _it was oky_

_____

I see you really did some thinking, today Paxton

Diarama Evaluation   Feb.

Names: _____ _____ _____

Subject: _____

I (we) want the viewer to see the following things
when they look at our diarama : _____
_____
_____
_____

I am very pleased about this specific thing
about my diarama : _____
_____

I am disappointed about this specific thing about
my diarama : _____
_____
_____

I think that most of the work was done by
_____

I enjoyed working with _____ because
_____

My craftsmanship is good, medium, poor
I have made a diarama before it was better, worse
This will be a good teaching tool for me to explain
      my subject to my buddy. (True? False? Sort of?)
I wanted to do a really good job on this (True or False)
I did an excellent good fair poor bad job of my diarama.

Providing forms for comments can be helpful to keep students' focus on the specific work at hand.

Such comments acknowledge the students' work and effort, steps forward, and ventures into new territory. Taking that kind of descriptive approach when using the writing folders as a basis for conferences makes writing both safe and productive.

Reading response journals are another valuable source of student-supplied information. Along with comments about their reading, students are expected to keep a running list of the books they read within a term or throughout the year. Again, not all records will be complete, but between the lists of books and students' comments about the reading, the journals provide a record that reflects both volume of work and level of sophistication. Here, as in the writing folder, noting the variety of material read, the students' willingness to try new topics and genres, and their honesty about likes and dislikes offers insight into student learning and personal preferences. (See chapter 5.)

Student folders that include records of singing, artwork, and project work flesh out the documentary evidence of their work. Descriptions of dioramas and other project materials help serve as reminders of these displays once they have been removed

```
                        Contract

   1. I have read my paragraphs and have made sure that each paragraph is
      about one main topic. If my paragraph has unnecessary information
      or it if is disorganized, I have rewritten it.

   2. I have proofread and corrected my rough draft career reports.

   3. I have made sure that they are neatly written. If they were not
      neat, I have rewritten them.

   4. I have the following reports:

      Mr. Matthews — Careers
      Mr. O'Toole — Customs Officer
      Mr. Ferguson — Engineer/Astronaut/Pilot
      Mr. Devitt — Cartoonist
      Mr. Czarnecki — The Performing Arts
      Mr. Stewart — Marine Specialist
      Dr. Moisey — Doctor
      Mrs. Czarnecki — Writer
      Ms. Harper — Museum Careers
      Special Constable Perlin — R.C.M.P./Pilot
      Mrs. Peterson — Lawyer
      Mr. Batchelor — Geologist
      Mrs. Ingalls — Teacher/Superintendent
      Mr. Mercredi — Professional Hockey Player

      If I do not have the reports, I have given the reason and will
      accept any discipline measure required. (If reasons are adequate,
      no disciplinary measure will be taken.)

   5. I have put all my reports in order and stapled them together.

   6. I have prepared a detailed report concerning ONE career and have
      included appropriate illustrations. My report has several headings
      and the material has been collected into paragraphs under the
      headings. I have proofread my report and have had someone else
      proofread it. It does not, to my knowledge, contain any errors in
      punctuation or spelling. My report has a neat cover. My report has
      my name on it. My report is ready for you to grade.

            * * * * * * * * * * * * * * * * * * * * * * *

   I have read and completed the above checklist. My assignment has been
   completed to the best of my ability.



            Signed: _____
```

*Anne Davies' contract
re: a careers research and
writing assignment.*

Nov 11

Things Katherine Can Do As A Writer
· write good sentences (capitals, periods)
  with compound + simple structures
· gives lots of information —
· keeps the story sequential

Katherine — regarding Henry's Vacation :
  Please take this piece + make it into a
chapter of a book. Stop the trip and just
take the Airport part and polish it :
    · paragraphs
    · take out extra stuff
    · make it really clear
    Then Land in your 2ND Draft
Otherwise you will be stuck for a long
time. Perhaps you could get to Morocco
after that (another project)

Write to me + tell me what you think
                    Mame.

                        Oct 9
    Katherine
      Please finish your Inftnatting
letter so we can act on it (send in
whatever your plans are.)

                    M.

Things Morgan   Can Do As A Writer
· Can check for all the senses in her
  writing
              smell
              hear (sounds)
              seeing (sights)
              touch (feeling)
              taste
              emotions (how you feel)
· paragraph
· capitals at beg. of sentences

Can-do lists note particular landmarks and give the teacher the opportunity to extend student work.

Comments:

Terrific, Cindy. It was carefully
written and had lots of information.
I appreciated your last sentence. You
do have a long time to choose. Also
you don't have to choose only modeling
as a career. You can plan to have
more than one career!

Well done Cindy –

*Students will follow the
teacher's model when they
are asked to comment on
their classmates' work.*

from the classroom. Photographs and drawings connected with
special events add pictorial evidence to your assessment work.

OBJECTIVE MARKING
OF FACTUAL INFORMATION

Though much of assessment and reporting at the intermediate
level is kept in anecdotal and descriptive form (containing more
detail), the requirement to assign grades and number values to
work has not yet vanished from the scene, particularly at the
upper grade levels. As students prepare to move into junior high
school, marks and letter grades are often requested by the
students themselves and may be required by the receiving
school. Parents may also feel that they would have a more
conventional way of assessing their child's standing when
report cards show letter grades as well as descriptive comments.
If there is an option, and neither the school board nor the junior
high school demands letter grades, a meeting and discussion
among teachers, students, and parents can serve as the final
determinant in opting for letter grades or staying with purely
anecdotal comments on the report cards.

Name: Meg   June Report
Please comment on the strengths and weakness of these events:
[Safety Events] ① Health Fair I did a poster about
Drinking and Driving conterataK I enjoyed
sorting the foods into the food grops in
Kern's class ② Fire Safety House Liz's and our class went
through the fire safety House and some fire men
came and talked to us about fire saftey.
            ③ Small Craft Safety I enjoyed the
funny skit the red cross did and the life joke
and P.F.D. fashin show.
            ④ Bicycle Education I was sick.

[Environmental Events]
            ① Litter pick-up in James Bay - Earth Day Preparation
Our class did neighbourhood clen up We
sure got a lot of tigeritte buttsllespecally
around the James bay Inn!! ② Environment Fair: Our class made
rewrap for the enviroment fair and I made a
poster with Chrissy and Rhionnan about Rewrap
            ③ Driftnet Mural and Float I was not
on the flot and I did not make eanything
for the mural but I went on the peace
walk and saw the ④ Lost Lake Seed Orchard Our grop went
flot] inside first, and we took apert pride cones
and conter the rings on tress. Afer, we went outside
and identifed tress. ⑤ Sewer system (Mr. Austin) Mr. Austin
took us on a walk througn the park to
the beach (we did not get to the beach)
He showed us the sewer outlets.

At the end of the year Marne collected student comments on the year's events. These will be used in planning for the following year.

Contract work, special projects, and studies in the traditional content areas offer ample scope for setting specific criteria to be met in order for students to qualify for designated letter grades. See pages 296 and 297. Working in the integrated classroom with two or more grade levels offers a greater challenge, but Sylvia, whose class opted for letter grades, overcame the difficulty by assigning very specific information-finding tasks and offering full marks for fulfilling those tasks.

Making choices between numbers and commentary

Early during the school year Sylvia's class presented news reports each morning as part of their social studies work. The students worked in groups of six. One student acted as anchor person for the presentation and each other member reported on one area – international, national, local news, weather, and sports. At first, to keep track of the work and to assign marks, Sylvia produced an evaluation sheet that she marked during each newscast. Then she had second thoughts. As Sylvia describes it:

After a while I decided that marks were really irrelevant and that immediate oral feedback would be much better for the kids. To begin with I had wanted to be fair, feeling that if I jumped in and coached one group that would give an advantage to the next one. But then I focused on the fact that they were doing the presentations to learn, not simply to chalk up marks. And the oral comments provided after each presentation were far better for promoting learning.

Regardless of their writing ability, all students are able to dig out the factual information required and get ten out of ten for the unit. They feel successful, look for an A as a mark, and then are quite happy to exert themselves when launching into the writing work connected with the project. Here the divergence in age and level of maturity leaves full scope for the more advanced students to prepare reports that extend over several pages, while some of their classmates may write no more than a paragraph or two. Depth and understanding of the content of the unit will be different for individual students, but each of them will have covered the basic content and will have something to build upon.

In line with the open climate of teaching the learners' way, contracts offer students choices of working to the levels that they wish to achieve. After introducing the topic to be studied and brainstorming with the students to generate areas of interest, the teacher draws up a list of topics they can choose to include in their work and then negotiates with individual students to arrive at mutual agreements about their projected work. Age, prior experience, learning style and pace, interest in the topic, and other commitments in classroom work are factors in negotiating contracts. Within the contract, students have

Name: _____

CAPITAL CITY

Factual information: - location - country, continent   2
                         - size - population   2
                         - language   1
                         - industries/occupations   5
                         - unique features eg. food, music   15
                                             25

Presentation: Map   10
                  Pictures   5
                  Neatness   5
                  Organization
                  Mechanics — punctuation, grammer, spelling   5
                                             25

You may be as creative as you like. The report does not have to be long, (2 pages is enough), but it must attempt to convey the spirit and flavor of the city. What does it feel like, smell like, taste like, look like, sound like .....?

Total Marks: 50
Due Date : —MONDAY, SEPT. 18th

Maximum marks assigned to specific aspects of the project give students a base line for working on their project contracts.

many options of topics, manner of research and presentation of materials, and depth or sophistication of information. After the work begins, contracts can be renegotiated so that students move up a mark if they become excited about their research or down a mark if they have overestimated their ability and/or willingness to invest themselves in the work. The contract provides a framework for ongoing evaluation to students and teacher alike, but the flexibility of negotiating for marks removes feelings of anxiety or pressure.

As the teacher makes the guidelines concrete and is available for consultation, contract work gives the students solid information against which to compare their progress toward completing their contract. Negotiations about grades may become part of other work as well, and both teacher and students learn the art of examining work and describing it dispassionately to arrive at agreement.

```
                      News Report

        Name    _____

        Date    _____    Category  _____

        Preparation

            Content—factual and comprehensive    10  _____

            Clear notes                            5  _____

            Variety of sources                     3  _____

            Documentation of sources               2  _____

                          Sub-total   20  _____

        Presentation

            Voice—audible and expressive           5  _____

            Poise—body language—speaking not reading   10  _____

            Visual aids                           10  _____

                          Sub-total   25  _____

        Cooperation in Group                       5  _____

                          Total       50  _____

                          Percent     10  _____ %

                          Grade           _____
```

To assign specific marks to the students' news reports, Sylvia designed this form. She later abandoned its use in favor of oral comments to students. (See page 295.)

SYLVIA: [Talking to student who wants to renegotiate his writing mark] *O.K. Convince me that I should give you a higher mark.*

ROLAND: *Well, I felt that I had a really good point of view and put in a lot of effort. Ten out of ten?*

SYLVIA: *Would you read it to me?* [As Roland reads his composition, Sylvia interjects comments and questions to clarify ambiguities in the text.] *In what respect is it good? How is it good?*

ROLAND: *The words and selection . . .*

SYLVIA: *Yes, I think you have selected some good words. I particularly like "A strong scent of dead mushrooms filled the air." That's a powerful expression.*

ROLAND: *Are you going to put it up five marks?*

SYLVIA: *Now, where could you have filled it out a bit more?*

ROLAND: *In the battle?*

SYLVIA: *Yes.*

ROLAND: *But I didn't want to.*

SYLVIA: *Right. My reasons for giving you five were: You've made a token effort . . . you've got a little bit of everything here, which is worth five. But I did not know whose point of view it was . . .*

ROLAND: *But I rewrote that.*

SYLVIA: *. . . There were a lot of spelling errors here, and this section here was unintelligible.*

ROLAND: *I know.*

SYLVIA: *So I thought it was worth five out of ten. Because I know what neat careful work you are capable of doing, I thought, "This gives me the impression that Roland has done this very quickly. He only took about five minutes."*

ROLAND: *No, I was working on it for hours. And I thought about it for days.*

SYLVIA: *All right. Go and correct the things we discussed, and I'll reconsider.*

Using standardized tests

To check your students' performance or to fulfill the requirements of your school board or district, you may want or need to administer standardized tests from time to time. If there have been no multiple-choice tests in the work you have been doing, then you will want to give students a number of practice sessions to familiarize them with the format and intent of multiple-choice tests. Discussing results and showing ways of eliminating choices that are obviously wrong provide a good lesson in reasoning skills and minimize random guessing. At times we find that we also need to remind students that when we give them a test we want to find out what *each* student can do. A test is not the time to use their usual cooperative ways of working together.

We have found that students who learn skills in global ways are nevertheless able to focus in on fine detail. They are confident about their knowledge and have developed ways of thinking about what they know. After a brief introduction to the mechanics of multiple-choice tests, students usually do well with them. In fact, on reading comprehension tests they often score particularly well. The vast amount of reading and writing practice stands them in good stead, and your records will be enhanced by grades that will not be challenged by any of those who may have expressed doubts about the validity of your anecdotal comments.

INFORMAL QUIZZES

Grades or comments may also be given for on-the-spot quizzes in any topic in which you want to know how much information students have taken in and retained. Examples we have observed include: spelling checks done at intervals during the year; math exercises and quizzes; checks on subject information about a country, a science, or social studies topic. While such spot checks can be both revealing and reassuring, we find that they are needed only now and then. Most checking on students' knowledge is done more effectively in the context of their work where they can demonstrate not merely the acquisition of facts but understanding, integration, and application of what they know. But for ease and assurance of record keeping, tests and quizzes have a definite place in noting and recording student progress.

Conferences form an important part of evaluation

WRITING CONFERENCES

Writing conferences are part of the ongoing evaluation of student progress throughout the year. They also supply information for term-end or year-end report cards. As you discuss their writing with students, you will get a feel for their understanding of the conventions of writing that transcends what they are showing on paper. Quite often you will find that their thoughts are ahead of their ability to express them. When you discuss their writing with them you will not only extend their ways of expressing themselves but open them to new areas of thinking about or organizing ideas. You can reflect your assessment of their latent thinking and writing powers in positive ways both during the conference and in your written reports:

- "Katherine's imagination has blossomed, and she is exploring interesting ways of expressing herself through legends and fairy tales."
- "Ariel has expanded her writing into non-fiction reports. She is now working on organizing her writing into paragraphs."
- "Nathan has done a wonderful job of information gathering. He is now branching out into oral presentations of his knowledge. In the process he is developing wonderful leadership qualities."
- "James has produced an excellent radio play and is now refining his editing skills, learning to sift the important from the extraneous."

Such comments not only give credit for what has been done, but acknowledge the direction that further work will take.

The benefit of writing conferences clearly lies in the two-way communication between teacher and students that reveals underlying thoughts, feelings, and trends. As Marne puts it, "When students read their written work to me, I understand far more of what they are trying to say or imply. When they add their voices to the stories or poems, the written words come alive for me." So writing conferences offer in-depth assessments of where students are at any given point and the trends in their writing development. If you can remember the frustration of handing in papers written against deadlines and then having your writing ability judged on the basis of that one-time effort, you will know that neither you nor your instructor had the opportunity to probe more deeply into what it was you were intending to convey, and you rarely had the opportunity to upgrade your writing. In that truncated interaction, not only did your marks fail to reveal what you were truly capable of producing, but the experience probably put a damper on your willingness and desire to expand your writing and to branch out into unexplored areas. The safety provided and the supportive ways of interacting during writing conferences, on the other hand, extend and encourage writing.

TERM-END STUDENT CONFERENCES

Before completing and sending home report cards at the end of each term, the teacher sits down with students to discuss their work, areas of progress, and areas of difficulty or need. As they look back over the months just past, highlights and successes come into focus. The student folder you have kept will help you to remind them of some of the specifics that bear reflecting upon. Asking students to assess their own performances will generate honest answers and opinions. Actually, the more advanced students are, the more likely they are to undervalue rather than overvalue their achievements. They have set themselves high standards and often feel they would have liked to have done better. Vicki Green comments that it is wise to listen to students' self-assessments and to acknowledge the expressed feelings. Rather than say, "Oh, but you did a beautiful job!" ask them, "What would you have done differently?" or "Where do you think you could have improved your work?" or "How can you move in the direction that you want to take?"

As you discuss past achievements and their relative merits to arrive at appropriate comments and/or marks for the report card, you may want to amend or expand your report-card notes. You will also want to discuss plans for the forthcoming term and ask each student to look ahead in light of what he or she has done so far. Between the two of you, you will know which areas have gone well and which areas need special attention. The meeting is also a time to encourage students to commit themselves to venturing a little further afield. If personal narratives have been the sum total of their writing, imaginative work, reports, letter writing, or descriptions may be among your subjects for discussion. If reading has been slow or heavily weighted toward Garfield or simple stories, the student may agree to select at least two novels during the upcoming term and to read them with the help of someone at school and/or at home. If spelling continues to be rough despite excellent composition, specific ways of working to enhance awareness of spelling patterns and ways of checking for accuracy would certainly form part of the goal setting for the new term.

PARENT CONFERENCES

Once parents become familiar with the positive nature of evaluating progress that characterizes working the learners' way, much of the worry and tension that may accompany meetings between parents and teachers vanishes. Reports that focus on steps forward, backed up by the evidence from students' work collected in their individual folders, set the tone for the discussions. Most parents are open to following your lead in looking at steps forward and focusing on progress more than on gaps in their children's learning. However, they may have specific concerns, and accurate spelling is one that comes up regularly. Another is the lack of grades, which may seem confusing to them. Parents may want to know not only where their children are in respect to the other students but also in respect to some norm they perceive to exist for that particular grade or age level. Here, as in student conferences, it is a good idea to ask parents for opinions and input. If parents voice concerns or even disapproval, give them the opportunity to explain fully what they have on their minds and acknowledge the validity of their concerns. Rather than contradicting them and stating flatly that their child "is doing fine," give descriptive comments that clearly demonstrate that the student is progressing in the right direction:

At the beginning of the year Paxton was writing only a line or two; now he is writing two and three pages each day in writer's workshop. His spelling has improved a lot. Here he was purely guessing at some of the vowels, now he is using the words he knows to guide his spelling of new words. He is thinking about the words and beginning to use a dictionary. If you look at his sentences, you will notice that he uses quite a variety and that they are nicely connected to make a flow of writing. So while he is working at becoming more accurate, he is definitely moving in the right direction and has made big strides during this term.

To make the parent interviews even more interactive, some teachers send home a note before the interview asking parents to jot down their impressions of their children's school work. Another alternative is to send home what amounts to a blank report card, and ask parents to write down their evaluation of their child's standing or progress in such areas as personal development, attitude toward learning, and anything else you can think of. Completing such a form gives parents the opportunity to take a close look at what their child is doing at home in connection with homework. This approach works well at South Park School because it is a "family school" in which close collaboration with parents is a given. When parents adopt the habit of observing the steps forward their child is taking, there is that much more encouragement for learning, and parents have the pleasure of watching their child's progress more closely.

Observations by **Parents**   Date:

Student: Teacher: Parent:

Teachers are interested in how you see your child at *home*. Please take a minute to make notes about his or her social
and academic development, interests, attitudes, strengths and special needs.
When you write, use phrases or brief comments.

Your child's interactions with other children or with siblings:

Your child's interests and activities at home:

Your child's previous or present experiences that you consider significant:

Your child's structured activities outside school (sports, music, art lessons…?):

Observations by Parents — page 1   © Linda Pierce Picciotto

*This form (continued on
next page) developed by
Linda Pierce Picciotto
invites parents to provide
observations about their
children.*

STUDENT-LED PARENT CONFERENCES

One way of assuring that parents become knowledgeable observers of their children's learning is to institute student-led conferences in which the students themselves conduct the after-report-card parent interview at school. Parents love it, students thrive on it, and teachers see far more parents – with far less anxiety and stress for everyone concerned. As students get ready for the big day, when they are to present their learning to

Observations by **Parents**

Date:

Student: Teacher: Parent:

Your child's attitude towards school and/or learning:

Your child's behaviour:

Your child's special needs (environment, rules, learning style ...):

Your child's physical development:

Anything else?

Thank You   **Parent Signature:**

© Linda Pierce Picciotto   Observations by Parents — page 2

their parents, their eagerness conveys itself and parents make sure they are there at the appointed time. No one wants to miss out on the fun. One teacher had twenty-seven eager participants attend the student-led parent conferences – a far cry from the three parents who came to the traditional parent-teacher interviews the year before.

The student-led conferences show evaluation to be an integral part of learning. For a month before the conferences, students collaborate with their teacher to plan the meeting.

They design and send out the invitations to the parents and later take charge of the conferences. In the meantime, they decide which centers to set up, which topics to include, and which of their own finished products they want to show or demonstrate – writing folders, artwork, science projects, social science dioramas, physical education activities, or reading abilities. Next they role-play guiding someone through the various centers and practice explaining what they know and what they can do. If at first they are hesitant and slow to speak up, practice builds confidence, and by the time their parents join them in the classroom, students demonstrate clearly who is in charge. They show confidence and pride in their work and leave the parents in no doubt about the learning that undergirds their accomplishments. Instead of the teacher talking *about* the children's learning, the students give concrete demonstrations of their work and amaze their parents with their aplomb in asking politely, "What would you like to know about my learning?" then, "What concerns you about my learning?" and finally, "Tell me what you think I do well."

Parents wholeheartedly enter into the fun and mirror the enthusiasm of their children. What used to be an exhausting, dreaded chore becomes a rewarding, warm-hearted time for sharing. At South Park School, the gym became the focus for the spontaneous organization of all kinds of ball games with parents, with students from a variety of grades and teachers joining in to form teams to try out some of the skills the students were demonstrating. The sharing of juice and cookies – prepared in advance by the students – had to wait till later.

If turning the traditional parent-teacher interview over to the students seems like a risky step, we can only assure you that our risk-taking was richly rewarded. Once the South Park teachers took the plunge, the benefits become apparent quickly. The students' learning expanded and deepened. They not only reinforced their already acquired skills and knowledge by working at their presentations, but they added interpersonal skills, gained immensely in confidence and poise, and also learned how to organize and structure successful meetings.

For the teachers, the student-led conferences turned what had traditionally been an exhausting, marathon talking session into an easy flowing social event. The sign-up sheet for conferences assured an appropriate flow of visitors to the classroom, and the worksheet that parents used as a guide to the various centers provided room for parent feedback that often led to in-depth discussions about a student's progress or needs. Though parents had the option of signing up for a private parent-teacher interview, only two did so, but when it came time to meet, they commented that all of their questions had already been answered by following their children's presentation. The follow-up questionaire sent to parents to get their reactions and suggestions for the future brought a 100 percent return and a 100 percent "yea" vote for more student-led parent conferences in the future. Try them, and you'll never go back to traditional parent-teacher interviews.

Student—Led Parent Conference

April 11 and 12

Student Name _____

Parent(s) _____

Please go to each of the following centers during your visit to discuss each area of your schooling with your parent or parents. You may visit the centers in any order.

Centers	Parent Comments
Reading Share your present book. - describe the plot - describe the main characters - read a paragraph out loud	
Writing - Share your response journal. - Show your writing folder or your favorite piece of writing. - Show your research notes.	
Math - Solve the fraction problems. - Show how to convert to decimal fractions. - Solve one multiplication problem. Check your answer with the calculator.	
Social Studies - Explain three reasons for the exploration of Canada by the Europeans. - Tell who were the first peoples to explore Canada and where they came from. - Explain the significance of the Hudson Bay Company. - Explain why the exploration stopped at the Rockies while other explorers came to the west by sea.	

This form (continued next page) provided space for their comments, and acted as a road map to parents as they moved from center to center..

Centers	Parent Comments

Science
  - Explain these jobs for working in
    your cooperative groups
    - reader
    - writer
    - organizer
    - proofreader
    - materials
    - presenter
  - Explain what is meant by
    "All for one, and one for all."
  - Read the questions you answered
    about the beaver.
  - Give a brief description of the
    beaver and tell why it became
    endangered in Europe.	

Art
  - Show and discuss your artwork
    that is displayed in the room.	

P.E.
  - Demonstrate the following skills
    in volleyball.
    - volleying
    - bumping
    - serving	

Have a talk with Liz at the conference table and show your parents your self-evaluation.	
When you are finished, serve your parent(s) juice and cookies, and enjoy some yourself!	

PEER CONFERENCES

Like the student-led parent conferences, peer conferences integrate learning with assessment – in this case student-to-student assessment. Peer conferences may not add much to your evaluation records, but they do help students obtain feedback on their progress. During writer's workshop, peer conferences bring students together to critique each other's drafts and to ask leading questions that help the student authors expand on points that seem obscure to the listener. Discussions during

Practice with the teacher prepares the way for the meeting with parents.

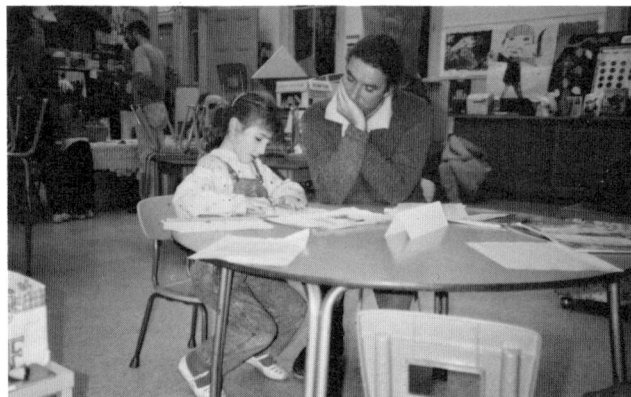

projects help to clarify the students' thoughts, and if you have been modeling thoughtful questioning, questions raised by their classmates can lead students to expand on their writing. Marking each other's math or spelling can result in students checking their own work more closely, learning to explain reasons for doing things a particular way, and eventually becoming more accurate. Modeling polite, matter-of-fact ways of probing and commenting is an essential starting point. Laying down some definite rules about what is and what is not an acceptable way to talk to each other may become necessary. To give all students the chance to voice their feelings and thoughts, these rules may need to be discussed as a class. But in a friendly, open climate of learning, peer conferences will be valuable adjuncts to evaluation.

Self-evaluation is an ongoing process

Since the teacher is sharing his or her ongoing observations with students many times during the day, students, too, get in the habit of assessing their own progress. Keeping folders on their various activities gives them the opportunity to look back to see how much progress they've made. Extensive reading gives the students models for their writing, and a good number of students turn to pattern writing in which they strive to emulate their favorite writers or genres – mystery novels, fairy tales, poetry, cartoon strips. As they try to match them, they refer back to their models and set high standards for themselves.

By the time students reach adolescence and the upper levels of elementary school, many struggle with their self-image and the problems associated with leaving childhood behind. Learning to do fair and accurate self-evaluations can be a wonderful balm for tender feelings. When you model the approach that focuses on what is going right and what is getting better and how to turn errors into new learning, students are less likely to dwell on their own shortcomings or the shortcomings of their work. As we pointed out earlier in this chapter, they will be aware that some of their work falls short of their self-generated standards or ideals. Turning negative self-criticism into questions about how to improve, what to do next, and what direction to take can be helpful and does not deny their self-evaluation.

1. Camping trip to Parksville (every year trip, this one Jul. 21 - Jul. 29)

2. Wake up one day, ~~say~~ I have shrunk.

3. Aventure - fantasey in the land of Englakii

4. ~~Recombitfon~~

5. tunnel adventure

6. poem? Description?

7. my dog - going on an adventure.

Reactions from Meg

1. Good idea, interesting, would only make it one day.

2. Good idea, sounds funny.

3 Great, She likes fantasys.

5. Good, interesting, adventurous

6th good

7. great, she liked the other ones about him.

Following the teacher's model, peer comments are both positive and constructive.

Being accountable

TESTING

Administering tests in specified topics, doing unit tests for basal readers (if still in use), and giving required tests at prescribed intervals continue to be part of the classroom routine. In addition, specific diagnostic tests may be indicated for students who need extra help. No matter how effective our other assessment methods, we always comply with requirements laid down by the school administration. In fact, it becomes interesting to compare test results with our own assessment of students. At times we find that we can actually augment the results of diagnostic tests by using our own observations. Tests have been around for a long time and are likely to stay with us. We acknowledge and respect that fact – even though we would prefer not to use them.

RECORD KEEPING

Though a lot of ongoing observation will remain unrecorded, the need to maintain records that can be verified, and that have meaning to someone other than the teacher, remains as cogent as under more structured systems of instruction. We have discussed numbers of ways of keeping track of progress. Today the computer offers yet another way to maintain carefully detailed records that can be updated from day to day or at frequent intervals. Open learning and a focus on steps forward do not mean abandoning careful record keeping. Despite the focus on progress, records will also include notes on special needs and gaps in students knowledge or performance. Now, as always, it is crucial to maintain records in a manner that assures confidentiality, but that allows students access to the information through conferences with the teacher.

PREPARING REPORT CARDS

The quarterly reports to parents on their children's work may follow the traditional format that lists all the subjects. If your school or class opts for letter grades as the means of reporting progress, then the traditional form will be appropriate. In schools where anecdotal records and observations account for most of the day-to-day assessment, report cards are likely to be couched in descriptive language with separate headings and paragraphs on specific topics and skill development. Since British Columbia is in a period of transition and the Ministry of Education has not designed model report cards for the intermediate grades, schools are experimenting with their own formats as they try to match their report cards to the new ways of teaching. At South Park School the report card for intermediate students reflects the broad developmental areas noted in the new draft curriculum guide for the intermediate grades. Printed on a legal-size sheet, the entire back of the form is left open for comments, thus blending specific comments on student development with open-ended comments on the work through which the developmental goals were achieved. (See page 313.)

Whatever the form and format used, report cards and their content are intended to match the teaching/learning. Like all of assessment discussed above, they are intended to enhance and support further learning. If students and parents alike see assessing progress and being accountable in that light, then the learners' way of working truly pervades.

SOUTH PARK FAMILY SCHOOL

Teacher: _____

Student: _____

Div. _____ Date: _____

ATTENDANCE:	TERM	YEAR
DAYS ABSENT		
DAYS LATE		

SOCIAL AND PERSONAL DEVELOPMENT

Legend: ❑   √ - Yes   * - Refer to comment

❑ demonstrates a positive sense of self-worth, personal initiative, self-discipline and the importance of satisfaction gained through achievement.

❑ demonstrates an understanding of the importance of physical health, emotional well-being, and the importance of work and leisure activities in contributing to a quality of life.

❑ demonstrates strategies for dealing with change.

❑ demonstrates appropriate strategies and skills for dealing with conflicts.

❑ tolerates and respects the ideas and beliefs of other cultures, ages and sexes.

❑ follows directions.

❑ is developing the ability to organize own work.

❑ accepts and fulfills responsibilities.

❑ can work cooperatively in a group.

❑ demonstrates a sense of responsibility for the environment.

❑ is considerate of others.

❑ displays appropriate classroom behavior.

❑ displays appropriate behavior when out of the classroom.

❑ cares for personal and school property.

INTELLECTUAL DEVELOPMENT
MAJOR THEMES AND TOPICS COVERED THIS TERM

COMMUNICATION
(listening, speaking, writing, reading)

_____
_____
_____
_____

MATHEMATICS

_____
_____
_____
_____

SOCIAL STUDIES

_____
_____

SCIENCE

_____
_____

ART

_____
_____

MUSIC

_____
_____

PHYSICAL EDUCATION

_____

FAMILY LIFE (HEALTH)

_____

FRENCH

_____

OTHER

_____

The reverse of this form includes designated areas for comments and signatures of the teacher, principal, and parents.

PULLING IT ALL TOGETHER

9

REVIEWING OUR WORK of researching and writing *On The Move* once again confirmed the correctness of the theoretical framework that guided us in writing this book. We want to share that reflection with you. Having provided concrete, practical suggestions for applying whole-language teaching/learning, we now want to pull together the threads that tie the in-class work together. As we stated at the beginning of the book, whole-language teaching is more a philosophy or theory of learning than a method of teaching. So to offer you a framework for applying our suggestions in ways that fit your students, in this chapter we draw together our observations about intermediate learners, and how their natural learning fits the learning model that has guided both our research and practice.

Observing in intermediate classrooms ranging from grades 3–4 through grade 7 extended our earlier work in primary classrooms and quickly showed us that children growing toward adolescence make different demands on their teachers. Aside from the broader scope in curriculum and sophistication of work, teachers are faced with the need to acknowledge the individuality of their learners in more personal ways. Without submerging their own personalities, teachers need to consider their students' learning styles, levels of maturity, personality traits, special strengths or needs, and to be aware of the interests that fuel students' learning. Observing in these classrooms proved to be a special challenge as well.

Being in tune with the learners *and* the curriculum is the balancing act we saw teachers perform as they worked in open ways with their students, yet stayed in charge of the general area of learning. Flexible planning, going with sparks of interest, capturing teachable moments, setting interesting frameworks for learning, offering choices, and keeping work concrete and relevant kept both interest and productivity high.

As observers we had the opportunity to note how students responded to the teachers' ways of interacting with them and to test the fit between what we found and the model of language-learning strategies that had emerged from our earlier in-class observations in primary classrooms. Though the level of work is more sophisticated, the basic processes remain the same.

What does language learning have to do with intermediate teaching/learning?

Like many intermediate teachers who worry about the validity and workability of whole-language teaching, you may want a more holistic answer to your concerns. Now that we have pulled together the notes and examples of our in-class research and have had time to stand back and reflect on our findings, we can answer such questions as, "Just what does initial language learning have to do with teaching/learning in intermediate classrooms?" and "How is it possible for a model that deals with acquiring basic skills to answer the needs of teachers who are supposed to convey a body of knowledge with solid facts and sophisticated skills?"

LANGUAGE LEARNING BUILDS KNOWLEDGE AS WELL AS SKILLS

Language learning does not happen in a vacuum. Children learn to talk because they are curious about the world and want to communicate about it. They have an insatiable drive to learn and explore. So if you are worried about imparting knowledge about geography, history, science, mathematics, reflect on all a young child learns while growing up. Without specific instruction even babies learn about the geography of their homes, backyards, streets, the supermarket; they learn something about the history of their families – parents, grandparents, uncles, aunts, power struggles; and they gain important insights into the laws of physics as they manipulate things around them. They learn about gravity, energy, levers, laws of moving bodies and inertia. They count, divide, and estimate as they share food and toys.

They learn about hygiene, its pitfalls and benefits, and they develop excellent understanding of interpersonal relations. They may not be able to talk *about* that knowledge, but they nevertheless demonstrate that they have made it their own. While acquiring all this solid information, they also learn the *how* of learning. They observe, classify, compare, hypothesize, experiment, revise previous impressions, and continue to observe and gather new information. In short, they do all the things a scientist does when exploring new data. Bruner has commented on the remarkable job young children do and figure 4 (page 316) provides a more detailed list of all the effective activities young learners engage in. Because they learn so competently, and apparently without effort, we tend to overlook the magnitude of the learning they accomplish; yet they are truly scientific explorers who daily make new discoveries and integrate those discoveries with what they have gathered in before. They are constantly on the move.

LANGUAGE LEARNERS INTEGRATE
NEW INFORMATION TO MAKE IT THEIR OWN

Because the young scientists select what they want to investigate, they give their research their full attention and make the new learning truly their own. Think of the absorption with which a child will explore the qualities and possibilities of a mud puddle, remember the perseverance and thought invested in building a sand castle, recall the wonder at observing the locomotion of a caterpillar, the satisfaction of creating interesting squishy noises by sloshing around in boots half-filled with rainwater. As a parent you may not have regarded these scientific explorations with unreserved joy, but as a teacher you will agree that they attest to a marvelous drive and self-initiated capacity for learning and exploring. And that is what the language-learning model is all about: *the conscious acknowledgement that young students have a well-functioning system of learning, tremendous capacity to assimilate and accommodate new information, and an innate drive to explore and understand the world around them.*

Observing intermediate students at work confirmed that if they are given the chance to explore and discover, they function in just that way. They search for meaning and patterns, and in the process they acquire a host of skills as a by-product to building up their knowledge base. In class, as at home, skills are not learned out of context. Experienced teachers commented

FIGURE 4
METHODS OF RESEARCH AND ENQUIRY USED BY SCIENTISTS
DOING RESEARCH AND CHILDREN EXPLORING THEIR WORLD

Both will -

Decide what *they* want to investigate, what is important to *them*

Observe, listen, physically examine, test, use all their senses to gain knowledge

Use prior knowledge and previous experience to aid information gathering

Follow the lead of their peers

Draw on the experience of others to aid research, ask questions

Note recurring patterns, similarities, differences, predictable patterns

Develop hypotheses about the materials or activities they are testing

Experiment to test hypotheses

Draw inferences on the basis of experiments and observations

Make retests to confirm or deny findings

Anticipate what will happen next

Generate rules and theories based on observed patterns

Update or correct previous findings on the basis of new evidence

Refine knowledge and test its fit with prior information

Consider the entire situation or context to interpret findings

Work actively to acquire new knowledge

Use imagination and intuition to further their research

Stay with a problem of their choice

Take risks in exploring and putting forth new findings

Are curious and love to explore unknown territory

Work hard to solve problems and overcome obstacles

From *The Learners' Way*, 1989.

that students will readily learn quite sophisticated skills if they are needed to satisfy the students' eagerness to explore topics of their choice.

Conditions that foster learning

Acknowledging the students to be capable, independent learners makes teaching more a matter of creating the right learning environment than one of presenting facts and information. The exciting aspect of that shift is that the learning climate you create will be as interesting and relevant to you as it will be to your students. *Genuine communication, solving real problems, and meeting everyday needs* become the foundation of learning for you and your students. Comparisons of the conditions that foster learning at home and in intermediate classrooms confirm that the language-learning model has much to offer.

LEARNING IS CONCRETE AND RELEVANT

Since parents seldom present specific lessons to their children, learning springs directly from the physical environment of the home. Without textbooks, lectures, or tests, children learn about the world around them – what things are, how they work, and what they are used for. They learn to speculate about differences and similarities, about possible outcomes – If I do this, is that likely to happen? They solve real problems – How can I reach the cookie jar? They experiment – How can I make that ball bounce the right way? They look at cause and effect – Why do kites fly?

Visitors sense that same air of purposeful activity and intense concentration when they enter classrooms of intermediate teachers who draw upon their students' knowledge and interests to make learning concrete and relevant – connecting writing to students' personal experience; selecting reading material that touches upon their current concerns; tapping their personal talents or interests as a basis for projects; looking at their home community to study history, the effects of pollution, the impact of government decisions; finding ways to demonstrate that the abstract laws of science or difficult rules of math have some very practical applications that are of importance to students.

LEARNING INVOLVES HANDS-ON WORK

Practical learning at home involves all the senses. Children learn by trying things out, manipulating, taking apart, rebuilding, and just plain messing about. As children get older, trial-and-error learning leads to adventure and thoughtful testing of new and different ways of working. Both the level of learning and the materials used become increasingly sophisticated. And hands-on work remains just as important as learners mature. For intermediate students it produces intense involvement and effective learning that moves well beyond rote memory. Using layers of construction paper to create contour maps of a treasure island has students develop a sense of the full scope of map-making that no amount of atlas study could achieve. Constructing dioramas of the environmentally safe home or displays of living rooms of ten, twenty, thirty years ago generates enthusiastic participation. Running science experiments, cooking, or dealing with money make abstract concepts tangible. Students discuss such work eagerly, compare notes, play with the materials, and enjoy the results of their cooking efforts. Their whole beings – not just the left hemispheres of their brains – are involved in learning.

LEARNING IS SET IN A FRAMEWORK

The familiar setting of the home becomes the starting point and backdrop for new learning. Everyday events help learners connect new experiences to existing knowledge, and participating in familiar activities offers a solid base for further explorations. Providing familiar frameworks for new learning can be just as productive in class. Field trips, special in-school settings – the library, gym, music room – set the scene for meaningful research on local businesses, on wildlife, or on topics of students' choice. But setting mental frameworks can be equally effective – using the Olympics as a framework for studying ancient Greece yielded enthusiastic participation and wonderful learning; studying the personal backgrounds and writings of Canadian authors made geography come alive; folk dancing in the gym sparked imaginative artwork.

LEARNING IS INTERACTIVE

At home, working together on everyday jobs – cooking, cleaning, shopping, gardening – is a natural avenue for learning. Talking together, reading aloud, discussing thoughts and problems, weighing the pros and cons of vacation trips or family outings get everyone involved. Learning is by no means a one-way street.

As teachers participate in students' projects, discuss the various aspects of the work or ways of presentation, or confer with students about their writing, there is a mutuality of learning that makes the classroom a community abuzz with excitement. At times students take on the role of teacher and present special knowledge to their peers, and in writer's workshop peer editing and conferencing form a viable part of moving students' writing through the initial rough drafts to a more finished product. Learning is neither a solitary nor a unidirectional activity. Just as information sharing and joint work spark ideas and creativity for adults, so does the interactive work in intermediate classrooms.

The South Park staff room was turned into a tortilla factory.

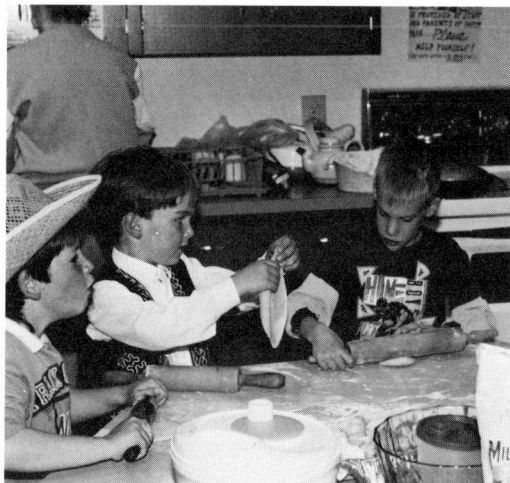

LEARNING EVOLVES OVER TIME

Parents accept that learning takes time and that their children grow and mature at differing rates. They have neither timetables nor predetermined schedules for monitoring their children's learning. When teachers in intermediate classrooms abandon fixed time frames for learning, work in their classrooms takes on greater depth. Jobs and projects – writing, artwork, and special research – move through several drafts and become enriched far beyond work that must be completed according to a set timetable. The open time frame makes full allowance for differences in students' pace and styles of learning whether you work with a single grade or with multi-age grouping.

LEARNING INTEGRATES KNOWLEDGE AND SKILL BUILDING

Reality-based learning at home is embedded in everyday living and does not involve worksheets or special exercises. Instead, learning to talk and then improving that skill go hand in hand with everyday communication and learning. Much of what is learned is implicit yet nonetheless profound. Quite young children learn to recognize body language, tone of voice, and facial expression as "storm ahead" or "all's well" signals. In the course of learning to feed themselves they develop manual dexterity, and while learning to walk they find out about balance and staying upright.

Integrative learning in the whole-language classroom works in much the same way. Reading and writing are not treated as separate subjects but as means of communication. While distinct blocks of time are set aside for practice, both reading and writing have solid meaning and purpose. Projects and field trips not only integrate reading, writing, and research but also cut across subject areas to draw upon science and social studies. Because information and subjects are not compartmentalized, both students and teachers experience the joy of studying topics in depth. Science teachers are free to draw on literature and history to enrich their discussions; art teachers expand the scope of their lessons to include examinations of myths, traditions, and cultural factors that have influenced specific genres of painting or sculpture.

Inherent in all these examples is the fact that with the use of a whole-language model the role of the teacher changes from that of being the chief information giver to that of being the person who creates an environment conducive to learning.

Just as the parent at home sets the learning environment and provides the learning materials for young children, so the teacher creates the setting that invites learning in class. But in an intermediate classroom the whole-language teacher is not so much in a parent–child role with the student as in a master–apprentice relationship. As the master learner in the classroom he or she models learning, enquiry, interest, skillful work, and a positive attitude toward the jobs at hand. He or she also supplies materials, subject matter to work on, expertise in handling the materials, and intense involvement with learning. The classroom becomes akin to a workshop where serious, meaningful work is done throughout the day. If you think of the popularity and success of some of the co-op programs at colleges and universities, you will have an idea of the effectiveness of turning the responsibility for classroom jobs and projects connected with learning over to the students. They rise to the challenge of responsibility and work harder and more effectively than seemed possible under the traditional teacher–pupil relationship. As Judy Woodward, a grade 7 Victoria teacher, puts it:

Looking at students in new ways has got us away from the structured approaches we used to follow. When I look back I realize how rigid we were in defining lessons as "The Learner Will . . . ." I thought it might be more realistically expressed, "The Learner Might . . . ." We used to use the abbreviation TLW and then write down our objectives, but I always felt that I was counting my chickens before they hatched. I put it down knowing that they just might do whatever it was if I was lucky; in fact, they'd probably do even *more* if I was lucky.

And so they do when the teacher turns control for learning over to the students.

BECOMING A "LEAD TEACHER"

The openness of learning and flexibility of planning in whole-language classrooms often lead to questions about discipline and keeping control. Just as at home the parents remain in charge, so the teacher remains in charge in the classroom. Taking the role of a lead teacher means fostering responsible behavior in class. Like lead parents who have high expectations

Trevor   Div.5

The people of the eagle greet you.
You have taught us so much while you
have been Principle of south Park. Our
Play Ko-'shintm it and son of eagle dramitizes
two very important leson's. You have taught
us to be proud of are tallentts and that we
don't always have to be like other people
We need to be ourselves.

                Thank you

Knowledge of legends and metaphors aided students in composing their farewell messages to their principal. Such patterns enriched the very personal expressions of their affection for Trevor.

of their children, the lead teacher has high expectations of students and involves them in setting and enforcing rules of behavior. The climate of delight rests on trust in the students' ability to function well on all levels, including social behavior. Cooperation and purposeful learning pervade the school day.

Patterns of learning that emerged from in-class observations

When we started our initial research in Margaret's kindergarten–grade 1 class, we were looking for the ways in which young children move from not reading and writing at all to a modicum of fluency. As we observed children work in class, we noted some well-defined landmarks: knowing about books and print, developing a feel for book language, beginning to acquire a sight vocabulary, using language patterns to make meaning, and the gradual emergence of spelling and knowledge of letter-sound correspondence. As there were fairly clearcut *yes/no* answers when looking for children's ability to read, write, and spell, we evolved a definite sense of the developmental sequence of reading and writing and were able to draw close parallels between the stages of development in oral language development and those of written language learning (Forester 1975).

Researching in intermediate classrooms proved more of a challenge. Most intermediate students already know how to read and write and have at least a rudimentary knowledge of spelling. So what are their signposts of new learning? What major milestones are there along the way? And what do our observations tell us about the ways in which students learn – not just memorize but truly internalize and connect material to existing knowledge? What is it that keeps alive or reawakens that natural curiosity and drive to learn that very young children bring to their explorations of the world around them?

As happens to us so often, we found that our own learning followed the learning patterns of the students. It took time – over two years – to gain insights and to detect patterns. We needed to accumulate a lot of experience and look at the transcripts of our in-class recordings again and again to understand their significance. We needed to talk about what we had observed in order to extract the deeper meaning of the concrete, day-to-day work. In short, our own work, like that of the students *moved from taking in whole patterns to abstracting parts, from looking at lots of concrete work to deriving abstract concepts, from gross processing of the data to finer discrimination of its meaning.* Here are the patterns we observed.

STUDENTS ARE ACTIVE LEARNERS

Practice and immersion in the work – much more than lessons taught by the teacher – produced new learning. Skills and knowledge emerged as students spent time on reading, writing, working on projects.

CONCRETE PRACTICE BUILDS
ABSTRACT KNOWLEDGE

Abstract lessons *about* paragraphs, literary terms, scientific principles, math took on meaning only *after* the students had accumulated a large stock of practical experience. No description – no matter how clear and practical – about what constituted a paragraph elicited that gleam of understanding in the students' eyes – or practical application by the students – until *after* their own writing had naturally progressed to a length and complexity that required paragraphing to make the writing more understandable. Explanations about the need to hold printing blocks firmly in order to make well-defined prints fell on deaf ears until students themselves had experimented with printing and noted the problem of smudging. Students need lots of building blocks and hands-on work to construct knowledge.

STUDENTS NEED TO GENERATE THEIR OWN LEARNING

To make knowledge or concepts their own, students need to discover the information themselves. *They* need to experiment, accumulate a large body of experience, discuss what they are working on, and *then* have the teacher help them express their knowledge. Examining patterns, overgeneralizing known patterns, experimenting with sounds become the prelude to accurate spelling. Manipulating blocks, pie shapes, weights or measures forms the basis of understanding math and answering problems effectively. In math we particularly noticed how in the absence of concrete practice students can be coaxed into providing "right" answers without understanding the how and why of the work. And the same kind of empty verbalism could be elicited by presenting textbook lessons about longitude and latitude or about rules of grammar.

On the other hand, reality-based learning and discussions elicited rapt attention and eager participation. Solving real problems – How do we convey math to young buddies? What can we do to influence our environment positively? What went wrong in this project and what can we do to make it better next time? – changed students from listless foot shufflers to bright-eyed, eager participants. Like adults, students resent and resist work that appears irrelevant. Like initial language learners, students need to generate the information and rules that make learning uniquely their own.

MEANING AND THE SEARCH FOR PATTERNS GUIDE LEARNING

These observations about intermediate students' learning are similar to those we noted about the learning of primary students. The most important aspect of our early work many years ago was the discovery that while Margaret was basing her reading lessons on letters, sounds, and the particles of speech, the children were searching for meaning. That search became manifest as they converted the stilted language of the basal reader into a more normal pattern of speech, read *mother* as *mom*, and looked ahead to see if the context would yield clues about unfamiliar words. They were using patterns of language rather than sounds in isolation. In spite of the teacher's emphasis on sounding words out, they were moving directly to the heart of reading – making meaning. Like experienced readers, they used their knowledge of language and how it works to aid the process of deriving meaning, and that, more than any lessons on phonics, moved them toward reading with comprehension and fluency. More important, it infused excitement and a sense of discovery and joy into their learning. A look at what we noted about intermediate students' learning confirms that for them, too, the search for meaning is central. Like their younger peers, they do not respond well to abstract lessons but seek to connect what they know to the lessons at hand; they need to be active participants in that learning. They, too, work with patterns, hence the need for a wealth of experience to draw upon. Patterns do not exist in isolated, abstract lessons; they emerge from a knowledge base that is varied and broad.

Where primary children draw upon their knowledge of patterns of spoken language to help them learn to read, intermediate students internalize and draw upon the patterns of written language. As their writing evolves, it begins to reflect the vocabulary, style, and structure of book language. Their stories

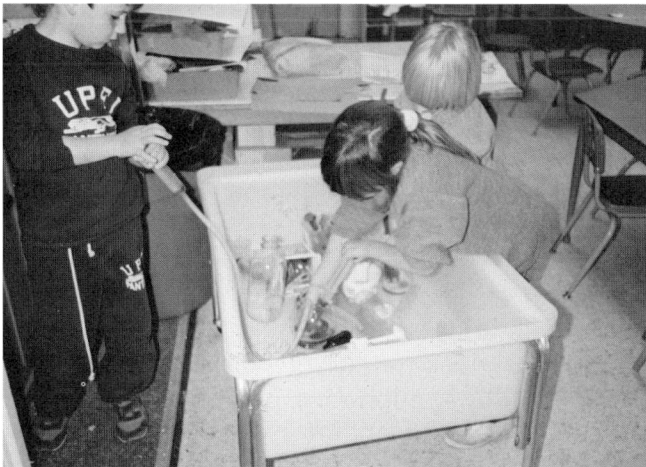

Joining their younger buddies, intermediate students "work" at the watertable to learn firsthand about hydraulic pressure, flow, syphoning, and capillaary action. No amount of lecturing could equal the depth of learning achieved by such personal exploration.

reveal that they are aware of the patterns of story grammars, and their writing is enlivened by phrases, metaphors, and stylistic devices that they have encountered in their reading. Extensive reading, written exchanges with the teacher, and open discussions about the books and stories they read establish patterns of thought and language that move beyond those of the primary grades. Because the students have ample opportunity to choose their own reading material and are not limited to either grade-level basal readers or to fiction, the patterns of written language that students internalize are enhanced by the range of factual information they gain.

To the degree that lessons in content areas offer the opportunity, the students draw upon both their reading and their everyday knowledge to imbue the material with meaning. Like the primary children, they respond with alacrity to the opportunity to discover and explore the concrete world, to question and hypothesize about what they see, manipulate, and hear. When encouraged to do their own research for projects or reports, students become keen observers and careful recorders of information. Because they involve all their senses and draw upon prior experience, they relate to the work on a very personal level.

So the sign posts of learning are not so much the information students take in but the way in which they approach learning and information gathering. As students engage in active experiments in science, explore math materials, try out new genres of writing, or venture into non-fiction reading they are synthesizing a wealth of material and are generating their own patterns of learning. Moving well beyond the acquisition of facts from textbooks or lectures, they create knowledge and express it in very personal ways – through writing, in displays, through drama, in pictures.

The process of constructing knowledge remains the same

The milestones of learning show themselves in bursts of writing in sudden "aha" breakthroughs when students tell you, "Oh now I know what I need here!" when they make the connections between the world outside and the world in the classroom. The concentration, attention, and care they lavish on their work mark them as active learners who know the how of gathering knowledge and skills and revel in it. They are on the move in their learning in ways that meet their individual needs and learning styles. In intermediate classes as in the primary grades,

Potlatch

Artwork enhances the writing as students prepare for the all-school Farewell Trevor Potlatch that included parents as well as students and staff.

the learning climate that invites learners to work in their own natural ways produces rich rewards. Though it may seem that by the time they reach the intermediate grades young learners will have outgrown these very fundamental principles, our observations have shown us that the basic patterns of learning remain the same. The process of constructing knowledge is universal no matter what the age of the learner.

CONCLUSION –
THIS IS JUST
THE BEGINNING

FOR YOU, AS FOR US, the end of the book is just the beginning. The can-do attitude of whole-language learning will keep you and your students moving along without any thoughts of barriers or upper limits. The energy flowing from the excitement of discovery learning will carry you right through the year without plateaus or troughs. As Marne put it the day before summer vacation, "We're still on high energy! There hasn't been any letdown or drop in commitment. We've kept right on going to the last minute!"

As you shift to whole-language teaching, the same boundless energy will fill your classroom and will create that feeling of continuous flow. Freedom to learn and explore will work as well for you as for your students. As you become a co-learner in your classroom, you will recapture the excitement of teaching. You will be free to share your interests and feelings. Instead of hugging the curriculum, you will be giving your affection to the students. Instead of focusing on the products of learning, you will be focusing on the students and getting to know them more deeply and personally than was possible when you had to direct your energy within narrowly defined guidelines.

The wonderful bonus for you will be that by shifting the focus to fulfilling the needs of students, you will also be fulfilling your own needs. Like your students, you will enter upon a path of never-ending growth and discovery. Each day will bring interesting work because the students collaborate with you in shaping that learning. You and they together, not some chart handed down from a committee, will determine the direction and flow of the work to be done each day. In that climate, leadership qualities can emerge, and the sense of working together will engender mutual respect and caring. Far from creating chaos and diminishing learning, free-flowing collaboration that acknowledges everyone's contribution builds responsibility and attitudes of ownership in learning.

As you change your role from that of dispenser of knowledge and discipline to that of master learner and co-creator of the learning environment, you encourage the students to expand not only their learning but their social skills as well. Since conflict resolution is built into overall problem solving, students learn to make each conflict a learning experience. It may take a good deal of coaching from you – particularly at the outset – but the lifeskill of getting along and considering everyone else's point of view create harmony in class and excellent skills for the world beyond school. With a focus on strengths and successes, attention-getting through acting out is at a minimum both in school and at home.

Focusing on strengths and building on successes gives you every opportunity to reach all of your students, even those who may have been "written off" as slow learners, trouble causers, or even learning disabled. Your growing skills in observing students and noting *their* ways of working and *their* concerns will show you the way of empowering such students through their interests and their successes whether in math, writing, sports, the arts, or imaginative problem solving. Once you demonstrate to them that you truly value their unique contributions to the group, your students will show you their hidden potential and will share their excitement at their new growth with you. They may not grow in ways that follow your scope and sequence chart, but grow they do, and you will be secure in the knowledge that your work exerted a highly positive influence on the learners in your care.

If the new way of interacting does wonders for your students, it will do just as much for you. As you observe the growing spontaneity and creativity of your students, you will find that your own creative powers are expanding too. Once the pressures of having to follow specific time lines and sequences of work have been removed, you will experience as much release as your students. Modeling genuine enquiry behavior, doing a lot of "wondering about . . . ," feeling free to explore, make mistakes, and display not-knowing behavior will rekindle your interests

*At times, mutual enjoyment
of sharing expresses itself
in artwork. This drawing
was produced by Jessica to
let Anne know that her in-
class observations and
participation in activities
was welcomed.*

and special talents. And there is no need to wait until vacation time or weekends to indulge in your own interests or hobbies. Sharing them with your students is just another way of showing yourself to be a learner and explorer.

Along with intellectual and physical skills, you will find your intuition fine-tuned and expanded. The absence of strife and competition in your classroom creates the feeling of safety in which intuition has a chance to evolve. Tuning in to your student's needs and wishes will rekindle your ability to tune in to your own needs as well, and will help you to acknowledge that small inner voice that can be such an effective guide. As your intuition grows so does your ability to spot teachable moments, to notice the special needs of a student, to sense the right moment to introduce a concept you have been meaning to present.

The descriptions and models we have provided are just the indicators that the open whole-language ways *do* work in intermediate classrooms. But you will want to adapt the examples to fit your own interests and those of your students. Intuition, creativity, and imagination will help you and your students keep on the move. Making the shift in outlook and philosophy is just the beginning. Your own work and the joy and excitement of always-expanding learning will carry you forward. Enjoy!

SELECT BIBLIOGRAPHY

The books and articles in this bibliography are limited to those that are cited in the book. This bibliography is by no means a complete record of our reading.

Atwell, Nancie. "How We Learned to Write." *Learning,* (March 1985): 51–53.

_____. *In the Middle – Writing, Reading, and Learning with Adolescents.* Portsmouth, NH: Heinemann, 1987.

_____. (ed.). *Coming to Know – Writing to Learn in the Intermediate Grades.* Portsmouth, NH: Heinemann, 1990.

Baretta-Lorton, Mary. *Mathematics Their Way.* Reading, MA: Addison-Wesley, 1976.

Baumrind, Diana. "New Directions in Socialization Research." *American Psychologist* 35, no. 7, (1980) 639–652.

Bean, Wendy, and Chrystine Bouffler. *SPELL by Writing.* Rozelle, NSW: Primary English Teaching Association, 1987.

Davies, Anne, and Norma Mickelson. "A Whole Language Programme in the Intermediate Grades." *Reading Canada Lecture* 7, no. 3, (1989) 241–249.

Forester, Anne D., and Margaret Reinhard. *The Learners' Way.* Winnipeg, MB: Peguis Publishers, 1989.

Gentry, Richard R. *SPEL . . . Is a Four-Letter Word.* New York: Scholastic, 1987.

Glasser, William. "The Quality School." *Phi Delta Kappan* 71, no. 6, (1990) 424–435.

Goodlad, John I., and Robert H. Anderson. *The Non-Graded Elementary School.* New York: Teachers College Press, 1987.

Johnson, Terry D., and Daphne R. Louis. *Literacy Through Literature.* Melbourne: Methuen Australia, 1985.

_____. *Bringing It All Together – A Program for Literacy.* Richmond Hill, ON: Scholastic, 1990.

Kobrin, Beverly. *Eyeopeners! How to Choose and Use Children's Books About Real People, Places and Things.* New York: Viking Penguin, 1988.

Little, Nancy, and John Allan. *Student-Led Teacher Parent Conferences.* Toronto: Lugus Productions, 1988.

McMillan, Audrey. "Using Nancie Atwell's *In the Middle* in a Grade 7 Classroom." *Reading Canada Lecture* 7, no. 4, (1989) 254–258.

McNeil, Linda M. *Contradictions of Control – School Structure and School Knowledge.* New York: Routledge & Kegan Paul, 1986.

Moore, George N., Richard A. Talbot, and G. Willard Woodruff. *SPELLEX word finder.* N. Billerica, MA: Curriculum Associates, 1988.

Wasserman, Selma, and J. W. George Ivany. *Teaching Elementary Science – Who's Afraid of Spiders?* New York: Harper and Row, 1988.

BOOKS READ BY STUDENTS AND MENTIONED IN THE TEXT

Bradley, Marion Z. *The Mists of Avalon.* New York: Knopf, 1982.

Burnett, Francis Hodgson. *The Secret Garden.* London: Purnell, 1975.

Dahl, Roald. *James and the Giant Peach.* New York: Knopf, 1961.

_____. *The BFG.* New York: Farrar, Strauss, Giroux, 1982.

Frank, Anne. *Diary of a Young Girl.* Mattituck, NY: American Reprint Co., 1977.

Fritz, Jean. *The Good Giants and the Bad Puckwudgies.* New York: Putnam, 1982.

Gardiner, John Reynolds. *Stone Fox.* New York: Avon Camelot Books, 1978.

George, Chief Dan. *My Heart Soars.* Surrey, BC: Hancock House, 1989.

George, Jean. *Julie of the Wolves.* New York: Harper & Row, 1972.

Hayes, Barbara. *Folk Tales and Fables of the World.* New York: Portland House, 1987.

Milne, A. A. *Winnie-the-Pooh.* New York: E. P. Dutton, 1962.

Mowatt, Farley. *Owls in the Family.* Boston: Little, Brown, 1961.

Thomas, Dylan. *A Child's Christmas in Wales.* London: Caedmon, 1952.

Tolkien, J. R. R. *The Hobbit.* Boston: Houghton Mifflin, 1966.

_____. *The Lord of the Rings.* London: Unwin, Hyman, 1988.

White, E. B. *Charlotte's Web.* New York: Harper & Row, 1952.

BOOKS USED IN THE
BUDDY POETRY-WRITING SESSION

Bennett, Jill *Noisy Poems.* Oxford: Oxford University Press, 1987.

Hill, M. *Time for Poetry – A Teacher's Anthology.* Glenview, IL: Scott, Foresman, 1951.

Jacobs, Leland B. *Animal Antics in Limerick Land.* Champaign, IL: Garrard, 1971.

Lee, Dennis. *Alligator Pie.* Toronto: MacMillan, 1974.

Stevenson, Robert Louis. *A Child's Garden of Verse.* London: Gollancz, 1985.

DATE DUE

DEMCO 38-297